DIGGING DEEP
into
THE REVELATION
of
JESUS CHRIST

SECOND EDITION

A Study Guide (NKJV)

MICHAEL COPPLE

WESTBOW
PRESS®
A DIVISION OF THOMAS NELSON
& ZONDERVAN

WestBow Press books may be ordered through booksellers or by contacting:

WestBow Press
A Division of Thomas Nelson & Zondervan
1663 Liberty Drive
Bloomington, IN 47403
www.westbowpress.com
1 (866) 928-1240

ISBN: 978-1-9736-4917-5 (sc)
ISBN: 978-1-9736-4916-8 (e)

Library of Congress Control Number: 2018914958

Print information available on the last page.

WestBow Press rev. date: 03/19/2020

Acknowledgments

First and foremost I give thanks to our Triune God for saving my loved ones from the Great Tribulation and the Lake of Fire, and giving me eternal life with the Savior and with them. This new life and hope has motivated me to gather the truth of Scripture and consolidate it with explanations from gifted, solid brothers in Christ who have written commentaries, spoken at conferences, and have always been prepared to exercise their Spiritual gifts.

Our dear brother in the Lord Jesus, Randy Amos, was gracious to accept my request to edit the book for confirmation of truth. He is credited with suggesting the appropriate title. Two of brother Randy's books have left a profound, positive impact on my growth and walk with the Lord: *The counterfeit Jesus* and "*The Church*, a Discipleship Manual for the Body of Christ".

Brother Warren Henderson's recent completion of an 18 year Old Testament commentary project consisting of 14 volumes was of tremendous value. I am especially grateful for inspiring me with his "Bible Prophecy Overview" in his *Infidelity and Loyalty* commentary on the Books of Ezekiel and Daniel. Warren's way of teaching is comparable to a picture being worth a thousand words.

Another dear brother, Ralph Kirchhofer, who not only edited this study guide for truth, but he also has been my mentor for continuing my growth in faith. For the past 12 years Ralph has encouraged me moment by moment to take on more responsibilities, especially to spread the Gospel.

It's been a wonderful, encouraging experience to work with those at WestBow Press, such as John, DeeAnna and the ones behind the scenes in the production, printing and corrections departments.

My loving wife Elfriede Copple designed the cover and choreographed the layout so it would ease comparison of Scripture to commentary and be more appealing and acceptable to you, the reader. Elfriede's gift of service and effective communications with the WestBow publishing staff has been outstanding, and her measure of advice and support for me was incalculable.

I am grateful for my dad and mom (after much prayer and decades of patience) for instilling a foundation of moral values and faith; and for the way they raised my brother and sisters and myself with unfailing love and energy. I would not be the person I am today without what they have done for me. God has called both of them home. Without any doubt, I will see them again.

Introduction

The Book of Revelation reveals that the Lord Jesus Christ is Almighty Jehovah God (Revelation 1:8; 4:8; 11:17; 15:3; 16:7, 14; 19:15; {21:22}. See also: Exodus 3:14; 6:3; John 8:58); and that the Lord Jesus Christ is the King of kings and Lord of lords (Revelation 19:16).

Chronological Order of Events

A key to understanding Revelation is that it has a sequential order, but the chronological flow is often interrupted and begins over again by stern warnings given in some chapters. There is a definite beginning and end though somewhat vague if the "big picture" is not taken into consideration.

The general course of events is as follows:

- the instructions the Lord Jesus gives to John for what to write;
- the present Church Age;
- the coming of the Lord Jesus in the clouds to carry away and instantaneously gather His believers in the air—traditionally called the Rapture;
- the worshiping and praising in heaven of the Lord for redeeming His followers;
- the rewards given;
- the scroll being opened containing seven seals of warnings;
- the revealing of the Antichrist man on earth beginning the Seven-year Tribulation period;
- the salvation of the 144,000 Israelites;
- the prophecy of some others who will become believers during the Tribulation;
- the seven trumpets to sound more severe warnings and the command to charge the earth and its inhabitants;
- the two witnesses who prophesy for three and one-half years;
- then the two witnesses are killed and raptured three-and-a-half days later;
- the protection of the sealed Israelites from the woes of the last half of the Tribulation;
- the number of the beast (666—man—Antichrist);
- the false trinity made up of Satan, the Antichrist, and the False Prophet;
- the prophecy fulfilled for the ones who die in the Lord during the Tribulation;
- the seven plagues contained in seven vials (bowls) to be poured out bringing the wrath of God upon the earth and its inhabitants;
- the Mystery of Babylon; the fall of Babylon;
- the marriage of the Church to the Lamb;
- the marriage supper;
- Christ's Second Coming to earth;
- the overthrow of the Antichrist and False Prophet;

- the casting of Satan into the pit;
- the Millennial reign of Christ;
- the casting of Satan into the Lake of Fire;
- the Great White Throne of judgment for the unbelievers;
- the new heaven and new earth;
- and a glimpse of heaven.

Of the 404 verses in Revelation, 265 contain verses alluding to 550 Old Testament references. Certain numbers like seven, and twelve have special significances in Revelation: 7 churches (1:11), 7 lampstands (1:13), 7 stars (1:16), 7 messages (2:1-3:22), 7 Spirits (4:5), 7 seals (5:1), 7 trumpets (8:2), 7 bowls or vials (15:7), 7 mountains (17:9), and 7 blessings (1-22). The number 12, even 12 x 12=144,000 (7:4-8; 14:1), 12 gates, 12 angels at the gates, 12 tribe names, 12 foundations, names of the twelve apostles of the Lamb (21:12-14), and 12 fruits (22:2).

How to Use This Study Guide

This guide, first of all, contains the complete New King James Version Bible Scriptures of *The Revelation of Jesus Christ*. The guide has been prepared with four columns - Scripture verses and commentary are conveniently printed across both facing pages. When each page is turned the NKJV Bible Chapter will be on the left-most, column #1. In column #2, next to the Scripture will be commentary on that Chapter with references to other verses and passages within the Bible. To save the reader from searching and turning to those other Books, the reference verses and passages have been printed in column #3 on the side-facing page. Then column #4 consists of the commentary for the reference verses. Without turning any pages these four columns are side by side to use time more effectively and to promote and enhance ease of understanding. Being difficult to fit all explanation into 4 columns, *the purpose of this study is to promote learning, discussion, and blessing.*

In the 4th column, commentary of "Reference Verses", these verses have been <u>underlined</u> to lessen the need for "guessing" what is being referred to. There are some other <u>reference verses that are not underlined</u> because their sentences or phrases have not been printed nor commented on in this compilation. It is left up to each person's motivation to look up these verses and to keep them in proper context.

Some Scripture phrases have been **bold** printed or <u>underlined</u> for *emphasis only* since the original Scripture does not include this sort of highlighting. These are pointed out merely for enhancement of understanding the context correlation in the commentary columns.

When a comment of explanation is found in the Scripture verses (the first and third columns on the left side of each page), [brackets] are made use of indicating that <u>it is not an addition to the Bible</u>—it is merely for clarification and differentiation. The reason for the brackets is because actual (parenthesis) symbols will be found in some verses and passages in the Bible (i.e., 2 Kings; Romans 7:18; 10:7; 21:11; Revelation 21:25). On the commentary columns <u>for sentences not directly quoting Scripture</u>, normal (parenthesis) symbols are used.

This guide has been prepared and edited with careful and prayerful study comparing Scripture to Scripture to maintain our God's original intention on how to understand what is written. As Randy Amos says on page iv of *The Church—A Discipleship Manual for the Body of Christ* the "goal is to simply look at the Bible and with the Spirit's power, communicate what He says. If it cuts across man's interpretation, so be it."

Helpful Notes

Christ's Words "in Red" Changed to "Tekton Pro Font"

All Scripture has been taken from *The Holy Bible, New King James Version*, published by Thomas Nelson, Inc., Copyright 1994. In the original, the words of Christ were in red. For this study guide the color has been eliminated and replaced with Tekton Pro font.

Prophesy Timeline and Last Days Timeline

These two charts can be found at the back of this Study Guide!

The Revelation of Jesus Christ
Chapter 1 Verses 1-6

¹The Revelation of Jesus Christ, which God gave Him to show His servants —things which must shortly [quickly or swiftly] take place. And He sent and signified *it* by His angel to His servant John, ²who bore witness to the word of God, and to the testimony of Jesus Christ, to all things that he saw. ³Blessed *is* he who reads and those who hear the words of this prophecy, and keep those things which are written in it; for the time *is* near.

⁴John, to the seven churches which are in Asia: Grace to you and peace from Him who is and who was and who is to come, and from the seven Spirits who are before His throne,

⁵and from Jesus Christ, the faithful witness, the firstborn from the dead, and the ruler over the kings of the earth. To Him who loved us and washed us from our sins in His own blood,

⁶and has made us kings and priests to His God and Father, to Him *be* glory and dominion forever and ever. Amen.

Revealing the Revelation
Chapter 1 Verses 1-6
Commentary

The Revelation of Christ and What Must Happen

1:1-3

Christ's testimony reveals God Himself. The Revelation of Jesus Christ is both *from* Christ and about Christ. We see this also in Revelation 22:6, 16, and 20. **Things which must shortly take place** refers to the Rapture of the Church, and next, to "the Day of the Lord"—D*ay of the Lord* refers to any period when God acts in judgment—in this Book of *The Revelation,* especially at the ends of the Tribulation Period and Millennial reign. Although no one has seen God in all His essence, people did see God in Jesus Christ (John 1:18; John 14:9). Verse 3 gives the reason the Spirit motivates us to seek more deeply.

1:4-8

The greetings are from John and the Savior to the seven churches. Although the churches are named, the very words of the Head of the Church—the Lord Jesus Christ—should be heeded with all somberness by all local churches today: **"hear what the Spirit says to the churches."**

1:5

Jesus Christ is the witness of John's Book of *The Revelation* writing.

1:6

Jesus Christ has made believers to be kings and priests (1 Peter 2:5, 1 Peter 2:9a) while reminding us that all glory is given to our God—not ourselves.

Vv. 1-3

John 1:18 No one has seen God [God the Father] at any time. The only begotten Son, who is in the bosom of the Father, He has declared *Him*.

John 14:9 Jesus said to him [Philip], **"Have I been with you so long, and yet you have not known Me, Philip? He who has seen Me has seen the Father; so how can you say, 'Show us the Father'?"**

Vv. 1-3

John 1:18 combined with John 14:9 tells us that the Father is seen and heard *in* His only begotten Son because the Father sent Him to be alive in us. The Lord Jesus Christ said to the Jews who sought to kill Him: **John 5:37-38** [37] **"And the Father Himself, who sent Me, has testified of Me. You have neither heard His voice at any time, nor seen His form.** [38] **But you do not have His word abiding in you, because whom He sent, Him you do not believe."**

V. 6

1 Peter 2:5 you also, as living stones, are being built up a spiritual house, a holy priesthood, to offer up spiritual sacrifices acceptable to God through Jesus Christ. ...

1 Peter 2:9a But you *are* a chosen generation, a royal priesthood...

V. 6

1 Peter 2:5, 1 Peter 2:9a: *The **spiritual house** is built up of all believers in Christ, and is therefore the same as the Church.* All believers are saints and priests—representatives of the Head of the Church, the Lord Jesus.

⁷Behold, He is coming with clouds, and every eye will see Him, even they who pierced Him. And all the tribes of the earth will mourn because of Him. Even so, Amen. ⁸ **"I am the Alpha and the Omega, _the_ Beginning and _the_ End,"** says the Lord, **"who is and who was and who is to come, the Almighty."**

1:7-8

He will be seen by all at His Second Coming, whether then or during His Millennial reign or at the Great White Throne of judgment (Zechariah 12:10). Jesus Christ is the equal Almighty God with the Father (Revelation 15:3; 16:7; 19:15, 19:11). The Lord Jesus Christ is referred to as the great I AM when referred to in John 8:58 with Exodus 3:14, and YHWH, (Jehovah in NKJV margin of Exodus 6:3). See also Isaiah 41:4; Isaiah 48:12.

1:9-20

These verses give John's vision of the **Son of Man** (Revelation 1:13)—a title the Savior gave for Himself especially in the Gospel of Luke.

⁹I, John, both your brother and companion in the tribulation and kingdom and patience of Jesus Christ, was on the island that is called Patmos for the word of God and for the testimony of Jesus Christ.

1:9

John writes of his tribulation on the Island of Patmos off the SW coast of today's Turkey.

¹⁰I was in the Spirit on the Lord's Day, and I heard behind me a loud voice, as of a trumpet,

¹¹saying, **"I am the Alpha and the Omega, the First and the Last,"** and, **"What you see, write in a book and send _it_ to the seven churches which are in Asia; to Ephesus, to Smyrna, to Pergamos, to Thyatīra, to Sardis, to Philadelphia, and to Lāodicēa."**

1:11

*Jesus tells John to **write** the vision he had seen.* What John wrote, we are reading today: In Chapter 1, **"which are"** were the churches of the early part of the Church Age addressed in Chapters 2 and 3. The seven churches in Chapters 2 and 3 are typified in today's churches.

Christ's accolades and rebukes are still relevant today.

Vv. 7- 8

Isaiah 41:4 "Who has performed and done *it*, calling the generations from the beginning? 'I, the LORD, am the first; and <u>with the last</u> I *am* He.'" [See also the prophecy of Zechariah 12:10].

Vv. 7-8

<u>Isaiah 41:4</u>: The passage (Isaiah 41:2-4) which contains this verse 4 *is about Jehovah raising up Cyrus to decree that the Jews be released from captivity. The Lord raised up Cyrus to have one generation succeed another, but even with the <u>last</u> generation, the Jehovah Lord Jesus <u>is still the same</u>.* Jeremiah 52:27-30 gives the prophesy of the Jews being taken into captivity. 2 Chronicles 36:22-23, Ezra 1:1-4 and Isaiah 44:28-45:1 provide further confirmation of the biblical prophesies and the historical fulfillments of these prophesies.

The fact that hundreds of past prophesies have come to fruition, lends incredible proof for knowing the prophesies in this *Revelation of Jesus Christ* will also surely be fulfilled.

¹²Then I turned to see the voice that spoke with me. And having turned I saw seven golden lampstands, ¹³and in the midst of the seven lampstands *One* like the <u>Son of Man</u>, clothed with a garment down to the feet and girded about the chest with a golden band. ¹⁴His head and hair *were* white like wool, as white as snow, and His eyes like a flame of fire; ¹⁵His feet *were* like fine brass, as if refined in a furnace, and His voice as the sound of many waters; ¹⁶He had in His right hand seven stars, out of His mouth went a sharp two-edged sword, and His countenance *was like* the sun shining in its strength.

1:12-16

John describes Jesus in his vision. John's vision resembles Ezekiel's more detailed vision, with angels as well, in Ezekiel 1:4-28. (<u>Ezekiel 1:4;</u> <u>Ezekiel 1:7; Ezekiel 1:10; Ezekiel 1:13; Ezekiel 1:24;</u> <u>Ezekiel 1:26-28</u>)

Chapter 1 Verses 12-16
References

Vv. 12-16

Ezekiel 1:4 Then I looked, and behold, a <u>whirlwind</u> was coming out of the north, a great cloud with raging <u>fire</u> engulfing itself; and <u>brightness</u> *was* all around it and radiating out of its <u>midst</u> like the color of amber, out of the midst of the <u>fire</u>. ...

Ezekiel 1:7 Their <u>legs</u> *were* <u>straight</u>, and the soles of their <u>feet</u> *were* like the soles of calves' feet. They sparkled like the color of <u>burnished bronze</u>. ...

Ezekiel 1:10 As for the likeness of their faces, *each* had <u>the face of a man</u>; each of the <u>four</u> had the face of a <u>lion</u> on the right side, each of the four had the face of an <u>ox</u> on the left side, and each of the four had the face of an <u>eagle</u>.

Ezekiel 1:13 As for the likeness of the <u>living creatures</u>, their appearance *was* like <u>burning coals of fire</u>, like the appearance of <u>torches</u> going back and forth among the <u>living creatures</u>. The <u>fire</u> was <u>bright</u>, and out of the fire went lightning. ...

Ezekiel 1:24 When they went, I heard the noise of their wings, like the <u>noise of many waters</u>, like the <u>voice</u> of the <u>Almighty</u>, a <u>tumult</u> like the noise of an army; and when they stood still, they let down their wings. ...

Ezekiel 1:26-28

-CONTINUED ON NEXT PAGE UNDER REFERENCES!-

Chapter 1 Verses 12-16
References Commentary

Vv. 12-16

<u>Ezekiel 1:4</u>: *The first Chapter of Ezekiel is taken up with a vision of the glory of God among the Jewish captives.* The **whirlwind** coming out of the north represents the Babylonians whom God used as agents of His judgment: **fire**—to punish the Jews by having them exiled.

<u>Ezekiel 1:7, Ezekiel 1:10</u>: The **four living creatures:** probably cherubim angels—represent God's majesty: **lion**; power: **ox**; swiftness: **eagle**; and wisdom: **face of a man**. The **straight legs** show strength, **calves' feet** point to stability and firm stance.

<u>Ezekiel 1:13</u>: The **burning coals of fire, torches** and **bright fire** convey God's **glory** and pure, burning justice.

<u>Ezekiel 1:24</u>: The **noise of many waters** in Ezekiel's time may be symbolic of many **living creatures** moving rapidly in reaction to Almighty God's sovereign authority. But, more specifically here in John's vision, the noise (or **tumult** in Ezekiel 1:24) may be the sound of an army, possibly the Christian warriors (Revelation 14:1-2). Isaiah 17:12-13 is also comparable with God's rebuking of the nations that exiled Israel in Isaiah's time.

-CONTINUED ON NEXT PAGE UNDER REFERENCES COMMENTARY!-

¹⁷And when I saw Him, I fell at His feet as dead. But He laid His right hand on me, saying to me, "Do not be afraid; I am the First and the Last. ¹⁸I *am* He who lives, and was dead, and behold, I am alive forevermore. Amen. And I have the keys of Hades and of Death.

<u>¹⁹</u>Write the things which you <u>have seen,</u> and the things <u>which are,</u> and the <u>things which will take place after this.</u>

1:19

*Jesus tells John to write of the past things <u>he has seen,</u> the things that <u>are presently happening</u> (the present church age), and **things which will take place after this** (after the Church is raptured; Chapters 4 to 22)*. John saw a soon coming Rapture, a Seven-year Tribulation, Christ's Second Coming, etc.

The **things** soon coming are the Rapture in Revelation 4:1 and then the Tribulation Period, Armageddon, and Christ's Millennial reign.

The Seven-year Tribulation is thoroughly described in Chapters 6 to 20. Chapter 16:16 begins the gathering for the Battle of Armageddon and it ends at the end of Chapter 19 and 20:2. Preceding that is the judgment seat of Christ (for rewards) in heaven. After that, the Tribulation Period on earth, and then the marriage of the Lamb and His Church in heaven. Then Armageddon and the marriage supper on earth. After that, the Millennial reign and Great White Throne (judging unbelievers), and the new heavens and new earth..

1:20

²⁰ The mystery of the <u>seven stars</u> which you saw in My right hand, and the <u>seven golden lampstands:</u> The <u>seven stars</u> are the <u>angels of the seven churches,</u> and the <u>seven lampstands</u> which you saw are <u>the seven churches.</u>

Jesus tells the mystery of **seven stars** and **seven golden lampstands**.

"The seven stars are the angels of the seven churches" in Chapters 2 and 3;

"The seven lampstands...are the seven churches."

-CONTINUED FROM PREVIOUS PAGE-

-CONTINUED FROM PREVIOUS PAGE-

Vv. 12-16

Ezekiel 1:26-28 ²⁶And above the firmament <u>over their heads</u> *was* the likeness of a throne, in appearance like a sapphire stone; on <u>the likeness of the throne *was* a likeness with the appearance of a man high above it</u>. ²⁷Also from the appearance of His waist and upward I saw, as it were, the color of amber with the appearance of fire all around within it; and from the appearance of His waist and downward I saw, as it were, the appearance of fire with brightness all around. ²⁸Like the appearance of a rainbow in a cloud on a rainy day, so *was* the appearance of the brightness all around it. This *was* the appearance of the likeness of the <u>glory</u> of the LORD. So when I saw *it*, I fell on my face, and I heard a voice of One speaking.

Vv. 12-16

<u>Ezekiel 1:26-28</u>: The Godhead appears in the likeness of humanity, though *God is Spirit* (John 4:24) **the likeness of the throne *was* a likeness with the appearance of a man high above it**. The Messiah, God incarnate, Jesus, is the representative of the "fullness of the Godhead (Colossians 2:9), so this can be a prelude to the incarnation ("became flesh and dwelt among us" John 1:14) of Messiah in His character as Savior and Judge.

Jesus Speaks to the First Two of Seven Churches

"The Things Which are," is the Present Church Age

The number *seven* is God's number representing perfection and completion. The seven Churches here in chapters 2 and 3 could be representing all the churches of today's Church Age.

2:1-5

In verse 1 the Lord Jesus emphasizes the description of Himself in Chapter 1 (Revelation 1:13, Revelation 1:16). The message to the church at **Ephesus** who labored, were patient, could not stand those who **are evil**, **tested** spirits and **found** some to be **liars**, *******but* they **left** (*not necessarily lost nor have come back*) their **first love**** and must **repent**. *The Lord introduces Himself as the One **who holds the seven stars in His right hand, who walks in the midst of the seven lampstands**. Most of the descriptions of the Lord in these letters are similar to that which is found in Chapter 1*. After complementing the Ephesians for their **works, labor,** intolerance of **evil**, and ability to discern false **apostles** and deal with them accordingly, the Lord confronted them with their tragedy—*that they had **left** their **first love**. The fire of their affection had died down. They were still *mostly* sound in doctrine and active in service, but the true motive of all worship and service was missing* because, apparently, they were not in the whole counsel of God (Acts 20:27; Ephesians 6:13-14a). *If they would fail to **remember** and to **repent**, the Lord would **remove** the **lampstand** at Ephesus; that is, the assembly would cease to exist. Its testimony would die out.*

¹ To the angel of the church of <u>Ephesus</u> write, 'These things says He who holds the seven stars in His right hand, who walks in the midst of the seven golden lampstands; ²I know your works, your labor, your patience, and that you cannot bear those who <u>are evil</u>. And you have <u>tested</u> those who say they are apostles and are not, and have <u>found</u> them <u>liars;</u> ³ and you have persevered and have patience, and have labored for My name's sake and have not become weary. ⁴ Nevertheless I have *this* against you, that you have <u>left</u> your <u>first love.</u> ⁵ <u>Remember</u> therefore from where you have fallen; <u>repent</u> and do the first works, or else I will come to you quickly and <u>remove</u> your <u>lampstand</u> from its place—unless you repent.

V. 1-5

Revelation 1:13 and in the midst of the seven lampstands *One* like the Son of Man, clothed with a garment down to the feet and girded about the chest with a golden band. ...

Revelation 1:16 He had in His right hand seven stars, out of His mouth went a sharp two-edged sword, and His countenance *was* like the sun shining in its strength.

V. 1-5

Revelation 1:13, Revelation 1:16: *There was nothing between Christ the Lord and the individual lampstands; no agency, hierarchy, or organization. Each church was independent.* Local churches need no earthly head office with man to make inapt decisions and interfere with God's design. Satan can easily attack an earthly headquarters and that can affect many local churches, but it is more difficult for Satan to go after each self-sufficient local church which recognizes the only Head of the assembly to be the Lord Jesus Christ.

Acts 20:27 "For I have not shunned to declare to you the whole counsel of God."

Acts 20:27: God does not hide any of His Scripture and neither should we.

Ephesians 6:13-14a [13]Therefore take the whole armor of God, that you may be able to withstand in the evil day, and having done all, to stand. [14a]Stand therefore, having girded your waist with truth...

Ephesians 6:13-14a: *It isn't surprising that God's Word tells us the first piece of armor is **truth.** We must take the responsibility to seriously uphold His truth. But it is also necessary for the **truth** to hold us—accountable.*

2:6

⁶ But this you have, that you hate the deeds of the Nicōlāitans, which I also hate.

In verse 6 *we cannot be sure who the **Nicōlāitans** were.* However, they are mentioned again in Revelation 2:15 immediately following *the doctrine of Bālaam* in Revelation 2:14, and the Lord repeats His hatred of their deeds and their doctrine. Their teaching, it seems, is that of the false prophet Bālaam—the wicked apostate who loved the wages of unrighteousness (Numbers 22:7; Numbers 25:1-2⁽³⁾; 2 Peter 2:15⁽³⁾).

2:7

⁷ He who has an ear, let him hear what the Spirit says to the churches. To him who overcomes I will give to eat from the tree of life, which is in the midst of the Paradise of God.'

The Ephesians' overcoming would prove the reality of their conversion experience. *In general, however, an overcomer is one who believes that Jesus Christ is the Son of God (1 John 5:4-5).*

V. 6

Revelation 2:14-15 ¹⁴ "But I have a few things against you [angel of the church of Pergamos], because you have there those who hold <u>the doctrine of Bālaam</u>, who taught Bālak to put a stumbling block before the children of Israel, to eat <u>things sacrificed to idols</u>, and to commit <u>sexual immorality</u>. ¹⁵ Thus you also have those who hold the doctrine <u>of the Nicōlāitans</u>, which thing I hate."

Numbers 22:7 So the elders of Mōab and the elders of Midian departed with the <u>diviner's fee</u> in their hand, and they came to Bālaam and spoke to him the words of Bālak.

Numbers 25:1-2 ¹Now Israel remained in Acacia Grove, and the people began to commit harlotry with the women of Mōab. ²They invited the people to the sacrifices of their gods, and the people ate and bowed down to their gods.

2 Peter 2:15 They have forsaken the right way and gone astray, following the way of Bālaam the *son* of Bēor, who <u>loved the wages</u> of unrighteousness;

V. 7

1 John 5:4-5 ⁴For whatever is born of God <u>overcomes</u> the world. And this is the victory that has overcome the world—our <u>faith</u>. ⁵Who is he who <u>overcomes</u> the world, but he who believes that Jesus is the Son of God?

V. 6

<u>Revelation 2 14-15</u>: **The doctrine of Bālaam** and **of the Nicōlāitans** are doctrines the Lord hates. This **doctrine** includes *****things sacrificed to idols** and **sexual immorality** and the practice of preaching for hire (<u>Numbers Chapters 22-25</u>).*****

In <u>2 Peter 2:15</u> the main reason the false teachers claim to teach the truth of God's Word is because they use their so-called ministry for financial gain. 1 Timothy 6:5b: *They suppose that godliness is a means of gain.*

V. 7

*****The world's methods are a monstrous scheme of temptations, always trying to get us to lose our focus on God and from what is eternal, and seeking to occupy us with what is temporary and sensual. People of the world have become the victims of temporary, passing things. Only the believer **who is born of God** can actually **overcome the world**, because by **faith** (<u>1 John 5:4-5</u>) he is able to rise above the *temporary*, perishing things of this world and to see things in their true, *eternal* perspective. It is not the great scientist or philosopher or psychologist, but the simple believer who realizes the difference between things which are <u>temporary</u> and things which are <u>eternal</u>.***** The scientist might know a lot of information, but the difference between knowledge and wisdom is this: A knowledgeable man can know a lot of information, but with wisdom from God a man can tell what is true or false about the things he knows.

⁸ And to the angel of the <u>church</u> in <u>Smyrna</u> write, 'These things says the First and the Last, who was dead, and came to life:

2:8

This message is to the **church** at **Smyrna** who will be tested in **tribulation** by the **devil** for **ten days** in **prison**, <u>but **he who overcomes**</u> will <u>**not** be hurt **by the second death**</u> (hell, the lake of fire) and <u>will receive the</u> **crown of life**.

⁹ I know your works, <u>tribulation,</u> and poverty [lack of money and temporary material things] (but you are rich [**but** these saints are "rich" in spiritual blessings]); and *I know* the blasphemy of those who say they are Jews and are not, but *are* a synagogue of Satan.

2:9

The Lord encourages us *to be willing to die rather than deny our faith in* Him (<u>Matthew 10:22b</u>).

¹⁰ Do not fear any of those things which you are about to suffer. Indeed, the <u>devil</u> is about to throw *some* of you into <u>prison,</u> that you may be tested, and you will have tribulation <u>ten days.</u> Be faithful until death, and I will give you the <u>crown of life.</u>

2:10

The **crown of life** is for human testing even to martyrdom. The Lord Jesus commends the church in Smyrna and lets them know they will be persecuted (<u>John 15:20</u>), but He holds nothing against them.

¹¹ He who has an ear, let him hear what the Spirit says to the churches. <u>He who overcomes shall <u>not be hurt by the second death</u>.</u>'"

2:11

Again the willing hearer is encouraged to listen to the Spirit's advice (<u>Psalm 27:14</u>). *Here an overcomer is one who proves the reality of his faith by choosing to go to heaven with a good conscience rather than stay on earth with a bad one. He will not be affected by **the second death**, the doom of all unbelievers (<u>Revelation 20:6</u>, <u>Revelation 20:14</u>).*

V. 9

Matthew 10:22b "But he who endures to the end will be saved."

V. 9

"He that endures to the end will be saved". This is a promise of perseverance not a teaching that salvation may be lost. Rather, it indicates that those who are truly saved will indeed endure to the end.** John 10:28-29 confirms the believer's life is eternal. Nothing can change this fact. (Romans 8:38-39)

V. 10

John 15:20 "Remember the word that I said to you, 'A servant is not greater than his master.' If they persecuted Me, they will also persecute you. If they kept My word, they will keep yours also."

V. 10

We can expect to be persecuted (John 15:20), no matter how slight or how severe. *But we cannot expect better treatment than our Lord Jesus received. Our word will be refused just as was the Savior's*—and still is rejected by many to this day.

V. 11

Psalm 27:14 Wait on the LORD; be of good courage, and He shall strengthen your heart; wait, I say, on the LORD!

Revelation 20:6 Blessed and holy *is* he who has part in the first resurrection. Over such the second death has no power, but they shall be priests of God and of Christ, and shall reign with Him a thousand years. ...

V. 11

The first resurrection
(Revelation 20:6) has three principal phases:

1) the resurrection of Christ;

2) the resurrection of His Church with the Rapture;

3) the resurrection of Old Testament and Tribulation martyred saints on earth.

Revelation 20:14 Then Death and Hādēs were cast into the lake of fire. This is the second death.

The second death is preceded by a resurrection of the unsaved to face the Lord at the Great White Throne. In this **second death** the unbeliever just keeps dying; it is **eternal punishment in the lake of fire** which will never be quenched (Isaiah 66:24; Jeremiah 7:20; Ezekiel. 20:47-48; Mark 9:44, Mark 9:46, Mark 9:48; Jude 7).

Jesus Speaks to the Third and Fourth of Seven Churches

¹² "And to the angel of the church in <u>Pergamos</u> write, 'These things says He who has the <u>sharp two-edged sword:</u>

2:12

The message to the **church** at **Pergamos** who held **fast** to the **name** of Jesus *but* <u>ate things sacrificed to idols</u> and <u>committed sexual immorality</u> must **repent**. *The sharp two-edged sword** is the word of God (<u>Hebrews 4:12-13</u>) and represents Jesus Christ as Judge* (<u>John 5:22</u>, <u>John 5:27</u>).

¹³ I know your works, and where you dwell, where <u>Satan's throne</u> *is*. And you hold fast to My name, and did not deny My faith even in the days in which <u>Antipas</u> *was* My faithful martyr, who was killed among you, where Satan dwells.

2:13

The reason **Pergamos** was called the place of **Satan's throne** in verse 13 was because *Pergamos** was the Asia Minor headquarters for the cult of emperor-worship. **Antipas** was of this assembly, and he was martyred for his confession of the Lord Jesus. He was the first known Asian to die for refusing to worship the Roman emperor.

¹⁴ <u>But</u> I have a few things against you, because you have there those who hold <u>the doctrine of Bālaam</u>, who taught Bālak to put a stumbling block before the children of Israel, to eat things sacrificed to idols, and to commit sexual immorality. ¹⁵ Thus you also have those who hold <u>the doctrine of the Nicōlāitans</u>, which thing I hate. ¹⁶<u>Repent</u>, or else I will come to you quickly and will fight against them with the sword of My mouth. ¹⁷ He who has an ear, let him hear what the Spirit says to the churches. To him who overcomes I will give some of the hidden manna to eat. And I will give him a white stone, and on the stone a new name written which no one knows except him who receives *it*.'

2:14-17

But the Lord reprimanded them in verses 14-15 for permitting men with evil **doctrine** to attempt to continue in Christian fellowship.* Some have said that **The doctrine of Bālaam** written in 1400 BC (Numbers Chapters 22-25; 31) indoctrinates flocks of the churches still today (<u>2 Peter 2:15</u>; <u>Jude 11b</u>). Also **the doctrine of the Nicōlāitans** could possibly be pointing to those who serve for monetary gain as well as eating things sacrificed to idols and to committing sexual immorality (1 Timothy 6:3-5, <u>1 Timothy 6:10</u>). So additional to the problems mentioned, this refers to <u>the practice of preaching for hire</u> (<u>John 10:11-13</u>).

V. 12

Hebrews 4:12-13 ¹²For the <u>word</u> of God *is* living and powerful, and sharper than any two-edged sword, piercing even to the division of soul and spirit, and of joints and marrow, and is a discerner of the thoughts and intents of the heart. ¹³And there is no creature hidden from His sight, but all things *are* naked and open to the eyes of Him to whom we *must* give account.

John 5:22 "For the Father judges no one, but has committed <u>all judgment</u> to the Son."...
John 5:27 "and has given Him authority to execute judgment also, because He is the Son of Man."

V. 12

<u>Hebrews 4:12-13</u>: *The Greek here for <u>*word*</u> is *logos*. This refers, not to the living Word <u>Jesus</u>, but to the <u>living written word</u>, the Bible.* It is the Word that judges us, not we who judge the word. Nothing escapes our Creator's notice; He, *being omniscient, is constantly aware of all that is going on in the universe.* Unbelief is detected by the living Lord.

<u>John 5:22, John 5:27</u>: <u>All things</u> <u>now</u> *and* at the <u>final judgment</u> are <u>committed to the Son</u>, as we honor the Father. And every one who does not thus honor the Son, does not honor the Father who sent Him (1 John 2:23).

Vv. 14-17

2 Peter 2:15 They have forsaken the right way and gone astray, following the way of Balāam the *son* of Bēor, who loved the wages of unrighteousness;
Jude 11b ...have run greedily in the error of Balāam for profit, ...

1 Timothy 6:10 For <u>the love of money is the root of all kinds of evil</u>, for which some have strayed from the faith in their greediness, and pierced themselves through with many sorrows.

John 10:11-13 ¹¹ "I am the good shepherd. The good shepherd gives his life for the sheep. ¹² But a <u>hireling</u> [**hired man**], *he who is* not the shepherd, one who does not own the sheep, sees the wolf coming and leaves the sheep and flees; and the wolf catches the sheep and scatters them. ¹³ The hireling flees because he is a hireling and does not care about the sheep."

Vv. 14-17

In Revelation 2:15 <u>**the doctrine of the Nicōlāitans, which thing I hate**</u> it is interesting to note that hate is the antonym of love. **The love of money is the root of all kinds of evil.**

[18] And to the angel of the church in <u>Thyatīra</u> write, 'These things says the Son of God, who has <u>eyes</u> like a flame of fire, and His <u>feet</u> like fine <u>brass</u>: [19] I know your works, love, service, faith, and your patience; and *as* for your works, the last *are* more important than the first. [20] Nevertheless I have a few things against you, because you allow that woman Jezebel, who calls herself a prophetess, to teach and seduce My servants to commit sexual immorality and eat things sacrificed to idols. [21] And I gave her time to repent of her sexual immorality, and she did not repent. [22] <u>Indeed I will cast her into a sickbed, and those who commit adultery with her into great tribulation, unless they repent of their deeds.</u> [23] <u>I will kill her children with death,</u> and all the churches shall know that I am He who searches the minds and hearts. And I will give to each one of you according to your works. [24] Now to you I say, and to the rest in Thyatīra, as many as do not have this doctrine, <u>who have not known the depths of Satan,</u> as they say, I will put on you <u>no other burden</u>. [25] But hold fast what you have till I come. [26] And <u>he who overcomes, and keeps</u> My <u>works until the end,</u> to him I will give <u>power over the nations</u>— [27] 'He shall rule them with a rod of iron; they shall be dashed to pieces like the potter's vessels'—as I also have received from My Father;

2:18-27

*The **eyes** speak of piercing vision, and the **feet** of **brass** threaten judgment.* The message to the church at **Thyatīra** who had works of love, faith, and patience *but* had a <u>woman</u> called Jezebel *teaching* (<u>Numbers 16:3</u>, <u>Numbers 16:31-32a</u>; <u>Isaiah 3:12b</u>) and seducing Christ's servants to commit sexual and spiritual immorality (Revelation 2:20) and eat things sacrificed to idols. Christ gave her time to repent, but she did not repent. Therefore Jesus says, "**Indeed I will cast her into a sickbed** (in place of her bed of lust), **and those who commit adultery with her into great tribulation** (they will not be raptured), _**unless**_ they _**repent**_ of their deeds. I will kill her children with death**"...*Those **who have not known the depths of Satan** will receive **no other burden, and** to **he who overcomes, and keeps** Christ's **works until the end will** receive **power over the nations**. Then **all the churches** would **know that** the Lord is watching and that He rewards **according to** man's deeds.

Vv. 18-27

Numbers 16:3 They [250 Israelites of the congregation] gathered together against Moses and Aaron, and said to them, "You *take* [assume too much for] too much upon yourselves, for <u>all</u> the congregation *is* holy, every one of them, and the LORD *is* among them. Why then do you exalt yourselves above the assembly of the LORD?"...

Numbers 16:31-32a ³¹Now it came to pass, as he finished speaking all these words, that the ground split apart under them, ³²ᵃand the earth opened its mouth and swallowed them up...

Vv. 18-27

John 10:11-13; <u>Numbers 16:3, Numbers 16:31-32a</u>: Our Lord and Savior is tremendously serious about His prescription for how to conduct the church meeting. God's Word warns us that only men are to speak in the churches (1 Corinthians 14:34; 1 Timothy 2:11-12). Jesus also gave a warning that a **hireling** is one who serves for monetary gain. A **hireling** in any <u>*organizational*</u> occupation serves for pay. There are many hirelings in religious *organizations* that are <u>*run like businesses*</u> today. These are *men who choose the ministry as a comfortable occupation, without true love for God's sheep.* When danger approaches, the heart of the preacher will show who sincerely cares about the flock. Further, <u>hiring</u> women in religious leadership positions then doubly contradicts the Scriptures which prescribe separate essential roles for women than for men (1 Corinthians 14:34-35; 1 Timothy 2:11-14; 1 Timothy 3:1-13; Titus 1:5-9; Titus 2:1-5).

Isaiah 3:12b "And <u>women rule over them</u>. O My people! Those who lead you cause you to err, and destroy the way of your paths."

<u>Isaiah 3:12b</u>: **indicates the utter failure of male responsibility and spiritual leadership in their society as **women rule over them****...and **cause you to err**. Sadly, we see the same happening today which happened in Isaiah's time 2,700 years ago. The first time man letdown his wife was when Adam did not protect Eve when she took of the fruit and ate: Genesis 3:6: *So when the woman saw that the tree was good for food, that it was pleasant to the eyes, and a tree desirable to make one wise, she took of its fruit and ate. She also gave to her husband with her, and he ate.* Of course, Adam should have reminded her of when God commanded not to *eat of* that fruit or that they would *surely die.* (Genesis 3:17) But he did not take on the responsibility; rather he listened to her instead of listening to God.

2:28

The Lord Jesus is the Bright and Morning Star (Revelation 22:16). Just as the morning star appears in the heavens before the sun rises, so Christ will appear as the Morning Star to rapture His Church to heaven before His Second Coming when He will appear as the Sun of Righteousness to reign over the earth (1 Thessalonians 4:13-18; Malachi 4:2a).

²⁸ and I will give him the morning star.

²⁹ He who has an ear, let him hear what the Spirit says to the churches.'"

2:29

Thus the overcomer is promised a part in the Rapture. From this point on, only those who overcome are expected to have **an ear** to **hear what the Spirit says to the churches**.*

V. 28
Revelation 22:16 "I, Jesus, have sent My angel to testify to <u>you</u> these things in the churches. I am the Root and the Offspring of David, the <u>Bright and Morning Star</u>."

V. 28
The original Greek for **you in the <u>Revelation 22:16</u> is plural—the revelation is for <u>all</u> believers** T**he Bright and Morning Star**, Jesus, will soon rapture His bride. The Lord Jesus made known the surety of life and immortality: (2 Timothy 1:10b: *our Savior Jesus Christ, who has abolished death and brought life and immortality to light through the gospel.*).

1 Thessalonians 4:13-18 [13]But I do not want you to be ignorant, brethren, concerning those who have fallen asleep [died], lest you sorrow as others who have no hope. [14]For if we believe that Jesus died and rose again, even so God will bring with Him those who sleep in Jesus. [15]For this we say to you by the word of the Lord, that we who are alive *and* remain until the coming of the Lord will by no means precede those who are asleep. [16]For the Lord Himself will descend from heaven with a shout, with the voice of an archangel, and with the trumpet of God. And the dead in Christ will rise first. [17]Then we who are alive *and* remain shall be caught up together with them in the clouds to meet the Lord in the air. And thus we shall always be with the Lord. [18]Therefore comfort one another with these words.
1 Thessalonians 5:1-4 [1]But concerning the times and the seasons, brethren, you have no need that I should write you. [2]For you yourselves know perfectly that the day of the Lord so comes as a thief in the night. [3]For when <u>they</u> say, "Peace and safety!" then <u>sudden</u> destruction comes upon them, as labor pains upon a pregnant woman. And <u>they</u> shall not escape. [4]But <u>you</u>, <u>brethren</u>, are not in darkness, so that this Day should overtake you as a thief.
1 Thessalonians 5:9...For God did <u>not</u> <u>appoint us to wrath,</u> <u>but</u> to obtain salvation through our Lord Jesus Christ.

We know from the New Testament that all Church Age believers will be raptured before the Tribulation begins (<u>1 Thessalonians 4:13-18; 1 Thessalonians 5:1-4, 1 Thessalonians 5:9</u>; 2 Thessalonians 1:6-7; 2 Thessalonians 2:1-8; Romans 11:25-26; Revelation 4:1). When reflecting on the "Rapture Passage" in <u>1 Thessalonians 4:13-18</u> the reader needs to realize that in the original scroll there were no numbered chapters or verses. The message streams right along to <u>5:1-4 and 5:9</u>. The <u>day of the Lord</u> can refer to any day the Lord is to make judgment. Keeping the message in context, this time being spoken of is the judgment for rewards for the raptured believers. It is unlikely the Groom would allow *part of His bride* to be subjected to the wrath of Satan's Antichrist in any part of the Tribulation, and <u>verse 9</u> confirms we are <u>saved from wrath and saved for eternal life</u>. Romans 5:9 and 1 Thessalonians 1:10 further confirm this truth.

Malachi 4:2a But to you who fear My name <u>The Sun of Righteousness</u> shall arise with healing in His wings...

<u>Malachi 4:2a:</u> ****The Sun of Righteousness** is a figurative representation of the Messiah** Those who are born-again believers will overcome the world having been healed of their sin condition and *will triumph over their foes like ashes under their feet* (Malachi 4:3).

The Lord Jesus Christ Speaks to Two of the Last Three of Seven Churches

¹ "And to the angel of the church in <u>Sardis</u> write, 'These things says He who has the seven Spirits of God and the seven stars: "I know your works, that you have a name that you are alive, but you are <u>dead</u>. ² Be watchful, and <u>strengthen</u> the things which remain, that are ready to die, for I have not found your <u>works</u> perfect before God. ³ Remember therefore how you have received and heard; hold fast and <u>repent</u>. Therefore if you will not watch, I <u>will come upon</u> you as a <u>thief</u>, and you will not know what hour I will come upon you. ⁴ You have a <u>few</u> names even in Sardis who have not defiled their garments; and they shall walk with Me in white, for they are worthy.

⁵ He who overcomes shall be clothed in white garments, and I will not blot out his name from the <u>Book of Life</u>; but I will confess his name before My Father and before His angels. ⁶ He who has an ear, let him hear what the Spirit says to the churches.'"

3:1-4

The message is to the church at **Sardis** who have a name indicating they are **alive** (*Sardis* means *those escaping* or *renovation*), **<u>but</u>** they are **dead.** Perhaps they *simply went through a formal, dull routine and were not overflowing with spiritual life.* Obviously, their **works** are not perfect before God. They must have been so **dead** in spirit and **works** that some of them had no soundness of faith. Their belief in the genuine doctrines taught in the Scriptures must have become unrecognizable. So they must **repent** and watch for Christ's return or He **will come upon** them like **a thief**. Only a **few** of them were walking with the Lord and were worthy.

3:5-6

Those who have sincerely repented, and believe the Father sent His Son to shed His blood to forgive them, to die so that they can have life, and resurrected Him back to life will have their names written in **the Book of Life**. We all need to be constantly aware that authors of Bible commentaries, Bible dictionaries, and even churches that use the name of Jesus and Christianity can be controlled by Satan's tricks. We all need to <u>arm ourselves with the whole counsel of God</u>—that is, the entire Word of God—the Bible—and we need to pray without ceasing (<u>Ephesians 6:10-20</u>).

-CONTINUED ON NEXT PAGE
UNDER COMMENTARY!-

Vv. 5-6

Ephesians 6:10-20 ¹⁰Finally, my brethren, <u>be strong</u> in the Lord and in the power of His might. ¹¹Put on the <u>whole armor of God</u>, that you may be able to stand against the wiles [schemings] of the devil. ¹²For we do not wrestle against flesh and blood, but against principalities, against powers, against the rulers of the darkness of this age, against spiritual *hosts* of wickedness in the heavenly *places*. ¹³Therefore take up the <u>whole armor of God</u>, that you may be able to withstand in the evil day, and having done all, to stand. ¹⁴Stand therefore, having girded your waist with truth, having put on the breastplate of righteousness, ¹⁵and having shod your feet with the preparation of the gospel of peace; ¹⁶above all, taking the shield of faith with which you will be able to quench all the fiery darts of the wicked one. ¹⁷And take the helmet of salvation, and the sword of the Spirit, which is the word of God; ¹⁸praying always with all prayer and supplication in the Spirit, being watchful to this end with all perseverance and supplication for all the saints— ¹⁹and for me, that utterance may be given to me, that I may open my mouth <u>boldly</u> to <u>make known</u> the mystery of <u>the gospel</u>, ²⁰for which I am an ambassador in chains; that in it I may speak boldly, as I ought to speak.

Vv. 5-6

Christ <u>lives</u> in each and every believer. The <u>life</u> we now <u>live</u> in the flesh we live by faith in the Son of God. (Galatians 2:20). A church which follows Christ is a church that is <u>alive</u>. We are the <u>living body</u> of the <u>living Head</u>—the Lord Jesus Christ. Each <u>living</u> believer is a member of the <u>living</u> Body—the universal Church. An "*organization*" is **_not_** a "living thing". A church which is controlled by an organizational headquarters is a **dead** church (Revelation 3:1). A church that is "<u>alive</u>"—a <u>living</u> body—responds to the directions, the prescription and the commands, given by the <u>living</u> Head. Satan attacks the Body to kill Christianity, so each member of the Body is exhorted to put on the **whole armor of God** (<u>Ephesians 6:10-20</u>): When we are exhorted to **speak boldly** in Ephesians 6:19-20 we need not speak only to others **to make known**... **the gospel**, but we need also to **speak boldly** to our God. The indwelling Spirit of God within us helps us to remember to give Him **thanks always for all things...in the name of our Lord Jesus Christ**; because **all things** are made through Him (John 1:3).

-CONTINUED ON NEXT PAGE UNDER REFERENCES!-

-CONTINUED ON NEXT PAGE UNDER REFERENCES COMMENTARY!-

**-VERSES 5-6 REPEATED
FROM PREVIOUS PAGE-**

-CONTINUED FROM PREVIOUS PAGE-

[5] He who overcomes shall be clothed in white garments, and I will not blot out his name from the <u>Book of Life;</u> but I will confess his name before My Father and before His angels. [6] He who has an ear, let him hear what the Spirit says to the churches.'"

3:5-6

The Lord Jesus Christ who is the Judge will confess the name only of genuine believers (<u>Revelation 7:14b</u>; <u>Philippians 4:3d</u>; <u>Revelation 19:20b</u>, <u>Revelation 20:15</u>; <u>Matthew 10:32-33</u>). The Son of God is our Advocate who will confess our names before the Father. With the magnificent title of Mediator, the Spirit in God's Word instructs us to pray to the Father in the name of the Lord Jesus Christ (<u>Ephesians 5:20</u>).

-CONTINUED FROM PREVIOUS PAGE-

-CONTINUED FROM PREVIOUS PAGE-

Vv. 5-6
Revelation 7:14b "These are the ones who come out of the great tribulation, and washed their robes and made them white in the blood of the Lamb."

Vv. 5-6
Revelation 6:9; Revelation 7:14b: The unbelievers *prior* to the Rapture, but, who will become believers and be slain for maintaining their testimony during the Great Tribulation will come out of this horrific time wearing white robes which have been washed in the blood of the Savior. The 144,000 Jews become believers at this time.

Philippians 4:3d …whose names *are* in the Book of Life.

Philippians 4:3d: Their names will be in the **Book of Life** and they will live everlasting lives with the previously raptured saints.

Revelation 19:20b These two were cast alive into the lake of fire burning with brimstone
Revelation 20:15 And anyone not found written in the Book of Life was cast into the lake of fire.
Matthew 10:32-33 [32]"Therefore whoever confesses Me before men, him I will also confess before My Father who is in heaven. [33] But whoever denies Me before men, him I will also deny before My Father who is in heaven."

Revelation 19:20b; Revelation 20:15 Matthew 10:32-33: The individuals who take the mark of the beast and deny Jesus will also be resurrected—but resurrected to judgment at the Great White Throne and will be thrown into the lake of fire. The importance of listening—that is, absorbing and believing with a sincere heart—cannot be more emphasized than the Lord Jesus Christ has already done in Revelation 3:6.

Ephesians 5:20 giving thanks always for all things to God the Father in the name of our Lord Jesus Christ.

Ephesians 5:20: We overcome and win the battle by staying focused in the Word of God, spreading the Gospel message, and continuing endlessly in prayer **to the Father in the name of the Lord Jesus Christ.**

⁷ And to the angel of the church of <u>Philadelphia</u> write, 'These things says He who is holy, He who is true, *He who has the key of David, He who opens and no one shuts, and shuts and no one opens*": ⁸I know your works. See, I have set before you an open door, and no one can shut it; for you have a little strength, have <u>kept</u> My word, and have not denied My name. ⁹Indeed I will make *those* of the synagogue of Satan, who say they are Jews and are not, but lie—indeed I will make them come and worship before your feet, and to know that I have loved you. ¹⁰Because you have kept My command to persevere, I also will keep you from the hour of trial which shall come upon the whole world, to test those who dwell on the earth. ¹¹Behold, I am coming quickly! Hold fast what you have, that no one may take your crown. ¹²He who overcomes, I will make him a pillar in the temple of My God, and he shall go out no more. I will write on him the name of My God and the name of the city of My God, the New Jerusalem, which comes down out of heaven from My God. And *I will write on him* My new name. ¹³He who has an ear, let him hear what the Spirit says to the churches.'"

3:7-13

The message to the church at ****Philadelphia** (its name means "Brotherly Love")** who have faithfully **kept** God's Word and have been righteous and faithful in all the counsel of God. *By having been true believers they will be raptured, and they will be kept out of the Seven-year Tribulation Period.* This is the church which goes by the principles and prescriptions of the New Testament. This is the church we desire to emulate. Verse 7 repeats and fulfills the prophecy of Isaiah 22:22. We, like the church at **Philadelphia** want to be ever pleasing to our God (<u>Philippians 2:13</u>; <u>Colossians 1:10a</u>; <u>1 Thessalonians 4:1b</u>; <u>Hebrews 13:21</u>) and see every soul in His flock receive blessings referred to in the Book of Revelation (1:3; 19:9; 20:6; 22:7, 22:14). There are two more blessings in Revelation, but these refer to the saints who will come to believe during the Tribulation Period (<u>Revelation 14:13b</u>; <u>Revelation 16:15b</u>), and it is our prayer that all in our midst will be raptured, either from the grave or while still alive and will not have to go through the Tribulation Period.

Chapter 3 Verses 7-13
References

Vv. 7-13

Philippians 2:13 for it is God who works in you both to will and to do for *His* good pleasure.
Colossians 1:10a that you may walk worthy of the Lord, fully pleasing *Him*,

1 Thessalonians 4:1b you received from us how you ought to walk and to please God;
Hebrews 13:21 complete in every good work to do His will, working in you what is well pleasing in His sight, through Jesus Christ, to whom *be* glory forever and ever. Amen.

Revelation 14:13b "'Blessed *are* the dead who die in the Lord from now on.'"
Revelation 16:15b "Blessed *is* he who watches, and keeps his garments, lest he walk naked and they see his shame."

Chapter 3 Verses 7-13
References Commentary

Vv. 7-13

Sincere confession of Jesus Christ involves commitment to Him as Lord and the One and Only Savior. The indwelling Holy Spirit guides each believer to walk worthy of the calling and to be pleasing to Him (Philippians 2:13, Colossians 1:10a).

We need to stay focused and listen to and apply God's Word to be pleasing to Him (1 Thessalonians 4:1b; Hebrews 13:21). We also need to remember the price He paid for our souls.

And we need to stay motivated by the hope we have of His soon coming appearing to take us up alive forever (Revelation 14:13b; Revelation 16:15b).

Jesus Speaks to the Seventh of
Seven Churches

[1] 4"And to the angel of the church of the <u>Lāodicēans</u> write, 'These things says the Amen, the Faithful and True Witness, <u>the Beginning of creation of God</u>: [15] I know your works, that you are neither cold nor hot. I could wish you were cold or hot. [16] So then, because you are <u>lukewarm,</u> and neither cold nor hot, I will vomit you out of My mouth. [17] Because you say, 'I am rich [**rich** in temporary earthly things; the opposite of **rich** in spiritual blessings as we saw in Revelation 2:9], have become wealthy, and have need of nothing'—and do not know that you <u>are wretched, miserable, poor, blind, and naked</u>—

3:14-17

The message to the church at **Lāodicēa** who were only **lukewarm** will experience the Lord Jesus vomiting them out of His mouth...unless they **repent** (Revelation 3:19).

The very name *Lāodicēa means either *the people ruling* or *the judgment of the people*.* They did not credit the Lord Jesus Christ with being the Head of the church, the Almighty Creator, nor being the worthy Sovereign Righteous Judge.

The expression, **the Beginning of the creation of God"** means at the very least that Jesus began all **creation** (<u>Isaiah 44:24</u>; <u>Colossians 1:16-17</u>; <u>John 1:1-3</u>, <u>Hebrews 1:8-10</u>). He is the Head of the new creation: the church. He was never created; He is *eternal*. He is pre-eminent over all creation.

2 Corinthians 6:17a: *Therefore, if anyone is in Christ, he is a <u>new</u> <u>creation</u>;* In Revelation 5:11 the raptured Church believers are referred to as *<u>living creatures</u>. And the number of them was* [will be] *ten thousand times ten thousand, and thousands of thousands.*

The **Lāodicēans** are **rich**, have need of nothing, and do not even realize they **are wretched, miserable, poor, blind, and naked**. Those who listen and heed and overcome will be saved.

Vv. 14-17

Isaiah 44:24 Thus says the LORD, your <u>Redeemer</u>, and He who <u>formed you from the womb</u>: I *am* <u>the LORD</u>, who makes all *things*, who stretches out the heavens all alone, who spreads abroad the earth by Myself;

Colossians 1:16-17 [16]For by Him all things were created that are in heaven and that are on earth, visible and invisible, whether thrones or dominions or principalities or powers. All things were created through Him and for Him. [17]And He is before all things, and in Him all things consist.

John 1:1-3 [1]In the beginning was the Word, and the Word was with God, and the Word was God. [2]He was in the beginning with God. [3]All things were made through Him, and without Him nothing was made that was made.

Vv. 14-17

*God presents Himself to the faithful remnant as **Redeemer**, Jehovah (**the LORD**), our Creator* who started our life in the womb (<u>Isaiah 44:24; Colossians 1:16-17; John 1:1-3</u>). He loves us from eternal time past and expects our life on earth to last "from the womb to the tomb" (Alveda King).

Hebrews 1:8-10 [8]But to the Son *He says:* *"<u>Your throne, O God</u>, is forever and ever; A scepter of righteousness is the scepter of Your kingdom. [9]You have loved righteousness and hated lawlessness; therefore <u>God</u>, Your God, has anointed You with the oil of gladness more than Your companions."* [10]And: *"You, <u>LORD</u>, in the beginning laid the foundation of <u>the earth, and the heavens</u> are the work of Your <u>hands</u>."*

God the Father is quoted in <u>Hebrews 1:8-10</u> calling His Son "God" and "LORD". <u>The Father</u> even testifies that <u>His Son created</u> **the earth and the heavens** with <u>His</u> <u>own</u> **hands**.

¹⁸ I counsel you <u>to buy from</u> Me <u>gold refined in the fire,</u> that you may be <u>rich</u>; and <u>white garments,</u> that you may be clothed, *that* the shame of your nakedness may not be revealed; and <u>anoint</u> your <u>eyes with eye salve,</u> that you may see.

3:18

The Lord counseled them **to buy from** <u>Him</u> **gold refined in the fire**. *This could mean divine righteousness, which is bought without money or price (<u>Isaiah 55:1</u>). Or it may mean genuine faith, which when tested **in the fire**, results in praise, honor, and glory at the revelation of Jesus Christ* (<u>1 Corinthians 3:9-14</u>; <u>1 Peter 1:7</u>; <u>Romans 11:25b</u>; <u>Revelation 22:12</u>). ***White garments** refers to practical righteousness in everyday life. And they should **anoint** their **eyes with eye salve**, that is, gain true spiritual vision through the enlightenment of the Holy Spirit.* Here the expression is used metaphorically to remind us of Christ applying salve to the blind man's eyes so that he, physically, could see (Mark 8:23-25).

V. 18

Isaiah 55:1 "Ho! Everyone who thirsts, come to the waters; and you who have no money, come, buy and eat. Yes, come, buy wine and milk without money and without price.

1 Corinthians 3:9-14 ⁹For we are God's fellow workers; you are God's field, *you are* God's building. ¹⁰According to the grace of God which was given to me, as a wise master builder I have laid the foundation, and another builds on it. But let each one take heed how he builds on it. ¹¹For no other foundation can anyone lay than that which is laid, which is Jesus Christ. ¹²Now if anyone builds on this foundation *with* gold, silver, precious stones, wood, hay, straw, ¹³each one's work will become clear; for the Day will declare it, because it will be revealed by fire; and the fire will test each one's work, of what sort it is. ¹⁴If anyone's work which he has built on *it* endures, he will receive a reward. If anyone's work is burned, he will suffer loss; but he himself will be saved, yet so as through fire.
1 Peter 1:7 that the genuineness of your faith, *being* much more precious than gold that perishes, though it is tested by fire, may be found to praise, honor, and glory at the revelation of Jesus Christ.
Romans 11:25b until the fullness of the Gentiles has come in.

Revelation 22:12 "And behold, I am coming quickly, and My reward *is* with Me, to give to every one according to his work."

V. 18

*The Spirit of God sends out the evangelistic message for His mankind creation to return to Himself. He invites **everyone** everywhere to His free (**without money**), saving grace* (Isaiah 55:1). *All that's necessary is a consciousness of need (**thirst**).*

1 Corinthians 3:9-14; 1 Peter 1:7; Romans 11:25b; Revelation 22:12: The harvest **field** is the humankind of the world. Quoting Erdman, "We are fellow-workers who belong to God and are working with one another." In the phrase *you are* **God's building**, the word *you* is plural meaning all believers. In 1 Corinthians 3:16 it is again plural. The Holy Spirit indwells each individual believer and the body of Christ—the Church. Believers are Christ's representatives, His ambassadors; we carry His aroma and reflect His light to shine on those who might realize their life changing relationship with the Lord Jesus Christ. The ultimate result is the finished "building"—the last Gentile to fill the only remaining vacant slot for the last piece of **gold, silver,** or **precious stone** who will be the one to complete the building of His Church—His Body—the Bride of Christ. When this **fullness of the Gentiles has come in**, then Christ will descend to the clouds, and the voice which John heard say, **"Come up here"** (Revelation 4:1) will be heard like a trumpet by all believers as He calls us up to meet Him in the air (1 Thessalonians 4:13-18)! Upon being with the Lord face-to-face, He will test us at the judgment seat of Christ and we will be rewarded **according to** our **work**.

We will see the elders with crowns in Revelation 4:4, so it is possible that some of the raptured believers are rewarded by Christ at this time— right after the Rapture. Then in Revelation 22:12, we read of the Lord Jesus saying, *"And behold, I am coming quickly, and My reward is with Me, to give to every one according to his work."* Perhaps this is a second time He is on the judgment seat near the beginning of His Millennial reign. These could possibly be rewards for those who will be saved during the Tribulation and for the Old Testament believers.

¹⁹ As many as I <u>love,</u> I rebuke and chasten. Therefore be zealous and <u>repent.</u> ²⁰Behold, I stand at the door and knock. If anyone hears My voice and opens the door, I will come in to him and dine with him, and he with Me. ²¹To him who overcomes I will grant to sit with Me on my throne, as I also overcame and sat down with My Father on His throne.

²² He who has an ear, let him hear what the Spirit says to the churches.'"

3:19-21

The Lord's **love** for the Church is stated in verse 19 verifying the fact that He rebukes and chastens them. He genuinely, truly cares and loves us all. Those who follow the Lord Jesus Christ in humility, rejection, and suffering will also follow Him in glory.

3:22

After the last verse, 3:22, **the churches** are not mentioned again until the last Chapter, <u>Revelation 22:16</u>, because the churches that have overcome are about to be **RAPTURED** in the very next verse after 3:22—Chapter 4:1 (matches Romans 11:25 and 1 Thessalonians 4:16-17). Since these believers are being taken up to meet Christ in the clouds, and then right on up into heaven, they will not suffer the upcoming Tribulation period with its events back on earth. Chapters 4 and 5 speak about the raptured Church in heaven during the time the unbelievers on earth are experiencing the beginning sorrows of the Tribulation Period. Their Seven-year Tribulation experiences are described in Chapters 6 to 19.

V. 22

Revelation 22:16 "I, Jesus, have sent My angel to testify to you these things in the churches. I am the Root and the Offspring of David, the <u>Bright and Morning Star.</u>"

V. 22

Jesus, as **the Bright and Morning Star**, will rapture His Church. All believers will bow their knee to Him at the judgment seat of Christ. It is probable that at this time many who served Him well will receive rewards during this judgment. We will see in Revelation 4:4 that the elders are already wearing *crowns of gold on the heads*. After the Church is taken out of the way, the Antichrist will be revealed (2 Thessalonians 2:7-8), in Revelation 6:2-8. God will bring judgment onto unbelievers by way of the Seven-year Tribulation Period, and then the Battle of Armageddon. Following that will **be the new age: the Messianic Kingdom** (<u>Revelation 22:16</u>). The reason it is called the *new age* is because it is the age which follows the *church age*. At the end of the 1,000 year reign, all unbelievers will bow their knee to the Lord Jesus Christ at the Great White Throne and receive their due punishment for rejecting Him.

**First Half of the Seven-Year Tribulation Begins
The Church is Raptured
Rewards of Crowns are Issued**

Chapters 4 and 5 begin "the things that
shall be hereafter" (Revelation 1:19)

4:1-11 (-Introduction-)

-presents a picture of what is happening around
God's throne in heaven upon the Church being
raptured (Romans 11:25-26; 1 Thessalonians
4:13a, 1 Thessalonians 4:16-17; 1 Thessalonians
5:1-4; 1 Corinthians 15:52).
In Revelation 4:8 we see the second time in this
Book that the Lord Jesus Christ is revealed as being
equal to the Father and Holy Spirit as Lord God
Almighty.

¹After these things I looked, and behold, a door *standing* open in heaven. And the first voice which I heard *was* like a trumpet speaking with me, saying, "Come up here, and I will show you things which must take place after this." ²Immediately I was in the Spirit; and behold, a throne set in heaven, and *One* sat on the throne. ³And He who sat there was like a jasper and a sardius stone in appearance; and *there was* a rainbow around the throne, in appearance like an emerald. ⁴Around the throne *were* twenty-four thrones, and on the thrones I saw twenty-four elders sitting, clothed in white robes; and they had crowns of gold on their heads. ⁵And from the throne proceeded lightnings, thunderings, and voices. Seven lamps of fire *were* burning before the throne, which are the seven Spirits of God. ⁶Before the throne *there was* a sea of glass, like crystal. And in the midst of the throne, and around the throne, *were* four living creatures full of eyes in front and in back. ⁷The first living creature *was* like a lion, the second living creature like a calf, the third living creature had a face like a man, and the fourth living creature *was* like a flying eagle. ⁸*The* four living creatures [seraphim] each having six wings, were full of eyes around and within. And they do not rest day or night, saying: "Holy, holy, holy, Lord God Almighty, Who was and is and is to come!" ⁹Whenever the living creatures give glory and honor and thanks to Him who sits on the throne, who lives forever and ever, ¹⁰the twenty-four elders fall down before Him who sits on the throne and worship Him who lives forever and ever, and cast their crowns before the throne, saying: "¹¹You are worthy, O Lord, to receive glory and honor and power; for You created all things, and by Your will they exist and were created."

**-PRINTED VERSES OF
REVELATION 4:1-11
WITH DETAILED COMMENTARY,
REFERENCES AND REFERENCES
COMMENTARY
CAN BE FOUND ON THE
FOLLOWING SETS OF PAGES!-**

4:1-11 (-Introduction-)

Romans 11:25-26a ²⁵For I do not desire, brethren, that you should be ignorant of this <u>mystery</u>, lest you should be wise in your own opinion, that blindness in part has happened to Israel until <u>the fullness of the Gentiles has come in</u>. ^{26a}And so all Israel will be saved, as it is written: [in Isaiah 59:20-21 and see Zechariah 13:8-9]

1 Thessalonians 4:13a But I do not want you to be ignorant, brethren...

1 Thessalonians 4:16-17 ¹⁶For the Lord Himself will descend from heaven with a shout, with the voice of an archangel, and with the <u>trumpet</u> of God. And the dead in Christ will rise first. ¹⁷Then we who are alive *and* remain shall be caught up together with them in the clouds to meet the Lord in the air. And thus we shall always be with the Lord.

4:1-11 (-Introduction-)

Jesus said in Matthew 13:11 that the mysteries of the kingdom of heaven have been given now that He has come, but the **mystery** had not been given to those in the Old Testament ages. ****The fullness of the Gentiles** refers to the time when the last Gentile will have been saved and the church will be removed from the earth by the Rapture** **and so all Israel will be saved** (<u>Romans 11:25-26a</u>; 1 Thessalonians 4:13a, 1 Thessalonians 4:16-17). 1 Thessalonians 5:9 is noteworthy: *For God did not appoint us to wrath, but to obtain salvation through our Lord Jesus Christ.* This is in agreement with 1 Thessalonians 1:10 which tells us *Jesus delivers us from the wrath to come.* Also, Romans 5:9 tells us this: *Much more then, having been justified by His blood, we shall be saved from wrath through Him.* After the Rapture of the Church, and during the Seven-year Tribulation, national salvation will come to **the Twelve Tribes of Israel (12,000 from each tribe; 144,000** total newly converted Christian Jews, Revelation 7:4). God has temporarily blinded—or set Israel aside for the sake of the Gentiles, but He has not forgotten them because of His promise to their fathers. It is interesting to note that Romans chapters 9, 10 and <u>11</u> are respectively the Jews in the past, in the present, and in <u>the future</u>. The chronological order in Romans <u>11</u>:<u>25-26a</u> is in agreement with what we see here in Revelation. The Rapture is based upon the eye-witnessed fact that Jesus died and rose again. The certainty of every believer's hope is based on the resurrection of Jesus Christ.

1 Corinthians 15:52 in a moment, in the twinkling of an eye, at the <u>last trumpet</u>. For the <u>trumpet</u> will sound, and the dead will be raised incorruptible, and we shall be changed.

The **trumpet** in <u>1 Corinthians 15:52</u> is the same as we see in Revelation 4:1 and <u>1 Thessalonians 4:16</u>. It is called the <u>last trumpet</u> in <u>1 Corinthians 15:52</u> signaling the end of the Church age. There will be seven more trumpets sounding through the Tribulation period (Revelation 8:2, Revelation 8:6). Incidentally, the words "trumpet" and "trumpets" are in the Bible 110 times.

¹After these things I looked, and behold, a door *standing* open in heaven. And the first <u>voice</u> which I heard *was* like a <u>trumpet</u> speaking with me, saying, "<u>Come up here</u>, and I will show you <u>things</u> which must take place after this."

4:1

The Church is called **up**, that is, raptured. The words of this verse match directly with the words in other reference verses having to do with the Rapture: <u>1 Thessalonians 4:16-17</u>; <u>1 Corinthians 15:52</u>. In <u>Revelation 11:12a</u>, there is a loud voice telling the two witnesses to "Come up here". **Things** which must be hereafter will be shown through this Book; these "**things**" include His Judgment Seat, the Seven-Year Tribulation, the Second Coming of Christ, Armageddon, His Millennial reign, and the Great White Throne. All these and more will be revealed in the Chapters from here on.

²Immediately I was in the Spirit; and behold, a throne set in heaven, and *One* sat on the throne. ³And He who sat there was like a jasper and a sardius stone in appearance; and *there was* a rainbow around the throne, in appearance like an emerald.

4:2-3

John describes God much like Ezekiel does in <u>Ezekiel 1:22-28</u>. This being **in the Spirit** up at the **throne** in heaven is very similar to Paul the Apostle being *caught up to the third heaven* in 2 Corinthians 12:2.

Chapter 4 Verses 1-3
References

V. 4:1

1 Thessalonians 4:16-17a [16]For the Lord Himself will descend from heaven with a shout, with the voice of an archangel, and with the trumpet of God, and the dead in Christ will rise first. [17a]Then we who are alive *and* remain shall be caught up together with them in the clouds to meet the Lord in the air.

1 Corinthians 15:52 in a moment, in the twinkling of an eye, at the last trumpet. For the trumpet will sound, and the dead will be raised incorruptible, and we shall be changed.

Revelation 11:12a And they heard a loud voice from heaven saying to them, "Come up here"

Vv. 2-3

Ezekiel 1:22-28 [22]The likeness of the firmament above the heads of the living creatures [cherubim angels] *was* like the color of an awesome crystal, stretched out over their heads. [23]And under the firmament their wings *spread out* straight, one toward another. Each one had two which covered one side, and each one had two which covered the other side of the body. [24]When they went, I heard the noise of their wings, like the noise of many waters, like the voice of the Almighty, a tumult like the noise of an army; and when they stood still, they let down their wings. [25]A voice came from above the firmament that *was* over their heads; whenever they stood, they let down their wings. [26]And above the firmament over their heads *was* the likeness of a throne, in appearance like a sapphire stone; on the likeness of the throne *was* a likeness with the appearance of a man high above it. [27]Also from the appearance of His waist and upward I saw, as it were, the color of amber with the appearance of fire all around within it; and from the appearance of His waist and downward I saw, as it were, the appearance of fire with brightness all around. [28]Like the appearance of a rainbow in a cloud on a rainy day, so *was* the appearance of the brightness all around it. This *was* the appearance of the likeness of the glory of the LORD. So when I saw *it*, I fell on my face, and I heard a voice of One speaking.

Chapter 4 Verses 1-3
References Commentary

V. 4:1

We are told the Rapture begins with a voice and the trumpet both in Revelation 4:1 and here in 1 Thessalonians 4:16. The trumpet is repeated twice in 1 Corinthians 15:52, the first time being referred to as the *last trumpet*. The *last* trumpet is most likely referring to the *last trumpet* of the Church Age, since the Church is being raptured. It is obviously not the last trumpet ever, since the words *trumpet* and *trumpets* are repeated in the last Book of the Bible six more times, and appear in the Bible 110 times. In Revelation 11:12a the two witnesses are seen ascending to heaven.

Vv. 2-3

****The firmament** here (Ezekiel 1:22-28) comes from the same Hebrew word in Genesis 1:6-7 for the expanse created by God on the second day. Its dazzling brilliance was an appropriate reminder of God's holiness and awe-inspiring majesty.** **The noise of many waters** could refer to *the multitude of many people who make a noise like the roar of the seas* and God Almighty's voice rebuking them (Isaiah 17:12-13). But the **voice from above the firmament** was no doubt the **voice of the Almighty** (Ezekiel 1:24). The Godhead appears in the likeness of humanity. The Messiah (Christ Jesus) God incarnate is the representative of the "fullness of the Godhead" (Colossians 2:9). **The glory of the LORD** is that glory which shines fully in the person of Jesus Christ (2 Corinthians 4:6) and is a constant theme in the Book of Ezekiel.

⁴Around the throne *were* twenty-four thrones, and on the thrones I saw <u>twenty-four elders</u> sitting, clothed in <u>white robes</u>; and they had <u>crowns</u> of gold on their heads. ⁵And from the throne proceeded lightnings, thunderings, and voices. <u>Seven lamps</u> of fire *were* burning before the throne, which are the <u>seven Spirits</u> of God.

4:4-5

****Twenty-four elders** are probably the representatives of the raptured Church in heaven. They are wearing **crowns** of reward from the judgment seat of Christ.** Romans 14:10b tells us we (believers) *shall all stand before the judgment seat of Christ.*
(<u>1 Corinthians 3:12-15</u>; <u>2 Corinthians 5:10</u>)

The **white robes picture their righteousness which has now been judged and purified,** and they are wearing **crowns** showing they have been judged at the Judgment Seat of Christ. Their sanctification process has been completed.

**David divided the Levitical priesthood into 24 sections in 1 Chronicles 24:7-19. Believers here in the church age were seen as a kingdom of priests (Revelation 1:6).

Old Testament and Tribulation period believers are not yet included, since they will not be resurrected and rewarded until after the Tribulation period (Daniel 12:1-3;** Matthew 27:52-53; John 5:28-29).

Daniel 12:1-3 says: ¹*"At that time* [the Tribulation] *Michael shall stand up, the great prince who stands watch over the sons of your people* (Jews)*; and there shall be a time of trouble* (Tribulation)*, such as never was since there was a nation, even to that time. And at that time your people shall be delivered, every one who is found written in the book.* ²*And many of those who sleep in the dust of the earth shall awake, some to everlasting life, some to shame and everlasting contempt.* ³*Those who are wise shall shine like the brightness of the firmament, and those* (144.000 Jews) *who turn many to righteousness* [during the Tribulation] *like the stars forever and ever."*

The **seven lamps and **seven Spirits** symbolize the Holy Spirit of God (1:4;** Isaiah 11:2; Zechariah 3:9; Zechariah 4:10).

Vv. 4-5

1 Corinthians 3:12-15 [12]Now if anyone builds on this foundation *with* gold, silver, precious stones, wood, hay, straw, [13]each one's work will become clear; for the Day will declare it, because it will be revealed by fire; and the fire will test each one's work, of what sort it is. [14]If anyone's work which he has built on *it* endures, he will receive a reward. [15]If anyone's work is burned, he will suffer loss; but he himself will be saved, yet so as through fire.

Vv. 4-5

Each one's work will become clear: Romans 14:11 quotes Isaiah 45:23: For it is written: *"As I live, says the LORD, every knee shall bow to Me, and every tongue shall confess to God."* Philippians 2:10 also confirms: *that at the name of Jesus every knee should bow, of those in heaven, and of those on earth, and of those under the earth.* Both saints and, eventually, unbelievers will bow the knee: Acts 24:15 quotes Paul the apostle: *"I have hope in God, which they themselves also accept, that there will be a resurrection of the dead, both of the just and the unjust."* The justified ones who are viewed as righteous to receive eternal life are believers who will bend the knee at the judgment seat of Christ before His Millennial reign (1 Corinthians 3:12-15); the unjustified unbelieving ones who reject Christ will be judged at the Great White Throne at the end of the Millennial reign.

2 Corinthians 5:10 For we must all appear before the judgment seat of Christ, that each one may receive the things *done* in the body, according to what he has done, whether good or bad.

The just will be eternally with the Lord in heaven, and the unjust will then be eternally suffering in the lake of fire (2 Corinthians 5:10).

⁶Before the throne *there was* a <u>sea of glass, like crystal</u>. And in the midst of the throne, and around the throne, *were* <u>four living creatures</u> full of eyes in front and in back.

4:6

*The **sea of glass like crystal** tells us that the throne is located in a place undisturbed by the relentless temptations of this world, or by the opposition of the wicked, who are like a troubled sea* (<u>Ephesians 4:14</u>; <u>Hebrews 5:13-14</u>). **Four living creatures are probably cherubim angels** (<u>Ezekiel 1:5-6</u>) who guard God's throne.

[**Note** on Cherubim[1] and Seraphim: They are *created* beings just as we humans are *created* beings. Therefore, angels are not from eternity past nor are they, or we, omniscient as is our God. Cherubim in the Old Testament were all of <u>one piece at the two ends of the golden lid on the Ark of the Covenant inside the Holy of Holies</u>. This signifies that the redeemed and glorified <u>creatures</u>—both angelic and human—were <u>bound up with the sacrifice of Christ</u>. Being in union with Christ then proceeds out of the Mercy Seat. The function of the redeemed cherubim, seraphim, and humans is depicted as being in <u>fellowship with God</u> as well as being there for <u>serving Him</u>. The cherubim (cherubim is plural, with the letters *im* at the end, cherub is singular) compared to the seraphim are much the same except for primary duties. The cherubim are primarily guards, or attendants, "<u>attached</u>"—"*<u>united</u>*"—to God's throne (Exodus 25:18-19), whereas the seraphim flew above and around (Isaiah 6:2-7) to attend God's throne and offer praises to Him. God's angelic court serves as an example to each believer: As <u>redeemed created beings</u> who are eternally thankful for being *<u>united</u>* with our Savior—<u>in Him and Him in us</u>—our <u>primary purpose</u> <u>in our life</u> now and eternal is to serve and worship God.]

V. 6

Ephesians 4:14 that we should no longer be children, tossed to and fro and carried about with every wind of doctrine, by the trickery of men, in the cunning craftiness of deceitful plotting,

Hebrews 5:13-14 ¹³For everyone who partakes only of milk is unskilled in the word of righteousness, for he is a babe. ¹⁴But solid food belongs to those who are of full age, that is, those who by reason of use [practice] have their senses exercised to discern both good and evil.

V. 6

Believers avoid three dangers when exercising their Spiritual gifts in God's prescribed manner: Immaturity, instability, and gullibility. Most serious of all is the danger of deception (Ephesians. 4:14; Hebrews 5:13-14). *Saints will inevitably meet some false cultist who impresses them by zeal and apparent sincerity. Because he uses *religious* language, they assume he must be a true Christian. When we study the Bible for ourselves, we are able to see through the deceitful juggling of words* and we are able to discern false teachers and are able to avoid them and to withdraw ourselves from such (Proverbs 4:14-16; Romans 16:17; 2 Thessalonians 3:6; 1 Timothy. 6:5).

Ezekiel 1:5-6 ⁵Also from within it *came* the likeness of four living creatures. And this *was* their appearance: they had the likeness of a man. ⁶Each one had four faces, and each one had four wings.

Note the resemblances of the visions in the prophesies given by John in Revelation 4 verses 6 and 7 and Ezekiel's **four living creatures** and **likeness of a man** (Ezekiel 1:5-6).

⁷The first living creature *was* like a <u>lion</u>, the second living <u>creature like a calf</u>, the third living creature had a <u>face like a man</u>, and the fourth living creature *was* <u>like a flying eagle</u>.

4:7

The **lion represents strength** (Psalm 103:20: *Bless the LORD, you His angels, who excel in strength, who do His word, heeding the voice of His word*.); **the **calf** signifies service (<u>Hebrews 1:14</u>); the **face** of **a man** denotes *intelligence* (God the Son), and **eagle** swiftness (<u>Daniel 9:21</u>**<u>-27</u>).

V. 7
Hebrews 1:14: Are they [angel spirit beings] not all serving spirits sent forth to minister for those who will inherit salvation?

V. 7
Angels are inferior to the Son of God just as servants are inferior to the Universal Sovereign. (Hebrews 1:14).

Daniel 9:21-23: ²¹Yes, while I was speaking in prayer, the man Gabriel, whom I had seen in the vision at the beginning, being caused to fly swiftly, reached me about the time of the evening offering. ²²And he informed me, and talked with me, and said, "O Daniel, I have now come forth to give you skill to understand. ²³At the beginning of your supplications the command went out, and I have come to tell you, for you are greatly beloved; therefore consider the matter, and understand the vision:

Daniel 9:21-23: Daniel prayed for help to understand the vision. God sent **Gabriel** who *gave Daniel an outline for Israel's future* (Daniel 9:21-27). God's Word also gives us a prescription for eternal life.

Daniel 9:24: "Seventy weeks are determined for your people and for your holy city, to finish the transgression, to make an end of sins, to make reconciliation for iniquity, to bring in everlasting righteousness, To seal up vision and prophecy, and to anoint the Most Holy.

Daniel 9:24: Warren Henderson explains in his book *Infidelity and Loyalty* pg 391: "The Hebrew word *shabua* is translated "week," but literally means "seven", much like our English word dozen means twelve of something. The "something" is determined by the context. ... Based on how the final week is described elsewhere in Scripture, we are able to conclude that a week is speaking of seven years". So the first phrase **Seventy Weeks are determined** is actually 7 x 70 which equals 490 years. The first 483 of the 490 years began when Nehemiah started re-building the wall of Jerusalem, and ended at Christ's crucifixion. The rest of verse 24 explains the same thing Romans 3:21-22 reveals: When Christ is believed upon the believers will have the righteousness of God through faith in Jesus Christ. The anointing of the Most Holy means that the Father commissioned the Son to shed His blood and die for the sins of the world.

Daniel 9:25-27

-CONTINUED ON NEXT PAGE UNDER REFERENCES!-

-CONTINUED ON NEXT PAGE UNDER REFERENCES COMMENTARY!-

**-VERSE 7 REPEATED
FROMPREVIOUS PAGE -**

**-COMMENTARY REPEATED
FROM PREVIOUS PAGE-**

[7]The first living creature *was* like a <u>lion</u>, the second living <u>creature like a calf</u>, the third living creature had a <u>face like a man</u>, and the fourth living creature *was* <u>like a flying eagle</u>.

4:7

The **lion represents strength** (Psalm 103:20: *Bless the LORD, you His angels, who excel in strength, who do His word, heeding the voice of His word*.); **the **calf** signifies service (<u>Hebrews 1:14</u>); the **face** of **a man** denotes *intelligence* (God the Son), and **eagle** swiftness (<u>Daniel 9:21</u>**<u>-27</u>).

-CONTINUED FROM PREVIOUS PAGE-

-CONTINUED FROM PREVIOUS PAGE-

V. 7

Daniel 9:25-26: [25] "Know therefore and understand, t*hat* from the going forth of the command to restore and build Jerusalem Until Messiah the Prince, t*here shall be* seven weeks and sixty-two weeks; the street shall be built again, and the wall, even in troublesome times. [26]" And after the sixty-two weeks Messiah shall be cut off, but not for Himself; and the people of the prince who is to come shall destroy the city and the sanctuary. The end of it *shall be* with a flood, and till the end of the war desolations are determined.

Daniel 9:27: Then he shall confirm a covenant with many for one week; but in the middle of the week He shall bring an end to sacrifice and offering. And on the wind of abominations shall be one who makes desolate, even until the consummation, which is determined, is poured out on the desolate."

V. 7

Daniel 9:25-26: Gabriel explains that Nehemiah's rebuilding of Jerusalem shall be **seven weeks** or 49 years, and then **sixty-two** more **weeks** or 434 more years until the crucifixion of Christ. 49 years plus 434 years totals 483 years. The **prince who is to come** will happen at a presently undetermined time. He is the Antichrist. In AD70 Nehemiah's work was destroyed. **And till the end**: means the end of the Church Age—time of the Gentiles-rapture of the church—the time that only the Father knows (Matthew 24:36).

Daniel 9:27: **Then** means after the Father sends His Son to rapture the Church—he—the Antichrist—**shall confirm a covenant**—make a peace treaty—**with many**—all those who are left behind—for **one week**—seven years—signifying the beginning of the Tribulation period. But in the middle of the week—three-and-a-half years—the Great Tribulation begins.

NOTE
Ezekiel Chapters 38 + 39 prophesy the war of Armageddon at the end of the Seven-year Tribulation which matches what is coming in the Revelation of Jesus Christ (Revelation 19:13-21; 20:1-2).

[8]*The four living creatures [seraphim] each having six wings*, were full of eyes around and within. And they do not rest day or night, saying: "Holy, holy, holy, Lord God Almighty, Who was and is and is to come!"

4:8

Their **Eyes symbolize wisdom; the **wings** depict movement.** They worship God as did the seraphim in Isaiah's vision (Isaiah 6:1-3). The angelic vision is much like Ezekiel 10:15-22. Ezekiel 1:4-14 is printed here to provide the incredible similarities to Ezekiel 10:15-22 printed in the *Reference Column*.

Ezekiel 1:4-14 [4]Then I looked, and behold, a whirlwind was coming out of the north, a great cloud with raging fire engulfing itself, and brightness *was* all around it and radiating out of its midst like the color of amber, out of the midst of the fire. [5]Also from within it *came* the likeness of four living creatures. And this *was* their appearance: they had the likeness of a man. [6]Each one had four faces, and each one had four wings. [7]Their legs *were* straight, and the soles of their feet *were* like the soles of calves' feet. They sparkled like the color of burnished bronze. [8]The hands of a man *were* under their wings on their four sides; and each of the four had faces and wings. [9]Their wings touched one another. *The creatures* did not turn when they went, but each one went straight forward. [10]As for the likeness of their faces, *each* had the face of a man; each of the four had the face of a lion on the right side, each of the four had the face of an ox on the left side, and each of the four had the face of an eagle. [11]Thus *were* their faces. Their wings stretched upward; two *wings* of each one touched one another, and two covered their bodies. [12]And each one went straight forward; they went wherever the spirit wanted to go, and they did not turn when they went. [13]As for the likeness of the living creatures, their appearance *was* like burning coals of fire, like the appearance of torches going back and forth among the living creatures [conveying God's glory and pure, burning justice]. The fire was bright, and out of the fire went lightning. [14]And the living creatures ran back and forth, in appearance like a flash of lightning.

V. 8

Isaiah 6:1-3 ¹In the year that King Uzziah died, I saw the Lord <u>sitting on a throne, high and</u> lifted up, and the train of His *robe* filled the temple. ²Above it stood <u>seraphim</u>; each one had <u>six wings</u>: with two he covered his face, with two he covered his feet, and with two he flew. ³And one cried to another and said: Holy, holy, holy *is* the LORD of hosts; the whole earth *is* full of His glory!"

V. 8

In <u>Isaiah 6:1-3</u> Isaiah's vision was that of the Lord Jesus Christ, **sitting on a throne, high and** exalted. *The **seraphim** had four wings for reverence and two for service. These indicate the holiness of God and require that God's servants (us) be cleansed before serving Him.* We come each first day of the week with a clear conscience and clean heart to remember Christ's work with communion.

Ezekiel 10:15-22 ¹⁵And the cherubim were lifted up. This *was* the living creature I saw <u>by the River Chēbar</u> [a channel of the Euphrates River SE of Babylon]. ¹⁶When the <u>cherubim</u> went, the <u>wheels</u> went beside them; and when the cherubim lifted their wings to mount up from the earth, the same <u>wheels</u> also did not turn from beside them. ¹⁷When *the cherubim* stood still, *the <u>wheels</u>* stood still, and when *one* was lifted up, *the other* lifted itself up, for the spirit of the living creature *was* in them. ¹⁸Then <u>the glory of the LORD departed</u> from the threshold of the temple and stood over the cherubim [Ezekiel was saddened to witness the departure of **the glory of the LORD from the temple**]. ¹⁹And the cherubim lifted their wings and mounted up from the earth in my sight. When they went out, the wheels *were* beside them; and they stood at the door of the east gate of the LORD'S house [Ezekiel 11:23: *And the glory of the LORD went up from the midst of the city and stood on the mountain, which is on the east side of the city* {which is where Christ will land at His Second Coming when the Great Tribulation is ending.}], and the glory of the God of Israel *was* above them. ²⁰This is the living creature I saw under the God of Israel <u>by the River Chēbar</u>, and <u>I knew</u> they *were* <u>cherubim</u>. ²¹Each one had <u>four faces</u> and each one four wings, and the likeness of the <u>hands of a man</u> *was* under their wings. ²²And the <u>likeness of their faces</u> *was* <u>the same</u> *as* the faces which I had seen <u>by the River Chēbar</u>, their appearance and their persons. They each went straight forward.

<u>Ezekiel 10:15</u> emphasizes that **the cherubim** were the same as **the living creatures** he had seen **by the River Chēbar** in Chapter 1.

Following are comments on both <u>Ezekiel 1:4-14</u> (see opposite page for Scripture) and <u>10:15-22</u>:

*The **four living creatures**, *attached to God*, **had four faces (lion, ox, eagle, man)**, four **wings**, straight feet, and hands under its wings, all symbolizing those attributes of God which are seen in creation: His majesty (**lion**), power (**ox**), swiftness (**eagle**), and wisdom (**man**). (Many forget about the God above the cloud, who sits on the throne. They worship the creation rather than the Creator Himself.) Beside each living creature there was **a wheel**, or rather **a wheel** within a wheel (perhaps one wheel at right angle to the other like a gyroscope). Thus the vision seems to represent a throne-chariot, with **wheels...on the earth**, four living creatures supporting a platform, and the **throne** of God above it.* Ezekiel explains what he viewed in 43:3 as *"the vision which I saw when He came to destroy the city."* *In other words, the vision depicted God in His glory coming out of the north in judgment on Jerusalem, the Babylonians being the agents of His judgment.*

♦In Revelation 4:8 it is the second time that the Lord Jesus Christ is declared to be Almighty God (Revelation 1:8 was the first time).

4:9-11

⁹Whenever the living <u>creatures</u> give glory and honor and thanks to Him who sits on the throne, who lives forever and ever, ¹⁰the twenty-four elders fall down before Him who sits on the throne and worship Him who lives forever and ever, and cast their crowns before the throne, saying: "¹¹You are worthy, O Lord, to receive glory and honor and power; for You created all things, and by Your will they exist and were created."

All of heaven worship the Lord Jesus Christ (<u>Revelation 1:18</u>). The angels praise His character, and the **elders** (Church—we believers) praise His creative power. God has the right to rule and the sovereign authority to judge the earth, because He is both holy and the Creator of all (<u>Colossians 1:17</u>).

Vv. 9-11

Revelation 1:18 I *am* He who lives, and was dead, and behold, I am alive forevermore. Amen. And I have the keys of Hades and of Death.

Vv. 9-11

Christ is alive, and His body—the Church—is alive, and His Word is alive! (Revelation 1:18; Hebrews 4:12) Since He is alive, His body is also alive—His body of Church believers are alive in Him.

Colossians 1:17 And He is before all things, and in Him all things consist.

Jesus Christ is the Creator (Colossians 1:17; John 1:3; Colossians 1:16; Hebrews 1:10)

Sealed Scroll Tells of God's Tribulation Wrath

¹And I saw in the right *hand* of Him who sat <u>on the throne</u> a scroll written inside and on the back, sealed with seven seals.

5:1

John sees in God the Father's right hand the scroll sealed with seven seals. All the messages have been sealed by the authority of God. We know the Father is the One seated **on the throne**, because we learn in verse 6 that the Lord Jesus is standing **in the midst of the throne**, and He is **in the midst of the elders**. The breaking of the seals will reveal the message inside each part of the **scroll which <u>contains the Tribulation judgments</u> of God** (<u>Ezekiel 2:9-10</u>; <u>Daniel 12:4</u>; Revelation 6).

Daniel 8:26 *"And the vision of the evenings and mornings which was told is true; therefore seal up the vision, for it refers to many days in the future."*

²Then I saw a strong angel proclaiming with a loud voice, "Who is worthy to open the scroll and to loose its seals?" ³And no one in heaven or on the earth or under the earth was able to open the scroll, or to look at it. ⁴So I wept much, because no one was found worthy to open and read the scroll, or to look at it.

5:2-4

No one among mankind or angels could be found to remove the seals and read the scroll. Only Christ can do so. (<u>Isaiah 29:11</u>)

V. 1

Ezekiel 2:9-10 [9]Now when I looked, there was a hand stretched out to me; and behold, a scroll of a book *was* in it. [10]Then He spread it before me; inside and on the outside, and written on it *were* lamentations and mourning and woe.

V. 1

In Ezekiel 2:9-10 the prophet *was forewarned that his ministry would be unpopular. We too are forewarned that a true presentation of the Gospel will be offensive to the unsaved. It is commonly known as "the offenses of the cross." To some people we are the aroma of death* (2 Corinthians 2:15).

Daniel 12:4 "But you, Daniel, shut up the words, and seal the book until the time of the end; many shall run to and fro, and knowledge shall increase."

Daniel 12:4 teaches us that *(quoting Tregelles) "many shall scrutinize the book from end to end." Many will study the prophetic Word and **knowledge** of it **shall** surely **increase** during the Great Tribulation.*

Vv. 2-4

Isaiah 29:11 The whole vision [of the false seers—false prophets] has become to you like the words of a book that is sealed, which *men* deliver to one who is literate, saying, "Read this, please." And he says, "I cannot, for it *is* sealed."

Vv. 2-4

People's willful blindness brings judicial blindness upon themselves. God's Word is unintelligible—indiscernible—to them (1 Corinthians 2:14). To some it is a **sealed...book**, to others it is illegible. Everyone who does not accept it has an excuse. *The Revelation of Jesus Christ* is hereby opened.

5:5-7

⁵But one of the elders said to me, "Do not weep. Behold, the <u>Lion</u> of the tribe of Judah, the <u>Root of David</u>, has prevailed to open the scroll and to loose its seven seals." ⁶And I looked, and behold, in the midst of the throne and of the four living creatures, and <u>in the midst of the elders</u>, stood <u>a Lamb</u> as though it had been slain, having seven horns and seven eyes, which are the <u>seven Spirits of God</u> [the <u>complete fullness of God</u>] sent out into all the earth. ⁷Then <u>He</u> [the Son of God] <u>came and took the scroll</u> out of the right hand of Him [the Father] who sat on the throne.

Christ is presented both as a **Lion (Ruler) from the tribe of Judah (<u>Genesis 49:10</u>) and as **a Lamb** (Redeemer: <u>Isaiah 53:7</u>; <u>John 1:29</u>). The **Root of David** shows a Messianic connection with the Davidic covenant (<u>2 Samuel 7:16</u>; <u>Isaiah 11:1</u>)** and Christ the Lamb—the Messiah. The Savior took the scroll from the right hand of the Father who was sitting on the throne (Revelation 5:7).

The following verses should be repeated for emphasis:

Isaiah 53:7 *He was oppressed and He was afflicted, yet He opened not His mouth; He was led as a lamb to the slaughter, and as a sheep before its shearers is silent, so He opened not His mouth.*

2 Samuel 7:16 *"And your house and your kingdom shall be established forever before you. Your throne shall be established forever."*

Isaiah 11:1 *There shall come forth a Rod from the stem of Jesse, and a Branch shall grow out of his roots* (<u>Romans 11:16-24</u>).

Vv. 5-7

Genesis 49:10 The scepter [a symbol of kingship] shall not depart from Judah, nor a lawgiver from between his feet, until Shīlōh comes; and to Him *shall be* the obedience of the people.

Vv. 5-7

In <u>Genesis 49:10</u> *Shīlōh represents the Messiah (Christ).* Those who obey Him are those who love Him (John 14:15).

Isaiah 53:7 He was oppressed and He was afflicted, yet He opened not His mouth; He was led as a <u>lamb</u> to the slaughter, and as a sheep before its shearers is silent, so He opened not His mouth.

John 1:29 The next day John saw Jesus coming toward him, and said, "Behold! The Lamb of God who takes away the sin of the world!"

<u>Isaiah 53:7</u> and <u>John 1:29</u> take us back to *the blood of the lambs slain during the Old Testament period that did not put away sin. Those lambs were pictures or types, pointing forward to the fact that God would one day provide a **Lamb** who would actually *take away* the sin.* Only those sinners who receive the Lord Jesus as Savior are forgiven of their sins.

2 Samuel 7:16 "And your house and your kingdom shall be established forever before you. Your throne shall be established forever."

David's dynasty of <u>2 Samuel 7:16</u> has been interrupted since the Babylonians exiled the Jews, but it will be restored when Christ, the Seed of David, returns to govern over all the earth during His Millennial reign.

Isaiah 11:1 There shall come forth <u>a Rod</u> [Shoot] <u>from the stem</u> [stock or trunk] <u>of Jesse</u>, and a Branch shall grow [be fruitful] out of his roots.

The passage of <u>Isaiah 11</u> carries us forward to the Second Coming of Christ. Here in verse 1 we first see the lineage of the Son of David, **a Rod from the stem of Jesse**, who was David's father (1 Samuel 17:12).

Romans 11:16-24

CONTINUED ON NEXT PAGE UNDER REFERENCES!

CONTINUED ON NEXT PAGE UNDER REFERENCES COMMENTARY!

**-COMMENTARY REPEATED
FROM PREVIOUS PAGE-**

Isaiah 11:1 *There shall come forth a Rod from the stem of Jesse, and a Branch shall grow out of his roots* (<u>Romans 11:16-24</u>).

[8]Now when He had taken the scroll, the four living <u>creatures</u> and the twenty-four <u>elders</u> fell down before the <u>Lamb</u>, each having a harp, and golden bowls full of incense, which are the prayers of the saints. [9]And they sang a new song, saying: "You are worthy to take the scroll, and to open its seals; for You were slain, and have <u>redeemed us to God by Your blood</u> out of every tribe and tongue and people and nation, [10]And have made us kings and priests to our God; and we shall reign on the earth." [11]Then I looked, and I <u>heard the voice of many angels around the throne</u>, <u>the living creatures</u>, and <u>the elders</u>; and the number of them was <u>ten thousand times ten thousand, and thousands of thousands</u>, [12]saying with a loud voice: "Worthy is the Lamb who was slain to receive power and riches and wisdom, and strength and honor and glory and blessing!" [13]And every creature which is in heaven and on the earth and under the earth and such as are in the sea, and all that are in them, I heard saying: "Blessing and honor and glory and power *Be* to Him who sits <u>on the throne</u>, and to the <u>Lamb</u>, forever and ever! [14]Then the four living creatures said, "Amen!" And the twenty-four <u>elders</u> fell down and worshiped Him who lives forever and ever.

5:8-14

John heard **the voice of many angels around the throne**, he heard the voice of **the living creatures**, and he heard the voice of **the elders**. We human beings are living creatures. The living creatures represent the raptured Church. Some might have difficulty to realize that we are called *creatures*, but in 2 Corinthians 5:17a: *Therefore, if anyone is in Christ, he is a new <u>creation</u>...* and in James 1:18: *Of His own will He brought us forth by the word of truth, that we might be a kind of firstfruits of His <u>**creatures**</u>*. The <u>number of them</u> will be <u>ten thousand time ten thousand</u> (10 million) <u>and thousands of thousands</u>. **The **creatures** and the **elders** praise the **Lamb** for having been the Redeemer through His **blood** (verse 9) and for giving authority [in the future] to reign on the earth. Myriads of angels also praise the Lamb for His glory and wisdom, and every area of creation worships both the Father and the Lamb. The prayers are probably prayers of thanks for salvation and for the future fulfillment of the Messianic Kingdom.**

-CONTINUED FROM PREVIOUS PAGE-   -CONTINUED FROM PREVIOUS PAGE-

Romans 11:16-24 [16]For if the firstfruit *is* holy, the lump *is* also *holy*; and if the root is holy, so *are* the branches. [17]And if some of the branches were broken off, and you, being a wild olive tree, were grafted in among them, and with them became a partaker of the root and fatness of the olive tree, [18]do not boast against the branches. But if you do boast, *remember that* you do not support the root, but the root *supports* you. [19]You will say then, "Branches were broken off that I might be grafted in." [20]Well *said*. Because of unbelief they were broken off, and you stand by faith. Do not be haughty, but fear. [21]For if God did not spare the natural branches, He may not spare you either. [22]Therefore consider the goodness and severity of God; on those who fell, severity; but toward you, goodness, if you continue in *His* goodness. Otherwise you also will be cut off. [23]And they also, if they do not continue in unbelief, will be grafted in, for God is able to graft them in again. [24]For if you were cut out of the olive tree which is wild by nature, and were grafted contrary to nature into a cultivated olive tree, how much more will these, who *are* natural *branches*, be grafted into their own olive tree?

Two metaphors are used in the Romans 11 passage: the first metaphor is **the firstfruit** and **the lump**. *The **firstfruit** and **the lump** speak of dough, not of fruit. In Numbers 15:19-21 we read that a piece of dough was consecrated to the Lord as a heave offering—meaning that if the piece of dough is set apart to the Lord, so is all the dough that might be made from it. In this passage the **firstfruit** is Abraham. He was **holy** in the sense that he was set apart by God. The second metaphor is **the root** and **its branches**. Again Abraham is the **root**. The **branches** that **were broken off** picture the unbelieving portion of the twelve tribes of Israel. But only some of the **branches** were removed. A remnant, including Paul himself, had received the Lord. **With them** the Gentiles partook of the root and fatness of **the olive tree**.* The **olive tree** is not Israel, but rather God's line of privilege down through the centuries. It is also important to know that *the **wild olive** branch is not the church but the Gentiles viewed collectively.* (Interestingly, the next verse—Romans 11:25—reveals the Rapture of the Church by the last believer brought in, and verse 26 informs us that Israel will then be saved—during Tribulation.) We will see those 144,000 being saved and sealed in Revelation Chapter 7 after the church is raptured in Chapter 4 and praises Christ in Chapter 5, and Antichrist is revealed in Chapter 6.)

What is to Come in First Half of Seven-Year Tribulation

The Warnings of Christ's Day of Judgment Begins with the first 6 Seals being Opened

6:1

¹Now I saw when the Lamb opened one of the seals; and I heard one of the four living creatures saying with a voice like thunder, "Come and see."

**The seals describe what the beginning of Christ's judgment (a Day of the Lord) will be for unbelievers on earth during the Tribulation period. These judgments nearly mirror those predicted by Christ in Matthew 24:4-31. The purpose of the Tribulation period is to punish the unbelievers for their sin and rejection of Christ _and_ to bring a remnant to faith in the Lord Jesus Christ.

6:2

²And I looked, and behold, a white horse. He who sat on it had a bow; and a crown was given to him, and he went out conquering and to conquer.

The Antichrist man is now revealed. His seven year career is depicted by this white horse representing _peace_, and verses 4, 7, and 8, respectively: the red horse: upheaval and killings; the black horse: enormous inflation and famine; and the pale horse: death—to the Antichrist and his followers. The first seal initiates the conquest by the false savior—the false messiah, the Antichrist.** The first six of seven seals will be opened here in Chapter 6. **Matthew 24:5 "For many will come in My name, saying, 'I am the Christ,' and will deceive many."** The Antichrist will be the final Gentile world ruler [Revelation 13:7]. This _horseman_ is not the same as the one described in Revelation 19:11, who is Christ in His Second Coming. (2 Thessalonians 2:3c-4; Daniel 11:21b; Daniel 11:36-37)

**Still in the First Half of Tribulation
Seeing "Things to Come"**

V. 1

Matthew 24:3-31

—DUE TO THE LENGTH OF THE
SCRIPTURE, IT IS LEFT UP TO
THE READER TO REFER TO THE
BIBLE FOR THIS TEACHING.—

V. 1

Jesus explains the first half of the Tribulation in
Matthew 24:3-14 and the second half (the Great
Tribulation) in Matthew 24:15-28.

In the 28 verses of Matthew 24:4-31 Jesus also
explains the judgments.

V. 2

2 Thessalonians 2:3c-4 ³ᶜthe man of sin
[*lawlessness*] is revealed, the son of perdition, ⁴who
opposes and exalts himself above all that is called
God or that is worshiped, so that he sits as God in
the temple of God, showing himself that he is God.
Daniel 11:21b he shall come in peaceably, and
seize the kingdom by intrigue...
Daniel 11:36-37 ³⁶Then the king [the Antichrist]
shall do according to his own will: he shall exalt
and magnify himself above every god, shall speak
blasphemies against the God of gods, and shall
prosper till the wrath has been accomplished; for
what has been determined shall be done. ³⁷He shall
regard neither the God of his fathers nor the desire
of women, nor regard any god; for he shall exalt
himself above *them* all.

V. 2

The Antichrist is described in 2 Thessalonians
2:3c-4 in agreement with Daniel 11:36-37.
2 Thessalonians 2:3 and 2:7-8 confirm the
Antichrist will not be revealed until after the
falling away of faith by some and not until after
the Rapture:
2 Thessalonians 2:3b: ³ᵇ*that Day will not come
unless the falling away comes first...*
2Thessalonians 7-8a: ⁷*For the mystery* [hidden
truth] *of the lawlessness is already at work; only He
who now restrains will do so until He is taken out of
the way.* ⁸ᵃ*And then the lawless one will be revealed...*
He who is taken out of the way is the indwelling
Holy Spirit when the Church is raptured away to
heaven.

³When He opened the second seal, I heard the second living creature saying, "Come and see." ⁴Another horse, fiery red, went out. And it was granted to the one who sat on it to take peace from the earth, and that *people* should kill one another; and there was given to him a great <u>sword</u>.

6:3-4

The **<u>second seal</u> describes war and lack of peace. The **sword** is for conflict,** (<u>Ezekiel 33:1-6</u>; <u>Ezekiel 38:21</u>; <u>Joel 1:15</u>; <u>Ezekiel 39:23</u>; <u>Daniel 11:33</u>) and takes peace from earth.

Matthew 24:6-7 ⁶*"And you will hear of wars and rumors of wars. See that you are not troubled; for all these things must come to pass, but the end is not yet.* ⁷ *For nation will rise against nation, and kingdom against kingdom. And there will be famines, pestilences, and earthquakes in various places."*

⁵When He opened the third seal, I heard the third living creature say, "Come and see." So I looked, and behold, a black horse, and he who sat on it had a pair of scales [a symbol of famine since the grain was rationed] in his hand. ⁶And I heard a voice in the midst of the four living creatures saying, "A quart [about one quart] of wheat for a denarius [one day's wages for a worker—represents tremendous inflation]; and do not harm the oil and the wine."

6:5-6

The **<u>third seal</u> represents enormous inflation and famine. (Matthew 24:7) **

⁷When He opened the fourth seal, I heard the voice of the fourth living creature saying, "Come and see." ⁸So I looked, and behold, a pale horse. And the name of him who sat on it was Death, and <u>Hādēs</u> followed with him. And power was given to them over a fourth of the earth, to kill with sword, with hunger, with death, and by the beasts of the earth.

6:7-8

The **<u>fourth seal</u> describes death to a quarter of the earth's population through war, famine, and pestilence.**

Luke 21:11 *"And there will be great earthquakes in various places, and famines and pestilences; and there will be fearful sights and great signs from heaven."* **Death** takes bodies and **Hādēs** holds their spirits and souls for judgment.

Vv. 3-4

Ezekiel 33:1-6 ¹Again the word of the LORD came to me, saying, ²"Son of man, speak to the children of your people, and say to them: 'When I bring the <u>sword</u> upon a land, and the people of the land take a man from their territory and make him their <u>watchman</u>, ³when he sees the <u>sword</u> coming upon the land, if he blows the trumpet and warns the people, ⁴then whoever hears the sound of the trumpet and does not take warning, if the <u>sword</u> comes and takes him away, his blood shall be on his *own* head. ⁵He heard the sound of the trumpet, but did not take warning; his blood shall be upon himself. But he who takes warning will save his life. ⁶But if the <u>watchman</u> sees the <u>sword</u> coming and does not blow the trumpet, and the people are not warned, and the <u>sword</u> comes and takes *any* person from among them, he is taken away in his iniquity; but his blood I will require at the watchman's hand."

Vv. 3-4

<u>In Ezekiel 33</u> God is naming Ezekiel as the **watchman** and, if he doesn't warn the others, God is holding him responsible for Israel's destruction. Quoting MacDonald, *"The question arises for every believer: For whom will God hold us responsible? To whom shall we witness? Whom shall we warn? Our relatives, fellow workers, neighbors, friends? It is a solemn responsibility, and we do harm to our own soul if we do not fulfill it faithfully."* James 3:1: *My brethren, let not many of you become teachers, knowing that we shall receive a <u>stricter judgment</u>.*

Ezekiel 38:21 "I will call for a <u>sword</u> against <u>Gog</u> throughout all My mountains," says the Lord GOD. "Every man's sword will be against his brother."

The **sword** in <u>Ezekiel 38:21</u> consists of much more than only a sharp instrument: it is contained in the surrounding verses 17-23.

Joel 1:15 Alas for the day! For the <u>day of the LORD</u> *is* at hand; it shall come as destruction from the Almighty.

The prophet <u>Joel 1:15</u> confirms the destruction and repeats the call for the watchman in Chapter 2.

Ezekiel 39:23 "The Gentiles shall know that the house of Israel went into captivity for their iniquity; because they were unfaithful to Me, therefore I hid My face from them. I gave them into the hand of their enemies, and they all fell by the <u>sword</u>."
Daniel 11:33 "And those of the people who understand shall instruct many; yet *for many* days they shall fall by <u>sword</u> and flame, by captivity and plundering.

<u>Ezekiel 39:23</u> and <u>Daniel 11:33</u> speak of **Gog** forces swarming over the land and meeting with the blazing wrath and jealousy of God. There will **be a great earthquake, pestilence, bloodshed, flooding rain, hailstones, fire, and brimstone**.

⁹When He opened the fifth seal, I saw under the altar the souls of those who had been slain for the word of God and for the testimony which they held. ¹⁰And they cried with a loud voice, saying, "How long, O Lord, holy and true, until You judge and avenge our blood on those who dwell on the earth?" ¹¹Then a white robe was given to each of them; and it was said to them that they should rest a little while longer, until both *the number of* their fellow servants and their brethren, who would be killed as they *were*, was completed. ¹²I looked when He opened the sixth seal, and behold, there was a great earthquake; and the sun became black as sackcloth of hair, and the moon became like blood. ¹³And the stars of heaven fell to the earth, as a fig tree drops its late figs when it is shaken by a mighty wind. ¹⁴Then the sky receded [split apart] as a scroll when it is rolled up, and every mountain and island was moved out of its place.

6:9-14
The fifth seal presents the first martyrdom of the Tribulation saints throughout the world. The sixth seal describes huge natural disasters:**
Matthew 24:29 *"Immediately after the tribulation of those days the sun will be darkened, and the moon will not give its light; the stars will fall from heaven, and the powers of the heavens will be shaken."* [And the unbelievers will hate the believers because of Jesus' name (Matthew 24:9).] (Luke 21:25a; Joel 2:30-31)

Vv. 9-14
Matthew 24:9 "Then they will deliver you up to tribulation and kill you, and you will be hated by all nations for My name's sake."

Vv. 9-14
In Matthew 24:9 *faithful believers (who have come to believe during the Tribulation period) will experience great personal testing during the Tribulation. This verse seems to have particular reference to the 144,000 Jewish believers who will have a special ministry during this period.*

Luke 21:25a "And there will be signs in the sun, in the moon"

Luke 21:25a says *there will be disturbances involving **the sun...moon**, and stars that will be clearly visible on earth. Heavenly bodies will be moved out of their orbits. This might cause the gravitational pull to change and the earth could tilt on its axis.*

Joel 2:30-31 ³⁰"And I will show wonders in the heavens and in the earth: blood and fire and pillars of smoke. ³¹The sun shall be turned into darkness, and the moon into blood, before the coming of the great and awesome day of the LORD." [a judgment of the Lord = a Day of the Lord.]

[15]And the kings of the earth, the great men, the rich men, the commanders, the mighty men, every slave and every free man, hid themselves in the caves and in the rocks of the mountains, [16]and said to the mountains and rocks, "Fall on us and hide us from the face of Him who sits on the throne and from the wrath of the Lamb! [17]For the great day of His wrath has come, and who is able to stand?"

6:15-17

See Ezekiel 32:6-8, Joel 1:15; Joel 2:1, Joel 2:11 and Joel 2:31. People will want to die but can't. **The great day of His wrath** begins Christ's judgment—a "Day of the Lord."

Vv. 15-17

Ezekiel 32:6-8 [6]"I will also water the land with the flow of your blood, *even* to the mountains, and the riverbeds will be full of you. [7]When I put out your light, I will cover the heavens, and make its stars dark; I will cover the sun with a cloud, and the moon shall not give her light. [8]All the bright lights of the heavens I will make dark over you, and bring darkness upon your land," says the Lord GOD.

Vv. 15-17

Ezekiel 32:6-8 concerns the sun, moon and stars, and Ezekiel's prophecy lines up with the words of our Lord Jesus Christ.

Joel 1:15 Alas for the day! For the day of the LORD is at hand; it shall come as destruction from the Almighty.

In Joel 1:15 again the prophecies relating to the beginning of the Great Tribulation are all in miraculous agreement.

Joel 2:1 Blow the trumpet in Zion, and sound an alarm in My holy mountain! Let all the inhabitants of the land tremble; for the day of the LORD is coming, for it is at hand: ...

Joel 2:11 The LORD gives voice before His army, for His camp is very great; for strong *is the One* who executes His word. For the day of the LORD *is* great and very terrible; who can endure it? ...

Joel 2:31 "The sun shall be turned into darkness, and the moon into blood, before the coming of the great and awesome day of the LORD."

In Joel 2:1, 2:11 and 2:31 **the trumpet is used to alarm** the people to the seriousness of the crisis that is upon them. A double figure of locusts and a future invading army may be intended in verses 1-11. Nature has not gone awry; the locusts are not beyond God's control. They move at His specific command.** We read of this also in Exodus when Pharaoh's heart was hardened: Exodus 10:4: "Or else, if you refuse to let My people go, behold, tomorrow I will bring locusts into your territory." **The great and awesome day of the LORD** spoken of in verse 31 *will be preceded by wonders in the heavens. Some of these predicted signs are **blood**, fire, pillars of smoke, **the sun** turning **into darkness and the moon into blood**. All who turn to Jesus as Messiah (Christ, Savior), calling **on His name**, will **be saved** to enter the Millennium with Him.* Joel informs us of the breathtaking might **before the coming of the great and awesome day of the LORD.**

The Saved Ones During the Tribulation

Chapter 7, like a parenthesis, comes between the sixth and seventh revealing seals and shows God's grace and salvation during the Tribulation Period.

¹After these things I saw four angels standing at the four corners of the earth, holding the four winds of the earth, that the wind should not blow on the earth, on the sea, or on any tree. ²Then I saw another angel ascending from the east, having the seal of the living God. And he cried with a loud voice to the four angels to whom it was granted to harm the earth and the sea, ³saying, "Do not harm the earth, the sea, or the trees till we have sealed the servants of our God on their foreheads."

7:1-3

The four **winds depict God's judgment of the earth** (Daniel 7:2). **The four **angels** are restraining agents who are holding back judgment of the earth (Revelation 9:15) until God's special **144,000** Jewish servants can be sealed.** **They must be sealed with the seal of God on their foreheads before the Tribulation judgments begin**. The seal is Father God's name written on their foreheads. Jeremiah 32:37-41 tells how the LORD God promised to bring them back.

Vv. 1-3

Daniel 7:2 Daniel spoke, saying, "I saw in my vision by night, and behold, the <u>four winds</u> of <u>heaven</u> were <u>stirring up</u> <u>the Great Sea</u>.

Vv. 1-3

In <u>Daniel 7:2</u> *__the Great Sea__ is the Mediterranean* Sea and the **four winds** are obviously strong winds powered by God from **heaven**, coming from every direction to **stir up** the **sea**.

Revelation 9:15 So the <u>four angels</u>, who had been prepared for the hour and day and month and year, were released to kill a third of mankind.

The **four angels in <u>Revelation 9:15</u> are fallen angels or demons who have been temporarily bound up by God. They are let loose for the purpose of killing a "third" of the population of the world.**

Jeremiah 32:37-41 ³⁷'Behold, I will gather them out of all countries where I have driven them in My anger, in My fury, and in great wrath; I will bring them back to this place, and I will cause them to dwell safely. ³⁸They shall be My people, and I will be their God; ³⁹then I will give them one heart and one way, that they may fear Me <u>forever</u>, for the good of them and their children after them. ⁴⁰And I will make an <u>everlasting covenant</u> with them, that I will not turn away from doing them good; but I will put My fear in their hearts so that they will not depart from Me. ⁴¹Yes, I will rejoice over them to do them good, and I will assuredly plant them in this land, with all My heart and with all My soul.'

Jeremiah in <u>32:37-41</u> was probably concerned for getting the people back from Babylon, but the God of gods and Lord of lords goes beyond just getting them back home in this temporary life. He makes an <u>everlasting covenant</u> with them. He told Jeremiah in Jeremiah 32:26: *"Behold, I am the LORD, the God of all flesh. Is there anything too hard for Me?* Here in Revelation we see that God will continue as always to keep every one of His promises...forever."

⁴And I heard the number of those who were sealed. <u>One hundred *and* forty-four thousand</u> of all the tribes of the children of Israel *were* sealed: ⁵of the tribe of Judah twelve thousand *were* sealed; of the tribe of Reuben twelve thousand *were* sealed; of the tribe of Gad twelve thousand *were* sealed; ⁶of the tribe of Asher twelve thousand *were* sealed; of the tribe of Naphtalī twelve thousand *were* sealed; of the tribe of Manasseh twelve thousand *were* sealed; ⁷of the tribe of Simēon twelve thousand *were* sealed; of the tribe of Levi twelve thousand *were* sealed; of the tribe of Issachar twelve thousand *were* sealed; ⁸of the tribe of Zebūlun twelve thousand *were* sealed; of the tribe of Joseph twelve thousand *were* sealed; of the tribe of Benjamin twelve thousand *were* sealed.

7:4-8
The seal shows ownership and security, as a king's signet ring was used to authenticate and protect official documents (like a notary). **The **144,000** are all Jews from the twelve tribes** (<u>Genesis 49:1;</u> <u>Genesis 49:28;</u> <u>Romans 11:26</u>). There was always a remnant from all the tribes of the nation (<u>Acts 26:6-8;</u> <u>Acts 23:6</u>). <u>The **144,000** will be converted and be a light to the Gentiles during the Tribulation.</u>

Vv. 4-8

Genesis 49:1 And Jacob called his sons and said, "Gather together, that I may tell you what shall befall you in the last days. ...

Genesis 49:28 All these *are* the twelve tribes of Israel, and this *is* what their father spoke to them; he blessed each one according to his own blessing [much like believers will be blessed—or rewarded—at the judgment seat of Christ according to their service. The verses of Genesis 49 describe Jacob's vision of what will happen to his sons who are renamed in Revelation 7].

Vv. 4-8

Jacob's last words to his sons in Genesis 49 were both a prophecy (Genesis 49:1) and a blessing (Genesis 49:28).

In the last days refers to Israel's future in two ways:
1) the time of their occupation of Canaan, and
2) the status of Israel during the Great Tribulation. Deuteronomy 4:30:** *"When you are in distress, and all these things come upon you in the latter days, when you turn to the LORD your God and obey His voice"*

Romans 11:26 And so all Israel will be saved, as it is written: "The Deliverer will come out of Zion, and He will turn away ungodliness from Jacob;"

Romans 11:26: During the Tribulation all believing Israel saints will be saved before the second coming of Christ. But this will only happen after the Spiritual Temple—the Church—has been completed by the *fullness of the Gentiles* have come in—and the Church is raptured. (Romans 11:25)

Acts 26:6-8 ⁶"And now I stand and am judged for the hope of the promise made by God to our fathers. ⁷To this *promise* our twelve tribes, earnestly serving God night and day, hope to attain. For this hope's sake, King Agrippa, I am accused by the Jews. ⁸Why should it be thought incredible by you that God raises the dead?"

Acts 26:6-8 tells us that the *hope* and the *promise* is for the coming Messiah to deliver the nation of Israel and it is the hope in the resurrection of the dead. This "hope" *then, was Paul's crime! He asked Agrippa and all those who were with him, "What was so **incredible** about this?*

Acts 23:6 But when Paul perceived that one part were Sadducees and the other Pharisees, he cried out in the council, "Men *and* brethren, I am a Pharisee, the son of a Pharisee, concerning the hope and resurrection of the dead I am being judged!"

In Acts 23:6 *the **Sadducees** did not believe in the **resurrection**, and neither did they believe in the existence of spirits or angels. The **Pharisees**, being very orthodox, believed in both, so in Acts 23:8 some of the scribes of the **Pharisees** defended Paul's innocence.*

7:9-15

⁹After these things I looked, and behold, a <u>great multitude</u> which no one could number, of <u>all nations</u>, <u>tribes</u>, peoples, and tongues, standing before the throne and before the Lamb, clothed with white robes, with palm branches in their hands, ¹⁰and crying out with a loud voice, saying, "Salvation *belongs* to our God who sits on the throne, and to the Lamb!" ¹¹All the angels stood around the throne and the elders and the four living creatures, and fell on their faces before the throne and worshiped God,

Verses 9-14 compared to <u>Revelation 5:11</u> again confirm that the Rapture takes place prior to the Tribulation (<u>Colossians 1:23c</u>; <u>Romans 11:25-26a</u>). In Revelation 5:11, tens of thousands who had already been raptured will witness a new **great multitude** arriving before the throne. The ones who have been raptured are able to see the many Jews and Gentiles who will be saved <u>during the Tribulation</u>. **White robes portray a standing of righteousness and the multitude praises God for their salvation** (<u>Psalm 3:8</u>). They will be God's servants **day and night** and **God will wipe away every tear from their eyes**.

¹²saying: "Amen! Blessing and glory and wisdom, thanksgiving and honor and power and might, *be* to our God forever and ever. Amen."

Verse 12 has a noticeable seven-fold praise: As a hymn writer said, "Angels never felt the joy that our salvation brings." But they do chant His praises and pronounce Him worthy of seven distinct forms of honor.

¹³Then one of the elders answered, saying to me, "Who are these arrayed in white robes, and where did they come from?" ¹⁴And I said to him, "Sir, you know." So he said to me, "These are the ones who come out of the great tribulation, and washed their robes and made them white in the blood of the Lamb. ¹⁵Therefore they are before the throne of God, and serve Him <u>day and night</u> in His temple. And He who sits on the throne will dwell among them.

The <u>newly redeemed</u> multitude of <u>all</u> <u>nations</u> (Gentiles), <u>tribes</u> (including the one hundred and forty-four thousand of all the tribes of Israel—Romans 11:26) of this vision are new believers who will either be martyred of have survived the Tribulation and be on the earth upon Christ's return at His Second Coming. They will be left on earth for being Christ's servants during His Millennial reign (Ezekiel Chapters 40-44).

Vv. 9-15

Revelation 5:11 Then I looked, and I heard the voice of <u>many angels</u> around the throne, <u>the living creatures, and the elders</u>; and the number of them was ten thousand times ten thousand, and thousands of thousands,

Vv. 9-15

In <u>Revelation 5:11</u> even ***many angels** joined **the living creatures and the elders*** to praise the Lamb for His glory and wisdom.

Colossians 1:23c which was preached to every creature under heaven,

<u>Colossians 1:23c</u>: The creatures are the created and saved living creatures who have been raptured (Revelation 4:1; Revelation 5:11).

Romans 11:25-26a [25]For I do not desire, brethren, that you should be ignorant of this mystery, lest you should be wise in your own opinion, that blindness in part has happened to Israel until the fullness of the Gentiles has come in. [26a]And so all Israel will be saved...

<u>Romans 11:25</u> agrees with Revelation 4:1 that the Church has been raptured and will return with Christ to witness the multitude who will be saved during the Tribulation. And <u>Romans 11:26a</u> agrees with the chronological order that <u>after the fullness of the Gentiles</u> have <u>come in</u>—have come into the Church and have been raptured into heaven; then—<u>after</u> the last Gentile has <u>come in</u>, then <u>all Israel will</u> also <u>be saved</u>. Since the Church Age believers have already been praising the Lamb since chapter 5, here in chapter 7 are the 144,000 (and possibly others saved during the Tribulation) **arrayed in white robes who come out of the great tribulation** (Revelation 7:13-14).

Psalm 3:8 Salvation belongs to the LORD, Your blessing *is* upon Your people. Sēlah [*Selah*: is possibly a pause for action]

David is in prayer in <u>Psalm 3:8</u> asking God to bless His **people** by continuing to show them His marvelous deliverance.

[**Ezekiel** Chapters 38-39 describe scenes of Armageddon]

¹⁶They shall neither hunger anymore nor thirst anymore; the sun shall not strike them, nor any heat; ¹⁷for the Lamb who is in the midst of the throne will shepherd them and lead them to living fountains of waters. And <u>God will wipe away every tear from their eyes</u>.

7:16-17

The blessings will be great: no hunger, no thirst, perfect security as the sun shall not strike them, nor any heat; perfect guidance as the Lamb will be there to shepherd them and lead them; and perfect joy: **God will wipe away every tear from their eyes**. (<u>Psalm 23:1</u>; <u>Psalm 121:5-6</u>; <u>Isaiah 25:8a</u>; <u>Isaiah 49:10a</u>; <u>Matthew 5:4</u>; <u>Revelation 21:4</u>).

Chapter 7 Verses 16-17 References	Chapter 7 Verses 16-17 References Commentary

Vv. 16-17

Vv. 16-17

Psalm 23:1 The LORD *is* <u>my</u> shepherd; I shall not want [lack],

The <u>first verse</u> of the <u>23rd Psalm</u>, with the pronoun **my**, applies only to those who actually believe on Him to truly be their Shepherd.

Psalm 121:5-6 ⁵The LORD *is* your keeper; the LORD *is* your shade at your right hand. ⁶The sun shall not strike you by day, nor the moon by night.

<u>Psalm 121:5-6</u> guarantees that the great Sovereign of the universe is personally involved in the security of the most obscure saint, protecting us from every evil influence. These verses promise welcome protection and freedom from the chains of demon possession.

Isaiah 25:8a He will swallow up <u>death</u> forever, and the Lord GOD will wipe away tears from all faces; **Isaiah 51:**11 So the ransomed of the Lord shall return, And come to Zion with singing, With everlasting joy on their heads. They shall obtain joy and gladness; Sorrow and sighing shall flee away.

<u>Isaiah 25:8a and 51:11</u> tell us that Christ conquers **death** (by His resurrection and by raising the tribulation saints who have died), abolishes sorrow, and in <u>51:11</u> will summon all of Israel to return to the land.

Matthew 5:4 "Blessed are those who mourn, for they shall be comforted."

The mourning in <u>Matthew 5:4</u> does not refer to normal loss of human life. *It is the sorrow one experiences because of fellowship with the Lord Jesus. It is an active sharing of the world's hurting, killings, and sinning against Jesus. Therefore, it includes, not only sorrow for one's own sin, but also sorrow because of the world's rejection of the Savior.

Revelation 21:4 "And God will wipe away every tear from their eyes; there shall be no more death, nor sorrow, nor crying. There shall be no more pain, for the former things have passed away."

<u>Revelation 21:4</u>* confirms the last verse of this Chapter 7.

Seventh Seal is Opened

First Four Trumpets will Signal the Beginning of the Tribulation on the Earth

¹When He opened the <u>seventh seal</u>, there was silence in heaven for about half an hour. ²And I saw the seven angels who stand before God, and to them were given <u>seven trumpets</u>.

8:1-2

Beginning where Chapter 6 left off, the **seventh seal** contains the **seven trumpets**. The Lamb opens the seventh seal, and then silence is held for about half an hour to **indicate the beginning of these further series of judgments.** The first four trumpets will be blasted in this Chapter 8.

³Then another angel, having a golden censer, came and stood at the altar. He was given much <u>incense</u>, that he should offer *it* with the prayers of all the saints upon the golden altar which was before the throne. ⁴And the smoke of the incense, with the prayers of the saints, ascended before God from the angel's hand. ⁵Then the angel took the censer, filled it with fire from the altar, and threw *it* to the earth. And there were noises, thunderings, lightnings, and an earthquake. ⁶So the seven angels who had the seven trumpets prepared themselves to sound.

8:3-6

Incense is often an illustration of prayer (<u>Revelation 5:8</u>). The trumpet judgments may be God's response to the prayers of the saints in Revelation 6:10—a cry for revenge against the enemies of Christ (<u>Psalm 94:1</u>;** <u>Deuteronomy 32:35</u>; **<u>Romans 12:19</u>). The throwing of the censer to earth represents the coming judgment of the earth. Christ will use the angels to administer the trumpets. The blast of each trumpet symbolizes the execution of God's judgment.** (<u>2 Samuel 22:8-10</u>)

Vv. 3-6

Revelation 5:8 Now when He had taken the <u>scroll</u>, the four living creatures and the twenty-four elders fell down before the Lamb, each having a harp, and golden bowls full of incense, which are the prayers of the saints.

Psalm 94:1 O LORD God, to whom vengeance belongs—O God, to whom vengeance belongs, shine forth!

Deuteronomy 32:35 "<u>Vengeance</u> is Mine, and recompense; their foot shall slip in *due* time; for the day of their calamity *is* at hand, and the things to come hasten upon them."

Romans 12:19 Beloved, do not avenge yourselves, but *rather* <u>give place to wrath</u>; for it is written, "<u>*Vengeance* is Mine, I will repay</u>," says the Lord.

2 Samuel 22:8-10 [8]"Then the earth shook and trembled; the foundations of heaven quaked and were shaken, because He was angry. [9]Smoke went up from His nostrils, and devouring fire from His mouth; coals were kindled by it. [10]He bowed the heavens also, and came down with darkness under His feet.

Vv. 3-6

<u>Revelation 5:8</u> refers to coming judgment in the **scroll**. Due to His First and Second Comings—His work as Savior and as Sovereign Judge, Christ has the right to judge, possess, and rule the earth because of His submission to the death of the cross (Philippians 2:8-11).

The faithful remnant of Israel appeal to God in <u>Psalm 94</u> to bring His vengeance to reveal Himself in His hatred of evil. The gloating of the wicked will soon be silenced.

In <u>Deuteronomy 32:35</u> *God's **vengeance** upon the nations that were used to punish Israel was carried out. As a result, God's people and all the nations were to rejoice, because God avenged Himself and made atonement for His land and His people.*

Concerning <u>Romans 12:19</u>, *vengeance is God's prerogative. We **give place to wrath** because God will take care of it for us. Lenski writes, "God has long ago settled the whole matter about exacting justice from wrongdoers. Not one of them will escape. Perfect justice will be done in every case. If any of us interfered, it would be the height of presumption."*

<u>2 Samuel 22:8-10</u> describe the Lord's vengeance with **His triumphant march from Sinai to the Jordan River.** The description appears to be a prelude to the vengeance that He will be accomplishing prior to His Second Coming.

⁷The first angel sounded: And hail and fire followed, mingled with blood, and they were thrown to the earth. And a third of the trees were burned up, and all green grass was burned up.

8:7

The **first trumpet** brings literal **fire and hail**, and causes the destruction of much of the vegetation on earth. Famine and shortage of oxygen will result.** (Ezekiel 38:22)

⁸Then the second angel sounded: And *something* like a great mountain burning with fire was thrown into the sea, and a third of the sea became blood. ⁹And a third of the ships were destroyed.

8:8-9

The **second trumpet** turns one **third** of the **sea** into **blood** and one **third** of the sea creatures and **ships** will be **destroyed**.** Commerce will suffer.

¹⁰Then the third angel sounded: And a great star fell from heaven, burning like a torch, and it fell on a third of the rivers and on the springs of water. ¹¹The name of the star is Wormwood. A third of the waters became wormwood, and many men died from the water, because it was made bitter.

8:10-11

The **third trumpet** makes one **third** of the earth's fresh **water** turn bitter causing widespread thirst and death.** Prolonged sustainability of life on the earth's land will end. ***Wormwood** is literally *undrinkable*** (Deuteronomy 30:18-20).

¹²Then the fourth angel sounded: And a third of the sun was struck, a third of the moon, and a third of the stars, so that a third of them were darkened. A third of the day did not shine, and likewise the night.

8:12

The **fourth trumpet** takes away one **third** of the light from the heavens both **day** and **night** (Matthew 24:29; Luke 21:25).**

¹³And I looked, and I heard an angel flying through the midst of heaven, saying with a loud voice, "Woe, woe, woe to the inhabitants of the earth, because of the remaining blasts of the trumpet of the three angels who are about to sound!

8:13

The last three trumpets will bring such severity that trumpets five and six will be in Chapter 9, but **trumpet** *number seven* will be reserved until Revelation 11:15. **Here in 8:13 we find that these last three are so severe that there is a threefold **woe** expressed to initially describe them.** A single **woe** can be defined as sadness, despair, misery, distress, affliction, mournfulness...all due to a catastrophic calamity. A triple **woe** must be exceedingly miserable.

V. 7

Ezekiel 38:22 "And I will bring him to judgment with pestilence and bloodshed; I will rain down on him, on his troops, and on the many peoples who *are* with him, <u>flooding rain</u>, <u>great hailstones</u>, <u>fire</u>, and <u>brimstone</u>.

V. 7

<u>Ezekiel 38:22</u>: *depicting the destruction of the enemies of God's people reminds us of the Lord's promise in Isaiah 54:17:* *"No weapon formed against you shall prosper...This is the heritage of the servants of the LORD."* God's enemy will be unable to prevail against these supernatural disasters.

Vv. 10-11

Deuteronomy 30:18-20 [18]"I announce to you today that you shall surely perish; you shall not prolong *your* days in the land which you cross over the Jordan to go in and possess. [19]I call heaven and earth as witnesses today against you, *that* I have set before you <u>life</u> and <u>death</u>, <u>blessing</u> and <u>cursing</u>; therefore <u>choose life</u>, that both <u>you and your descendants may live</u>; [20]that you may love the LORD your God, that you may <u>obey His voice</u>, and that <u>you may cling to Him</u>, for He *is* your life and the <u>length of</u> your <u>days</u>; and that you may dwell in the land which the LORD swore to your fathers, to Abraham, Isaac, and Jacob, to give them."

Vv. 10-11

In <u>Deuteronomy 30:18-20</u> *the people were called to choose between **life** and good on the one hand, and **death** and evil on the other—**life** for obedience, but **death** for disobedience. Moses strongly pleaded with them to prefer **blessing** over **cursing**—to **choose life** so **that both** them **and** their **descendants may live**. The desired response (choosing to obey and live) brought good results, including **length of...days** and abundant spiritual **life**, implied by the words **that you may cling to Him**. The only alternative was that of **cursing**.*

V. 12

Matthew 24:29 "Immediately after the tribulation of those days the sun will be darkened and the moon will not give its light; the stars will fall from heaven, and the powers of the heavens will be shaken."
Luke 21:25 "And there will be signs in the sun, in the moon, and in the stars; and on the earth distress of nations, with perplexity; the sea and the waves roaring."

V. 12

<u>Matthew 24:29</u> and <u>Luke 21:25</u> promise a sad situation on this earth. *After the close of the Great Tribulation there will be terrifying disturbances in the heavens. Since the moon's light is only a reflection of the sun's, there will be only darkness—no **light**. The vast cosmic upheavals will undoubtedly affect the earth's weather, tides, and seasons.* We thank our God for the promise to send His Son to the air to take us up to be with Him prior to these seven years of Tribulation trials, temptations, deceptions, and persecutions; and before the last three-and-a-half years of enormous sufferings in the Great Tribulation.

**Trumpets Five and Six will Blast the
First Two Woes**

¹Then the fifth angel sounded: And I saw a star fallen from heaven to the earth. To him was given the key to the bottomless pit. ²And he opened the bottomless pit, and smoke arose out of the pit like the smoke of a great furnace. So **the sun** and the **air** were darkened, because of the **smoke** of the **pit**. ³Then out of the smoke locusts came upon **the earth**. And to them was given power, as the scorpions of the earth have power.

9:1-3

The **fifth** trumpet blasts a **star** (an angel) from **heaven to earth** that has been **given the key to the bottomless pit** (Hādēs—the *abyss* in Greek—the dwelling place of demons). The emitted **smoke** darkens the sun and air, (Joel 2:1-2, Joel 2:10-11; Matthew 24:29), locusts come out of the **pit** having the power of scorpions to torment, but not kill the unbelievers on the earth for five months. The locusts compare to those in the seventh plague against Egypt and the Pharaoh in Exodus 10:4.

⁴They were commanded not to harm the grass of the earth, or any green thing, or any tree, but only those men who do not have the seal of God on their foreheads. ⁵And they were not given *authority* to kill them, but to torment them *for* five months. Their torment *was* like the **torment** of a scorpion when it strikes a man.

9:4-5

The locusts' stings do not kill people, but it inflicts torment that lasts for five months. It produces such intense suffering that men will want to die, but they can't. The effect of scorpions will be brought out again in Revelation 16:2. However, the 144,000 men of Israel who **have the seal of God on their foreheads** (from Revelation 7:2-4) are not to be harmed.

Vv. 1-3

Joel 2:1-2 [1]Blow the <u>trumpet</u> in Zion, and sound an <u>alarm</u> in My holy mountain! Let all the inhabitants of the land tremble; for the day of the LORD is coming, for it is at hand: [2]A day of darkness and gloominess, a day of clouds and thick darkness, like the morning *clouds* spread over the mountains...

Joel 2:10-11 [10]The earth quakes before them, the heavens tremble; the sun and moon grow dark, and the stars diminish their brightness. [11]The LORD gives voice before His army, for His camp is very great; for strong *is the One* who executes His word. For the <u>day of the LORD</u> *is* great and very terrible; who can endure it?

Matthew 24:29 "Immediately after the tribulation of those days the sun will be darkened and the moon will not give its light; the stars will fall from heaven, and the powers of the heavens will be shaken."

Vv. 4-5

Revelation 7:2-4 [2]Then I saw another angel ascending from the east, having <u>the seal of the living God</u>. And he cried with a loud voice to the <u>four angels</u> to whom it was granted to harm the earth and the sea, [3]saying, "Do not harm the earth, the sea, or the trees till we have sealed <u>the servants of our God on their foreheads</u>." [4]And I heard the number of those who were <u>sealed</u>. One hundred *and* forty-four thousand of all <u>the tribes</u> of the children <u>of Israel</u> *were* <u>sealed</u>:

Vv. 1-3

In <u>Joel 2:1-2</u> **the **trumpet** is used to **alarm** the people to the seriousness of the crisis that is upon them.**

<u>Joel 2:10-11</u> predicts the greatness of **the Day of the Lord**.

<u>Matthew 24:29</u> previews beyond to the Second Advent—the Day of the Lord—at the close of the Great Tribulation. *There will be terrifying disturbances in the heavens. **The sun will be darkened, the moon will not** have the sun's **light** to give light at night, **the stars** will plunge from heaven and planets will be moved out of their orbits. Such vast cosmic upheavals will probably affect gravity, tides, seasons,* tsunamis, tornadoes, hurricanes, earthquakes, volcanoes and more.

Vv. 4-5

<u>Revelation 7:2-4</u> is John's vision of *the **four** (fallen) **angels** standing at the four corners of the earth and **holding** back **the four winds** that will burst a great storm onto the world. However, the angels are commanded to delay this terrible destruction until **the servants of God** have been given the seal **of God on their foreheads**. Twelve thousand persons from each of **the** twelve **tribes of Israel** are then **sealed**.* The believers of the Church Age are already sealed: 2 Timothy 2:19a: *Nevertheless the solid foundation of God stands, having this <u>seal</u>: "The Lord knows those who are His,"* Ephesians 1:13: *In Him you also trusted, after you heard* [absorbed] *the word of truth, the gospel of your salvation; in whom also, having believed, you were <u>sealed</u> with the Holy Spirit of promise.* (2 Corinthians 1:22)

9:6

⁶In those days men will not find it; they will desire to die, and death will flee from them.

In Revelation 9:6 [much like Revelation 6:15-17] the unbelievers wanted to hide and even choose **death** to escape the torment (Jeremiah 8:3). The king of those in the bottomless pit is named *Abaddon* (Destruction) in Hebrew, but *Apollyon* (Destroyer) in Greek. This would be Satan.

9:7-11

⁷The shape of the locusts was like horses prepared for battle. On their heads were crowns of something like gold, and their faces *were* like the faces of men. ⁸They had hair like women's hair, and their teeth were like lions' *teeth*. ⁹And they had breastplates like breastplates of iron, and the sound of their wings *was* like the sound of chariots with many horses running into battle. ¹⁰They had tails like scorpions, and there were stings in their tails. Their power *was* to hurt men five months. ¹¹And they had as king over them the angel of the bottomless pit, whose name in Hebrew *is* Abaddon [Hebrew for *Destruction*], but in Greek he has the name Apollyon [Destroyer].

Where here 9:7 says **like the faces of men** implies they were creatures of intelligence. **Hair like women's** suggests they were attractive and seductive. Lion-like **teeth** connotes they were ferocious and cruel. The **iron breastplates** made them difficult to attack and destroy. *Their noisy **wings** created a terrifying and demoralizing atmosphere. The **tails like scorpions** equipped them to torture both physically and mentally.

9:12

¹²One woe is past. Behold, still two more woes are coming after these things.

The first of three woes in Revelation 8:13 **is past**. The worst is yet to come. The judgments increase in intensity.* The second woe will end at Revelation 11:14. The third and final woe will end in Revelation 16:17.

V. 6

Revelation 6:15-17 ¹⁵And the kings of the earth, the great men, the rich men, the commanders, the mighty men, every slave and every free man, hid themselves in the caves and in the rocks of the mountains, ¹⁶and said to the mountains and rocks, "Fall on us and hide us from the face of Him who sits on the throne and from <u>the wrath of the Lamb</u>! ¹⁷For the great day of His wrath has come, and who is able to stand?"

V. 6

<u>Revelation 6:15</u> calls to our attention, *not surprisingly, all classes of society will be seized with panic. They prefer to be crushed by tumbling rocks than to endure the judgment of **the wrath of the Lamb!*** (<u>Revelation 6:16-17</u>)

Jeremiah 8:3 "Then death shall be chosen rather than life by all the residue of those who remain of this evil family, who remain in all the places where I have driven them," says the LORD of hosts.

In Jeremiah 8:1 *the Babylonian invaders dig up the graves of the previous believing kings, princes, priests, prophets, and inhabitants of Jerusalem exposing their bones to the heavens. Then in <u>Jeremiah 8:3</u> those Jewish observers who chose to sin and not to repent wished they could die.*

9:13-14

The **sixth** trumpet blasts and God commands the **sixth angel** to **release the four angels who are bound on the earth at the River Euphrates** (Revelation 16:12-14). We are reminded in Revelation 7:3 that they are not to harm the 144,000 of the tribes of Israel.

¹³Then the sixth angel sounded: And I heard a voice from the four horns of the golden altar which is before God, ¹⁴saying to the sixth angel who had the trumpet, "Release the four angels who are bound at the great river Eūphrātēs."

9:15-19

These **four angels** will be **released to kill** one **third of** remaining **mankind** with the use of three plagues from an **army**—the Lord's **army**—**of two hundred million horsemen**. The horses—*not the riders*—issue *three plagues: **fire**, **smoke**, and **brimstone** to kill one **third of mankind**. Not only do the **horses** kill with their **mouths**, but they also wound with their serpent-like **tails**.* This is the **power** of our God!

¹⁵So the four angels, who had been prepared for the hour and day and month and year, were released to kill a third of mankind. ¹⁶Now the number of the army of the horsemen *was* two hundred million; I heard the number of them. ¹⁷And thus I saw the horses in the vision: those who sat on them had breastplates of fiery red, hyacinth blue, and sulfur yellow; and the heads of the horses *were* like the heads of lions; and out of their mouths came fire, smoke, and brimstone. ¹⁸By these three *plagues* a third of mankind was killed—by the fire and the smoke and the brimstone which came out of their mouths. ¹⁹For their power is in their mouth and in their tails; for their tails *are* like serpents, having heads; and with them they do harm.

9:20-21

*But the remainder of mankind who were not killed by the plagues** still **do not repent**. They continue worshipping lifeless and impotent **idols** made with their own hands. And **they did not repent** of their **murders** or their **sorceries** (witchcrafts; pretenders to magic powers) or their **sexual immorality** or their **thefts**.* Only by believing, repenting and being born again with a new heart can a sinner's character change.

²⁰But the rest of mankind, who were not killed by these plagues, did not repent of the works of their hands, that they should not worship demons, and idols of gold, silver, brass, stone, and wood, which can neither see nor hear nor walk. ²¹And they did not repent of their murders or their sorceries or their sexual immorality or their thefts.

Vv. 13-14

Revelation 16:12-14 [12]Then the sixth angel poured out his bowl on the great river Eūphrātēs, and its water was dried up, so that the way of the kings from the east might be prepared. [13]And I saw three [false trinity] unclean spirits like frogs *coming* out of the mouth of the dragon [Satan], out of the mouth of the beast [Antichrist], and out of the mouth of the false prophet. [14]For they are spirits of demons, performing signs, *which* go out to the kings of the earth and of the whole world, to gather them to the battle of that great day of God Almighty.

Vv. 13-14

Here in Chapter 9 we read of the command for **the sixth angel** to sound his trumpet, and in Revelation 16:12-14 the situation is going to be, if one could possibly imagine, greatly worsened. Of course Chapter 16 is still to come, but here is a preview to see what happens when the sixth **bowl** is **poured out**. *The **water** of the **Eūphrātēs** River will be **dried up**, allowing the armies **from the east** to march toward the land of Israel. John sees **three** frog-like **spirits coming out of the mouth of the dragon, ... the beast and ... the false prophet**—Satan's false trinity*—Satan playing the part of God, the Antichrist man the part of Christ, and the false prophet the part of the Holy Spirit. These three counterfeits are *demonic **spirits, performing** miracles to deceive the world's rulers, and to lure them to a climactic soon coming **battle** against the Second Coming of the Lord Jesus Christ on the **great day of God Almighty**.* The seventh angel is yet to sound his trumpet...in Chapter 11:15. But first, in Chapter 10, the next chapter, *another angel* will cry out resulting in *seven thunders.*

Revelation 7:3 saying, "Do not harm the earth, the sea, or the trees till we have sealed the servants of our God on their foreheads."

Revelation 7:3 begins the protection of the saved Jews. Once saved, they are no longer appointed to wrath. In agreement, Revelation 9:4: *They were commanded not to harm the grass of the earth, or any green thing, or any tree, but only those men who do not have the seal of God on their foreheads.* God's protection continues throughout the Great Tribulation—the last three-and-a-half years as confirmed in Revelation 12:14: *But the woman* [the Israelites] *was given two wings of a great eagle, that she might fly into the wilderness to her place, where she is nourished for a time and times and half a time,* [3½ years] *from the presence of the serpent.* Therefore the demonic spirits of Chapter 16 will have no influence nor negative effect upon the 144,000 sealed forever believers.

Another Angel with the Little Book and Seven Thunders

[1]I saw still <u>another mighty angel</u> coming down from heaven, clothed with a cloud. And a rainbow *was* on his head, his face *was* like the sun, and his feet like pillars of fire. [2]He had a <u>little book</u> open in his hand. And he set his right foot on the sea and *his* left *foot* on the land, [3]and cried with a loud voice, as *when* a lion roars. When he cried out, <u>seven thunders</u> uttered their voices.

10:1-3

Another mighty angel comes down to earth **from heaven** *holding a **little book**—possibly containing a record of impending judgments.* **The description of this angel *resembles* that of Christ (<u>Revelation 1:13-16</u>),** but the text does not confirm it is Him. *The angel cries out in a loud voice and **seven thunders** are heard.*

Vv. 1-3

Revelation 1:13-16 ¹³and in the midst of the <u>seven lampstands</u> *One* like <u>the Son of Man</u>, clothed with a <u>garment</u> down to the feet and girded about the chest with a golden band. ¹⁴His head and <u>hair</u> *were* <u>white</u> like wool, as white as snow, and His eyes like a flame of <u>fire</u>; ¹⁵His feet *were* like fine <u>brass</u>, as if refined in a furnace, and His <u>voice</u> as the <u>sound</u> of many waters; ¹⁶He had in His right hand <u>seven stars</u>, out of His mouth went a sharp two-edged <u>sword</u>, and His <u>countenance</u> *was* *like* the <u>sun</u> shining in its strength.

Vv. 1-3

<u>Revelation 1:13-16:</u> **is a description of Jesus Christ as Judge (John 5:22, 27). The **seven lampstands** are identified in Revelation 1:20 as the seven churches mentioned in Revelation 1:11. **The Son of Man** is a Messianic title from Daniel 7:13,** and, since He, God Himself, was born in the flesh of Mary in the lineage to Adam through David, this ****Son of Man** was Jesus' most used designation for Himself.** However, He also referred to Himself as the *"only begotten Son of God"* (John 3:16). **The **garment** is a judge's robe. His **white hair** symbolizes justice, purity, and glory. **Fire** is also a symbol of judgment. The **brass** and the **sound** of the **voice** show Christ's authority and power. The **seven stars** are identified in verse 20 as the <u>angels</u> of the seven churches. The **sword** also represents Christ's judgment (Revelation 19:15) of the churches and the world through His Word. His **countenance** or face was **like the sun** as the glory of God shone forth.**

⁴Now when the seven <u>thunders</u> uttered their voices, I was about to write; but I heard a voice from heaven saying to me, "Seal up the things which the seven thunders uttered, and do not write them." ⁵The <u>angel</u> whom I saw standing on the sea and on the land raised up his hand to heaven ⁶and swore by Him who lives forever and ever, who created heaven and the things that are in it, the earth and the things that are in it, and the sea and the things that are in it, that <u>there should be delay no longer</u>, ⁷but in the days of the sounding of the <u>seventh</u> <u>angel</u>, when he is about to sound, the mystery of God would be finished, as He declared to His servants the prophets.

10:4-7

John is told not to write what he hears from the **thunders**. The **angel** swears to God in <u>heaven</u> that He has the authority to perform these judgments (<u>John 5:22</u>; <u>John 5:26-27</u>) because He is omnipotent (all powerful), omnipresent (everywhere all the time), omniscient (knowledgeable of all things past, present and future), even able to know our thoughts (Psalm 139:1-16; <u>Luke 5:22</u>; <u>Luke 6:8</u>; <u>Luke 11:17</u>; <u>Luke 24:38</u>), and because He is the Creator (<u>Psalm 19:1</u>; <u>Hebrews 1:8a</u>; <u>Hebrews 1:10</u>), and that **there should be no more delay**. The **seventh** and final trumpet will be blasted soon. (<u>Revelation 11:15</u>).

Here in 10:7, when the two prophet witnesses finish giving the testimony of the mystery of God, they will be killed, left to be seen for three-and-a-half days, and then be seen ascending to heaven (Revelation 11:3-12.)

Vv. 4-7
John 5:22 "For the Father judges no one, but has committed all judgment to the Son."
John 5:26-27 ²⁶ "For as the Father has life in Himself, so He has granted the Son to have life in Himself, ²⁷ and has given Him <u>authority</u> to execute judgment also, because He is the Son of Man."
Luke 5:22 But when Jesus perceived their thoughts, He answered and said to them, "Why are you reasoning in your hearts?"
Luke 6:8 But He knew their thoughts, and said to the man who had the withered hand, "Arise and stand here." And he arose and stood.
Luke 11:17 But He, knowing their thoughts, said to them: "Every kingdom divided against itself is brought to desolation, and a house *divided* against a house falls."
Luke 24:38 And He said to them, "Why are you troubled? And why do doubts arise in your hearts?"

Vv. 4-7
*For the Lord Jesus to be able to do this judging (<u>John 5:22; John 5:26-27</u>), He must also be God as the Father is God. He must have the knowledge, perfect righteousness, and **authority**. He must be able to discern the thoughts and motives of men's hearts* (Matthew 15:19; Mark 7:21; <u>Luke 5:22; Luke 6:8; Luke 11:17; Luke 24:38</u>; 1 Corinthians 3:20; Hebrews 4:12). *How strange it was that the Judge of all the earth should stand being judged before the Jews, asserting His authority, and yet they did not recognize Him!*

Psalm 19:1 THE heavens declare the glory of God; and the firmament shows His handiwork.
Hebrews 1:8a But to the Son *He says*: ...
Hebrews 1:10 And: "*You LORD, in the beginning laid the foundation of the earth, and the heavens are the work of Your hands.*"

<u>Psalm 19:1, Hebrews 1:8a and 10</u> not only tell us that God is our Creator, but the Father Himself is quoted in Hebrews 1 confirming that all of creation was done by the hands of God the Son, Jesus Christ. John 1:2-3 and Colossians 1:16-17 further clarify these truths.

Revelation 11:15 Then the <u>seventh</u> angel sounded: And there were loud voices in heaven, saying, "The <u>kingdoms of this world have become *the kingdoms* of our Lord</u> and of His Christ, and He shall <u>reign forever and ever</u>!"

The **seventh** trumpet in <u>Revelation 11:15</u> *reveals that the Great Tribulation is over (in this first chronological version) and the reign of Christ in His millennial kingdom has begun.* **The vials (or bowls; Revelation 16:1) are probably contained in the judgment of the **seventh** trumpet. They will occur in a very brief period of time at the end of the Great Tribulation. The Second Coming of Christ, while a great blessing for believers, will be God's most severe judgment of the earth. The **kingdoms of this world** will be completely overthrown by the coming kingdom of Christ (Revelation 19:11-21; Daniel 2:34-35; Daniel 2:44) who will **reign forever and ever** (Daniel 7:13-14; Daniel 7:27).**

10:8-10

The angel commanded John to **eat** the **little book** which would be **sweet** in his **mouth** but **bitter** in his **stomach**. The LORD caused Ezekiel to **eat** the scroll with writings on it, and it was like **honey** in sweetness in Ezekiel's **mouth** (Ezekiel 3:1-3). It is **sweet** to read of God's triumph over Satan and how all sin will be done away with, but it is **bitter** to contemplate the eternal doom of all who reject the Savior. We, too, need to *eat*, that is, absorb and digest God's Word. When we set our hearts to know and understand God, and pray to Him in His will, He hears us just as He did in Jeremiah 15:16 and Daniel 10:11-12. (Acts 8:30-31)

⁸Then the voice which I heard from heaven spoke to me again and said, "Go, take the little book which is open in the hand of the angel who stands on the sea and on the earth." ⁹So I went to the angel and said to him, "Give me the little book." And he said to me, "Take and eat it; and it will make your stomach bitter, but it will be as sweet as honey in your mouth." ¹⁰Then I took the little book out of the angel's hand and ate it, and it was as sweet as honey in my mouth. But when I had eaten it, my stomach became bitter.

10:11

¹¹And he said to me, "You must prophesy again about many peoples, nations, tongues, and kings."

John is told to **prophesy** a second time (key to understanding the *chronology* of the Book of Revelation is that the prophecy and its warnings will be repeated, but in more detail) to better enhance understanding of the personages and movements of the Tribulation period. Chapters 12 to 19 fulfill this repeated second prophecy mandate.

Vv. 8-10

Ezekiel 3:1-3 ¹Moreover He said to me, "Son of man, eat what you find; eat this <u>scroll</u>, and go, speak to the house of Israel." ²So I opened my mouth, and He caused me to eat that <u>scroll</u>. ³And He said to me, "Son of man, feed your belly, and fill your stomach with this <u>scroll</u> that I give you." So I <u>ate</u>, and it was in my mouth like honey in sweetness.

Vv. 8-10

Ezekiel **ate** the **scroll**, as commanded in <u>Ezekiel 3:1-3</u>. As we see here in Revelation 10:8-10, John did the same thing. *Every prophet, that is, preacher, needs to <u>absorb the Word of God</u>, making it part of his own life*—in order to be worthy and able to transmit it to others in truth which would please, honor, and glorify God.

Jeremiah 15:16 Your words were found and I ate them, and Your word was to me the joy and rejoicing of my heart; for I am called by Your name, O LORD God of hosts.

<u>Jeremiah 15:16</u> reveals that even though Jeremiah had been so faithful and yet suffered and was persecuted, he **found joy and rejoicing in** his **heart** with God's **words**.

Daniel 10:11-12 ¹¹And he [Michael the angel] said to me, "O Daniel, man greatly beloved, understand the words that I speak to you, and stand upright, for I have now been sent to you." While he was speaking this word to me, I stood trembling. ¹²Then he said to me, "Do not fear, Daniel, for from the first day that you set your heart to understand, and to humble yourself before your God, your words were heard; and I have come because of your words.

<u>Daniel 10:11-12</u> also depicts the tremendous value of us for being humble and hungering and thirsting for God's Word just as we are now doing in this study of *The Revelation of Jesus Christ*. It goes right back to Revelation 1:3: *Blessed is he who reads and those who hear the words of this prophecy, and keep those things which are written in it; for the time is near.*

Acts 8:30-31 ³⁰So Phillip ran to him, and heard him reading the prophet Isaiah, and said, "Do you understand what you are reading?" ³¹And he [the Ethiopian eunuch of great authority] said, "How can I, unless someone guides me?" And he asked Philip to come up and sit with him.

Acts 8:30-31 gives a perfect example of how all of us who need the help can benefit from gifted Bible teachers to better understand, know, and love our God.

The Seven Years Preview Ends in this Chapter

Then I was given a reed like a measuring rod. ¹And the angel stood, saying, "Rise and measure the temple of God, <u>the altar</u>, and those who worship there. ²But leave out the <u>court</u> which is <u>outside</u> the <u>temple</u>, and do not measure it, for it has been given to <u>the Gentiles</u>. And they will tread the <u>holy city</u> underfoot for <u>forty-two months</u>.

11:1-2

The temple that was built in 515BC (<u>Ezra 6:15</u>) was destroyed in AD 70 (<u>Luke 21:24</u>) and will be rebuilt during the Tribulation period (2 Thessalonians 2:4). ****The outer **court outside** the **temple** represents control of Jerusalem and Israel being trampled by **the Gentiles**.** (Ezekiel 40:3; Ezekiel 42:20) *The altar** probably pictures the means by which the worshipers approach God—that is—by believing in the work of Christ at Calvary.* **The **forty-two months** show that Jerusalem will be under **Gentile** control for the last three-and-a-half years of the Seven-year Tribulation period (<u>Daniel 9:24a</u>; <u>Daniel 9:26a</u>; <u>Daniel 9:27a</u>).** The **forty-two months** in verse 11:2 is exactly three-and-a-half years (the last half of the Seven-year Tribulation Period).

Vv. 1-2

Ezra 6:15 Now the temple was finished on the third day of the month of Ādar, which was in the sixth year of the reign of King Darīus.

Luke 21:24 "And they [the Jews] **will fall by the edge of the sword** [in AD 70 with the destruction of Jerusalem], **and be led away captive into all nations. And Jerusalem will be trampled by Gentiles until the** times of the Gentiles **are fulfilled."**

Daniel 9:24a "Seventy weeks [Each week represents one year; 7x70=490 years]...
Daniel 9:26a And after the sixty-two weeks Messiah shall be cut off, [434 years]
Daniel 9:27a Then he [the Antichrist] shall confirm a covenant with many for one week" [7 years].

Note:
Arriving here in Chapter 11 at the end of the first three-and-a-half years of the Tribulation, it would be well to look back concerning some of the sequence of events thus far:
2 Thessalonians 2:7-8 confirms that the Church indwelled by the Holy Spirit will be taken away before the Antichrist can be revealed. Further, once saved, Christ does not allow His betrothed bride to be handed over to wrath—neither the wrath of God nor the wrath of Satan and his Antichrist (Revelation 12:12).
Romans 5:9 Much more then, having now been justified [saved] by His blood, we shall be saved from wrath through Him.
1 Thessalonians 5:9 For God did not appoint us to wrath, but to obtain salvation through our Lord Jesus Christ.
1 Thessalonians 1:10 and to wait for His Son from heaven, whom He raised from the dead, *even* Jesus who delivered us from the wrath to come.

Vv. 1-2

Ezra 6:15 date: In his commentary *Revive Us Again*, pg. 66. Warren Henderson researched the exact date to be "March 12, 515 BC, approximately four and a half years after they had resumed construction (verses 15-16)."

In Luke 21:24 Jesus prophesies the destruction of the temple and fall of Jerusalem in AD 70. The ***times*** **of the Gentiles** is not the same as the *fullness* of the Gentiles. *The *fullness* of the Gentiles refers to the Rapture in Romans 11:25. The ***times*** **of the Gentiles** refers to the time which began with the Babylonian captivity in 586 B.C. and continues to the time when Gentile nations will no longer have control over Jerusalem.* So these ***times*** **of the Gentiles** control is still ongoing today.

Daniel 9:24a, 9:26a, and 9:27a is a highly complex and amazingly accurate prophecy including the Savior's death and beyond to the future-soon-coming Seven-year Tribulation period. The Hebrew context here of *seven weeks* is referring to *seven YEARS*. Daniel prophesied a total of 7 x 70 **weeks** = 490. (**Seventy** **weeks** translates to **490** *years*.) Seven weeks—or 49 years—after the release of the Jews from captivity in 468 BC brings us to 419BC when Nehemiah's work of rebuilding the Jerusalem wall was completed. Then 62 **weeks**—or 434 more years—from the end of Jerusalem being rebuilt (49 + 434 totaling 483 years from when the Jews were released) takes us to near the exact time of Christ's Triumphal Entry—the tenth day of the month of Nisan exactly four days before He was crucified or, as Daniel put it: **Messiah shall be cut off** (Daniel 9:26a). All that prophecy has been fulfilled. The Church Age follows Christ's death, resurrection, and ascension, and only the Father knows when He will send His Son to the air to rapture the saints. But, when the Rapture occurs, the last week—the seventieth week will begin. At the completion of those seven years—Daniel's prophecy will be fulfilled. Christ's Second Coming is based on the completion of seven years of Tribulation (Matthew 24:36; Mark 13:32; Zechariah 14:6-7).

God's Two Witnesses Testify (Vv. 3-12)

11:3-6

³And I will give *power* to my two witnesses, and they will prophesy one thousand two hundred and sixty days, clothed in sackcloth." ⁴These are the two olive trees and the two lampstands standing before the God of the earth. ⁵And if anyone wants to harm them, fire proceeds from their mouth and devours their enemies. And if anyone wants to harm them, he must be killed in this manner. ⁶These have power to shut heaven, so that no rain falls in the days of their prophecy; and they have power over waters to turn them to blood, and to strike the earth with all plagues, as often as they desire.

God gives power to **two witnesses for 1,260 days** (also three-and-a-half years based on prophetical years of 360 days each). **The **sackcloth** symbolizes mourning, confession, and repentance**—due to Israel's rejection of Jesus Christ during the entire present church age. **The witnesses** (possibly Moses and Elijah) **will proclaim a message of judgment and the need for repentance. They bear similarities to John the Baptist, and will be the ultimate fulfillment of the promised return of Elijah (Malachi 4:4-6). They are also identified as **the two olive trees and the two lampstands** (relating to Zechariah 4:2-3; Zechariah 4:9; Zechariah 4:12-14) where Zerubbabel and Joshua the priest are pictured as two olive trees for a lampstand (Israel). The two witnesses will perform miracles similar to those performed by *Moses* (Exodus 7:14-20; Exodus 9:33) *and Elijah* (1 Kings 17:1; 1 Kings 18:1; 2 Kings 1:10-12; Luke 4:25; James 5:17). They are protected from harm for three-and-a-half years. Their miraculous powers are apparently for the purpose of authenticating their divine message as in the case of Jesus and His apostles.** To this day no one has found the grave of Moses (Deuteronomy 34:5-6). Elijah was previously taken up (raptured) and seen ascending by Elisha in 2 Kings 2:11-12. Moses and Elijah actually appear during the Transfiguration in Matthew 17:3; Mark 9:4; Luke 9:32-33; 2 Peter 1:16. Peter, James and John also witnessed the appearance of Jesus and His garments being supernaturally changed; thus the Transfiguration named as it is. All this does not prove that the two witnesses are in fact Moses and Elijah, but these verses and passages certainly point to this possibility. We will only know when we meet them in heaven.

Vv. 3-6

Malachi 4:4-6 ⁴"Remember the Law of <u>Moses</u>, My servant, which I commanded him in Hōreb for all Israel, *with* the statutes and judgments, ⁵"Behold, <u>I will send</u> you <u>Elijah</u> the prophet before the coming of the great and dreadful day of the LORD. ⁶And he will turn the hearts of the fathers to the children, and the hearts of the children to their fathers, lest I come and strike the earth with a curse."

Vv. 3-6

The LORD is quoted in <u>Malachi 4:4-6</u> giving us the strong possibility that He will send <u>Moses</u> and <u>Elijah</u> as His two witnesses to proclaim a message of judgment and the need for repentance.

Zechariah 4:2-3 ²And he [the angel who talked with Zechariah] said to me, "What do you see?" So I said, "I am looking, and there *is* a lampstand of solid gold with a bowl on top of it, and on the *stand* seven lamps with seven pipes to the seven lamps. ³Two olive trees *are* by it, one at the right of the bowl and the other at its left."

Zechariah 4:9 "The hands of <u>Zerubbabel</u> have laid the foundation of this temple; his hands shall also finish it. Then you will know that the LORD of hosts has sent Me to you."

Zechariah 4:12-14 ¹²And I further answered and said to him, "What *are* these two olive branches that *drip* into the receptacles of the two gold pipes from which the golden <u>oil</u> drains?" ¹³Then he answered me and said, "Do you not know what these *are*?" And I said, "No, my lord. ¹⁴So he said, "These *are* the two anointed ones, who stand beside the Lord of the whole earth."

In <u>Zechariah 4:2-3, 4:9 and 4:12-14</u> <u>Zerubbabel and Joshua</u> (Joshua in Zechariah 3:7) the priest are pictured as the two olive trees for a lampstand (Israel). The 144,000 of Israel will witness to the world during the Tribulation period. They can only fulfill their function as a light to the world by the *oil*, i.e., by the Holy Spirit. The Holy Spirit will remove difficulties and Zerubbabel will finish rebuilding the temple. (Ezra 3:2; Ezra 3:8-10)

The Two Witnesses (Vv. 3-12)

11:7-10

⁷When they finish their testimony, the <u>beast</u> that ascends out of the bottomless pit will make war against them, overcome them, and kill them. ⁸And their dead bodies *will lie* in the street of the great city which spiritually is called <u>Sodom</u> <u>and Egypt</u>, where also our Lord was crucified. ⁹Then *those* from the peoples, tribes, tongues, and nations will see their dead bodies three-and-a-half days, and not allow their dead bodies to be put into graves. ¹⁰And those who dwell on the earth <u>will rejoice</u> over them, make merry, and send gifts to one another, because these <u>two prophets</u> tormented those who dwell on the earth.

The beast is the Antichrist (<u>Revelation 13:1**-2</u>; <u>Revelation 13:8</u>) or false messiah under the control of Satan. **At the end of the three-and-a-half years of preaching, the witnesses (Moses and Elijah) will finally be killed by the **beast** in the **holy city** (Jerusalem), *where also our Lord was crucified*** (just outside the wall of Jerusalem). Since it will be at this Tribulation time under the control of Satan, it will be **called **Sodom**, referring to uncleanness and immorality **and Egypt**, depicting oppression and bondage. Not allowing their dead bodies to be buried is the ultimate indignity. <u>The unbelievers of the earth</u>, having submitted to the authority of the beast, **will rejoice**, because they hate the plagues and the message of the **two prophets** (<u>1 Kings 18:17</u>; <u>John 16:20</u>).** The Antichrist will undoubtedly <u>rejoice</u> along with <u>those who dwell on the earth</u> because he has successfully silenced the Word of God just prior to the arrival of Satan to earth (having been defeated by Michael the archangel) in the next chapter: Revelation 12:12-13.

11:11-14

¹¹Now after the three-and-a-half days the breath of life from God entered them, and they stood on their feet, and <u>great fear fell</u> <u>on those who saw them</u>. ¹²And they heard a loud voice from heaven saying to them, "<u>Come up here</u>." And they ascended to <u>heaven</u> in a cloud, and <u>their enemies</u> saw them. ¹³In the same hour there was a great <u>earthquake</u>, and a tenth of the city fell. In the <u>earthquake</u> <u>seven thousand people were killed</u>, and the <u>rest</u> were afraid and gave <u>glory to</u> the <u>God</u> of heaven. ¹⁴The second woe is past. Behold, the <u>third woe</u> is coming quickly.

The two witnesses are <u>brought back to life</u> and taken up into **heaven. **Their enemies** react in **fear**, since the two witnesses' resurrection and ascension is absolute proof their message was true and Jesus is God and Messiah. An **earthquake** kills **seven thousand men**. Compare to the earthquake that opened tombs and allowed many to be raised after Christ's resurrection (<u>Matthew 27:51-53</u>). The **remnant** are those who are not killed by the earthquake. Many of them repent and give **glory to God**. The parenthesis begun with Chapter 10 ends here. The **third woe** begins with the **seventh trumpet** which comes next in v. 15.**

Of the 3 woes spoken of in Revelation 8:13, the
1ˢᵗ woe passed in Revelation 9:12, the
2ⁿᵈ ended here in Revelation 11:14, and the
3ʳᵈ ends in Revelation 16:17.

Vv. 7-10

Revelation 13:1-2 ¹Then I stood on the sand of the <u>sea</u>. And I saw a <u>beast</u> rising up out of the <u>sea</u>, having <u>seven heads</u> and <u>ten horns</u>, and on his horns <u>ten crowns</u>, and on his heads a blasphemous name. ²Now the <u>beast</u> which I saw was like a leopard, his feet were like *the feet of* a bear, and his mouth like the mouth of a lion. The <u>dragon</u> gave him his power, his <u>throne</u>, and great <u>authority</u>. ...

Revelation 13:8 All who dwell on the earth will <u>worship</u> him, whose names have not been written in the Book of Life of the Lamb slain from the foundation of the world.

Vv.7-10

In <u>Revelation 13:1-2 and 13:8</u> the **sea represents the Gentile nations of the world, from one of which the **beast**, the <u>Antichrist</u> comes.** The **seven heads** are said in Revelation 17:9-10 to be seven kings, or rulers, or seven different stages of the empire. **Ten horns** are predicted by Daniel 7:24 to be a ten-kingdom form. The **ten crowns** speak of the power to rule, from a **throne** with great **authority**, which was given to the Antichrist by Satan, the **dragon**. The Antichrist **beast** is **worshiped** by men. They are not only amazed at him; they actually worship him thinking he is God the Savior (2 Thessalonians 2:4-11). The **beast** will persecute the saints of God and all whose names are not in the Book of Life of the Lamb will be deceived and worship Satan and the Antichrist.

1 Kings 18:17 Then it happened, when <u>Ahab</u> saw Elijah, that Ahab said to him, "*Is that* you, O troubler of Israel?"

In <u>1 Kings 18</u> Elijah's prophecy defeated King **Ahab**'s false prophets.

John 16:20 "Most assuredly, I say to you [His disciples] that you will weep and lament, but <u>the world</u> will rejoice; and you will be sorrowful, but your <u>sorrow</u> will be turned into joy."

In <u>John 16:20</u> Jesus told them their future of which we read here in the Book of Revelation. "There will be no more **sorrow**" (Revelation 21:4).

Vv. 11-14

Matthew 27:51-53 ⁵¹Then, behold, the veil of the temple was torn in two <u>from top to bottom</u>; and the earth quaked, and the rocks were split, ⁵²and the graves were opened; and many bodies of the <u>saints</u> who had fallen asleep were raised; ⁵³and coming <u>out of the graves</u> after His resurrection, they went into the holy city and <u>appeared to many</u>.

Vv. 11-14

<u>Matthew 27:51-53</u> makes known two miracles: First, the curtain that blocked the entrance to the Most Holy place (Exodus 26:33; Hebrews 9:3) into God's presence was torn open **from top to bottom**, and now the way was opened by Him for a new and living way to God for believers. Matthew is the only writer to mention the **saints** who came **out of the graves** and nothing more is said about these believers except that they **appeared to many**. Great fear probably fell on those who saw them.

The First Prophecy Preview of the Seven Years End
The Seventh Trumpet and <u>Christ's Return</u>

11:15

¹⁵Then <u>the seventh angel sounded</u> [the <u>seventh trumpet</u>]: And there were loud voices in heaven, saying, "The <u>kingdoms of this world</u> have become *the kingdoms* of our Lord and of His <u>Christ</u>, and He shall <u>reign forever and ever!</u>"

<u>The **seventh trumpet brings closer the millennial kingdom of **Christ**</u>. The seven vials or bowls (<u>Revelation 16:1</u>) are probably contained in the judgment of the **seventh trumpet**. They will occur in a very brief period of time at the end of the Great Tribulation. <u>The Second Coming of Christ</u>, while a great blessing for believers, <u>will be God's most severe judgment of the earth</u>. The **kingdoms of this world** will be completely overthrown by the coming kingdom of Christ (<u>Revelation 19:11</u>; <u>Revelation 19:20-21</u>; <u>Daniel 2:34-35a</u>; <u>Daniel 2:44</u>), who will **reign forever and ever** (<u>Daniel 7:13a, 7:14b,</u> Daniel 7:27).**

V. 15

Revelation 16:1 Then I heard a loud voice from the temple saying to the seven angels, "Go and pour out <u>the bowls of the wrath of God</u> on the earth." ...
Revelation 19:11 Now I saw heaven opened, and behold, a <u>white horse</u>. And <u>He who sat on him *was* called Faithful and True</u>, and in righteousness He judges and makes war. ...
Revelation 19:20-21 ²⁰Then the beast was captured, and with him the false prophet who worked signs in his presence, by which he deceived those who received the mark of the beast and those who worshiped his image. These two were cast alive into the lake of fire burning with brimstone. ²¹And the rest were killed with the sword which proceeded from the mouth of Him who sat on the horse. And the birds were filled with their flesh.

V. 15

In <u>Revelation 16:1, 19:11 and 19:20-21</u> **the bowls of the wrath of God** represent the climax of God's punishment of sinners during the Tribulation period. **The **white horse** here is not the same one as in Revelation 6:2.** In 19:11 **He who sat on him *was* called Faithful and True** reveals that this is the Second Coming of Christ, arriving on earth for the Battle of Armageddon, to win the war and to begin His Millennial reign.

Daniel 2:34-35a ³⁴"You watched while <u>a stone was cut out without hands</u>, which struck the image on its <u>feet of iron</u> and <u>clay</u>, and broke them in pieces. ^{35a}Then the <u>iron</u>, the <u>clay</u>, the bronze, the silver, and the gold were crushed together, and became like chaff from the summer threshing floors; the wind carried them away so that no trace of them was found." ...
Daniel 2:44 "And in the days of these kings the God of heaven <u>will set up a kingdom which shall never be destroyed</u>; and the kingdom shall not be left to other people; it shall break in pieces and consume all these kingdoms, and it shall stand forever."
Daniel 7:13a "I was watching in the night visions, and behold, *One* like the Son of Man, coming with the clouds of heaven!
Daniel 7:14b His dominion *is* an everlasting dominion, which shall not pass away."

Daniel 2:34-35a, 2:44, 7:13a and 7:14b go with Daniel 7:27, preceded by Daniel 2:28 where Daniel informed King Nebuchadnezzar that God in heaven reveals the secrets of the king's dream of what will be occurring in *the latter days*. What we read in <u>Daniel 2:34-35</u> describe how **the feet of iron** foreshadow the Roman Empire and how the latter weakness is represented by poor mixture of **iron** and **clay**. The **stone** that was **cut out without hands** that will destroy the <u>last kingdom</u> represents Jesus Christ, who, at His return, will destroy Gentile world power, and in <u>Daniel 2:44</u> Christ **will set up a kingdom which shall never be destroyed**.

11:16-19

¹⁶And the twenty-four <u>elders</u> who sat before God on their thrones fell on their faces and <u>worshiped God</u>, ¹⁷saying: "We give You thanks, <u>O Lord God Almighty</u>, the One <u>who is</u> and <u>who was</u> and <u>who is to come</u>, because You have taken Your great power and reigned. ¹⁸The <u>nations</u> were angry, and Your <u>wrath</u> has come, and the time of the <u>dead</u>, that they should be <u>judged</u>, and that You should reward Your servants the prophets and the saints, and those who fear Your name, small and great, and should destroy those who destroy the earth." ¹⁹Then the temple of God was opened in heaven, and <u>the ark of His covenant</u> was seen in His temple. And there were lightnings, noises, thunderings, an earthquake, and great hail.

Verses 16 and 17 bring out the fact that not only is Jesus Christ called **God** with the Father, but also He is **Lord God Almighty.** This is the third of eight times in this last Book of the Bible that He is recognized as being **Almighty God**.

****God** is **worshiped** by the **elders** because what He promised is now accomplished. Their gratitude is for the establishment of the Millennial kingdom (1 Corinthians 15:24). The **dead** of <u>all</u> ages will be **judged** at the future Great White Throne (Revelation 20:11a, Revelation 20:15; Daniel 12:2; Matthew Chapter 25). Those who have tried to **destroy the earth** will themselves be destroyed by God. **The ark of His covenant** (testament) is a symbol of the presence of God and of His faithfulness in fulfilling His covenant promises.**

The Gentile **nations** will be overpowered. The **wrath** of God will take vengeance on His enemies (2 Thessalonians 1:7-8).

Old Testament and Tribulation saints who have died will be raised and rewarded (Isaiah 26:19a), and God will take revenge upon those who have rejected Him—their very Creator (Daniel 7:10).

Vv. 16-19

1 Corinthians 15:24 Then *comes* the end, when He delivers the kingdom to God the Father, when He puts an end to all rule and all authority and power.

Revelation 20:11a Then I saw a great white throne and Him who sat on it ...

Revelation 20:15 And anyone not found written in the Book of Life was cast into the lake of fire.

Daniel 12:2 And many of those who sleep in the dust of the earth shall awake, some to everlasting life, some to shame *and* everlasting contempt.

2 Thessalonians 1:7-8 7and to *give* you who are troubled rest with us when the Lord Jesus is revealed from heaven with His mighty angels, 8in flaming fire taking vengeance on those who do not know God, and on those who do not obey the gospel of our Lord Jesus Christ.

Isaiah 26:19a Your dead shall live; *together with* my [Isaiah's] dead body they shall arise.

Daniel 7:10 A fiery stream issued and came forth from before Him. A thousand thousands ministered to Him; ten thousand times ten thousand stood before him. The court was seated, and the books were opened.

Vv. 16-19

1 Corinthians 15:24, Revelation 20: 11a, 20:15, and Daniel 12:2 all refer to the following: At the end of Christ's Millennial reign, all who have died in unbelief will be resurrected to be judged at the Great White Throne to hear their doom. The reign of Christ will then give way to His eternal kingdom. 2 Peter 3:10-13 explains that His kingdom will not be on this present earth nor the present heaven: *10But the day of the Lord will come as a thief in the night, in which the heavens will pass away with a great noise, and the elements will melt with fervent heat, both the earth and the works that are in it will be burned up. 11Therefore, since all these things will be dissolved, what manner of persons ought you to be in holy conduct and godliness, 12looking for and hastening the coming of the day of God, because of which the heavens will be dissolved, being on fire, and the elements will melt with fervent heat? 13Nevertheless we, according to His promise, look for new heavens and a new earth in which righteousness dwells.*

2 Thessalonians 1:7-8 gives an example of those in the Church Age who are **troubled**—that is, persecuted—but makes known that we will be given rest and rewards **when the Lord Jesus is revealed from heaven**.

Isaiah 26:19a prophesied in about 700 BC could be giving the same kind of hope we have: Hope for not just rewards, but for life everlasting. But it could possibly be used metaphorically in speaking of Israel's restoration (Romans 11:26), so this could even refer to Christ's Second Coming with rewards for those who were saved during Tribulation.

Daniel 7:10 agrees with the numbers of saints who were praising the Lord at His throne in Revelation 5:11. Here they are seated within the court to watch **the books** being **opened** for the judgment of those who would be tried later at the Great White Throne (Revelation 20:12).

Satan Identified and Described Returning to Key Figures of the Last Half of the Tribulation

Chapters 12-14
These Chapters further explain prophesies pertaining to the major personages and movements of the latter half of the Tribulation period.

12:1-2

[1]Now a great sign appeared in heaven: a woman [Mary of Israel] clothed with the sun, with the moon under her feet, and on her head a garland of twelve stars. [2]Then being with child, she cried out in labor and in pain to give birth.

The **woman is Mary of Israel and her **Child** is Christ, the Messiah (Revelation 12:5; Isaiah 7:14; 9:6a; Isaiah 66:7-8; Micah. 5:2; Romans 9:4a-5). There is a comparison to see here: The **woman** can be visualized as Israel, and the **child** as the Jews (Isaiah 26:17-18). The woman is not the Church, since the Church did not bring forth Christ. Rather, Christ brought forth the Church. So her identification as the persecuted Jewish saints during the Tribulation period clearly proves the Church is no longer on earth** (Romans 11:25-26). When the fullness of the Gentiles comes in to the Church, Christ will then rapture the Church, and then *Israel will be saved*. *The **sun** depicts her as God's chosen nation, The **moon** alludes to God's promise of dominion, and **the** crown **of twelve stars** pictures royalty and relates to the twelve tribes of Israel. All combined together this portrays the glory and dominion which has been promised to her in the coming kingdom (John 16:21), just as they pictured Joseph's ultimate rule over his father, mother, and brothers (Genesis 37:9; Genesis 37:11).* **The **birth** pains refer to the period before the birth of Christ when Israel was waiting for redemption by the Messiah.** They themselves brought on their sharp pains with their stubbornness that led to much suffering during the Church Age as they rejected the Savior.

Vv. 1-2

Isaiah 7:14 "Therefore the Lord Himself will give you a sign: Behold, the virgin shall conceive and bear a Son, and shall call His name <u>Immanūel</u>."
Isaiah 9:6a "For unto us a Child is born, unto us a Son is given."

Micah 5:2 "But you, Bethlehem Ephrathah, *though* you are little among the thousands of Judah, *yet* out of you shall come forth to Me the One to be Ruler in Israel, whose goings forth *are* from of old, <u>from everlasting</u>.

Romans 9:4a who are Israelites ...
Romans 9:5 of whom *are* the <u>fathers</u> and from whom, according to the flesh, Christ *came*, who is over all, *the* <u>eternally blessed God</u>. Amen.

Isaiah 26:18 We [Israel] have been with child, we have been in pain; we have, as it were, brought forth wind; we have not accomplished any deliverance in the earth, nor have the inhabitants of the world fallen.

John 16:21 "A woman, when she is in labor, has sorrow because her hour has come; but as soon as she has given birth to the child, she no longer remembers the anguish, for joy that a human being has been born into the world."

Genesis 37:9 Then he [Joseph] dreamed still another dream and told it to his brothers, and said, "Look, I have dreamed another dream. And this time, the sun, the moon, and the <u>eleven stars</u> bowed down to me."
Genesis 37:11...And his brothers envied him, but his father kept the matter *in mind*.

Vv. 1-2

<u>Isaiah 7:14</u> and <u>Isaiah 9:6a</u> are two of the most heard verses during the celebration of Jesus' incarnate birth every Christmas. **In Isaiah's prophetic view the scene is present as he sees the pregnant virgin about to bear a Son. That this prophecy must refer to the virgin birth of Christ is obvious since the virgin is pregnant and is still a virgin! **Immanuel** is a symbolic name, meaning "God with us"**—in other words, the Divine Child. **Everlasting Father** (Isaiah 9:6b) literally means Father of Eternity. As the **Prince of Peace**, Christ Jesus will bring eternal peace to the hearts of all believers through the establishment of His kingdom.

<u>Micah 5:2</u> confirms the birth place of Jesus to be the same as David in Judah. ****From everlasting** clearly indicates the past eternality of Christ.**

<u>Romans 9:4a</u>, <u>Romans 9:5</u>: *Abraham, Isaac, Jacob, and the twelve sons of Jacob are the patriarch **fathers**. The Messiah is an Israelite from their lineage, but more, He is also the Sovereign of the universe, **the eternally blessed <u>God</u>**. This gives us a positive statement of the humanity <u>and</u> the deity of the Savior.*

<u>Isaiah 26:18</u>: But Israel's suffering was so drawn out that it seemed that she could give birth only to wind, meaning she could not deliver herself from her ongoing sorrows. (W. Henderson, "Sorrow And Comfort" A Devotional Study of Isaiah, pg. 161)

In <u>John 16:21</u> it's remarkable how quickly a mother can recover from the labor pains after giving birth to a child. It will also be so for the Israelites after the regret of being disconnected from our God for so long, but then how their sorrow will soon be forgotten and they will be comforted when they, the 144,00 are sealed.

<u>Genesis 37:9</u>; <u>Genesis 37:11</u>: As a "type" of the coming Messiah Joseph dreamt that the **eleven stars** were under his control. The Savior created the heavens with His own hands, and **eleven** of His disciples during His ministry on earth became apostles of the Lamb.

³And another sign appeared <u>in heaven</u>: behold, a great, <u>fiery red</u> <u>dragon</u> [Satan] having <u>seven heads</u> and ten horns, and <u>seven diadems</u> [crowns] on his heads [<u>seven world emperors</u> ruling <u>over ten nations</u>; the Antichrist is not one of the seven {Revelation 17:11}. Rather he is of their same reputation of being wicked and idolatress.]. ⁴His tail drew a <u>third of the stars of heaven</u> and threw them to the earth. And the dragon stood before the woman who was ready to give birth, to devour her Child [Jesus] as soon as it was born.

12:3-4

The **dragon,** dwelling <u>at this time</u> **in heaven**, **is identified as <u>Satan</u> in verse 9. His **red** color shows his <u>murderous</u> character (<u>John 8:44</u>). His **seven heads** and **seven crowns** depict the completeness and universality of his power and influence. His **ten horns** show Satan's connection with the fourth beast (the Roman Empire of <u>Daniel 7:7</u>; <u>Daniel 7:24</u>) and with the Beast from the sea (the Antichrist having seven heads and ten horns: Revelation 13:1; Revelation 17:3; Revelation 17:7; Revelation 17:9). The **third part of the stars of heaven** are probably the fallen angels who followed Satan in his original rebellion against God (<u>Isaiah 14:12-13a</u>; <u>Isaiah 14:14b-15</u>). Shortly after the incarnate birth of Christ, Satan was ready to kill Him (Matthew 2:13-16).**

Vv. 3-4

John 8:44 "You are of your father the devil, and the desires of your father you want to do. He was a <u>murderer</u> from the beginning, and does not stand in the truth, because there is no truth in him. When he speaks a lie, he speaks from his own <u>resources</u>, for he is a <u>liar</u> and the father of it."

Vv. 3-4

In <u>John 8:44</u> *Jesus does not "beat around the bush." He tells it like it is. He did not mean these Jews had been born of the devil in the way believers are born of God. Rather, it meant, as Augustine said, that they were children of the devil *by imitation*. The devil brought death to Adam and the whole human race. Not only was he a **murderer**, but he was also **a liar**. The Jews imitated Satan in those two ways, intending to kill the Son of God and saying that God was their Father. They pretended to be godly, spiritual men, but they were wicked.

Daniel 7:7 "After this I saw in the night visions, and behold, a fourth beast [Roman Empire], dreadful and terrible, exceedingly strong. It had huge iron teeth; it was devouring, breaking in pieces, and trampling the residue with its feet. It was different from all the beasts that *were* before it [Babylonian, Medo-Persian, Greek], and it had ten horns. ...
Daniel 7:24 The ten horns *are* ten kings *who* shall arise from this kingdom. And <u>another shall rise after them</u>; he [Antichrist] shall be different from the first *ones* and shall subdue three kings.

<u>Daniel 7:7 and 7:24</u> correctly predicted that the Roman Empire would follow the Grecian Empire, would cease, and then, after a considerable time (the present Church Age *is* this *considerable time*), Daniel also prophecies that the Roman Empire will be revived.*

Isaiah 14:12-13a [12]"How you are fallen from heaven, O Lūcifer, son of the morning! *How* you are cut down to the ground, you who weakened the nations! [13a]For you have said in your heart: 'I will ascend into heaven, I will exalt my throne above the stars of God;
Isaiah 14:14b-15 [14b]I will be like the Most High' [15]Yet you shall be brought down to Shēol, to the lowest depths of the Pit. [Ezekiel 28:12-16; 2 Peter 2:4; Jude 6]

<u>Isaiah 14:12-13a and 14:14b-15</u> describe how Satan was cast out of heaven in the beginning and how he will be defeated in the end.

The Old Testament Prophecies being in total agreement with the Book of Revelation prophecies just reinforce the purity and miraculous agreement of all these truths given by the Spirit in thousands of years wide time span.

⁵She bore a <u>male Child</u> who was to rule all nations with a rod of iron. And her Child <u>was caught up to God and His throne</u>. ⁶Then [right after the Church gets raptured] the woman fled into the <u>wilderness</u>, where she has a place prepared by God, that they should feed her there one thousand two hundred and sixty days [3½ years].

12:5-6

The **male Child is Christ the Messiah,** Almighty God (Revelation 19:15; <u>Psalm 2:7</u>). He **was caught up to God and His throne** (<u>Acts 1:9</u>; 7:55-56; <u>Mark 16:19</u>, Luke 24:51; <u>Psalm 2:8-9</u>). **The **wilderness** represents anywhere outside Israel (Some commentators believe their place of refuge will be in Petra about 55 miles south of the Dead Sea.). During the last half of the Tribulation period (1,260 days = 3 ½ years), Israel will take refuge among the Gentile nations, where God will care for them (possibly through Gentile believers**—Mark 9:41). Daniel 12:9 refers to the same 1,260 days as the **time of the end**—3½ years. Then Daniel 12:10-12 tell of the subsequent 30 and 45 days. **Chronologically, verse 6 occurs after verses Revelation 12:7-12, and is equivalent to verse 12:14.** (Verse 12:14 repeats verse 12:6.)

⁷And <u>war</u> broke <u>out in heaven</u>: <u>Michael and his angels</u> fought with the dragon; and <u>the dragon and his angels</u> fought, ⁸but they did not prevail, nor was a place found for them in heaven any longer. ⁹So the great dragon was cast out, that <u>serpent</u> of old [Genesis 3:1, 4], called the <u>Devil</u> and <u>Satan</u>, who deceives the whole world; he was cast to the earth, <u>and his angels</u> were cast out with him. ¹⁰Then I heard a loud voice saying in heaven, "Now <u>salvation, and strength, and the kingdom of our God, and the power of His Christ have come</u>, for the accuser of our brethren, who accused them before our God day and night, has been <u>cast down</u>."

12:7-10

In mid-tribulation **War** breaks out <u>in heaven</u> with **Michael and his angels** on one side and **the dragon, Satan** (who has been up in heaven acting like he is God) **and his angels** on the other. Michael is associated with the nation of Israel (<u>Daniel 12:1</u>). *The dragon* (**serpent**, **Devil**, deceiver) *is so thoroughly defeated that he and his followers are **cast down** to earth* where they will join the Antichrist and false prophet. (Revelation 19:20) *However, this isn't his final fate* as we will see when we arrive at Revelation 20:1-3; Revelation 20:10. The loud rejoicing in heaven is heard in the vision Christ has given to John to write.

Where verse 10 says **salvation, and strength, and the kingdom of our God, and the power of His Christ have come**, it is pointing toward Christ's soon coming Millennial reign. At the end of the Millennium He will raise the dead who rejected Him and judge them for their disobedience and immoral acts (<u>Revelation 20:11-12</u>).

Vv. 5-6

Vv. 5-6

Psalm 2:7 "I will declare the decree: The LORD has said to Me, 'You *are* My Son, today I have begotten You.

Christ was the **Son** of God from all eternity in Psalm 2:7, and the Psalm also means that Jesus was **begotten**—by His incarnate birth in the flesh. Jesus reminded His chosen apostles of all this before they witnessed Him ascending Acts 1:9; Mark 16:19; Luke 24:51.

Acts 1:9 Now when He had spoken these things, while they watched, He was taken up, and a cloud received Him out of their sight.

Mark 16:19 So then, after the Lord had spoken to them, He was received up into heaven, and sat down at the right hand of God.

Psalm 2:8-9 ⁸Ask of Me, and I will give *You* the nations *for* Your inheritance, and the ends of the earth *for* Your possession. ⁹You shall break them with a rod of iron; You shall dash them to pieces like a potter's vessel.'"

Psalm 2:8-9: Prior to Christ's inauguration as King, He will destroy those who do not know God and do not obey the gospel. Then, in the Millennium, He will rule **with a rod of iron**, punishing rebellion when it raises its head (Revelation 19:15-20:10).

Vv. 7-10

Vv. 7-10

Daniel 12:1 "At that time Michael shall stand up, the great prince who stands *watch* over the sons of your people; and there shall be a time of trouble [in heaven], such as never was since there was a nation, *even* to that time. And at that time your people shall be delivered, every one who is found written in the book.

In Daniel 12:1 **during the Great Tribulation there will be an unprecedented attack on the Jews, but **Michael** will deliver them.**

Revelation 20:11-12 reveals to us that it is a shocking, dreadful thing for a man to go to his grave with unforgiven sins. The dead who trusted in Him and believed in Him were already raised either with His Church at the Rapture or at the end of the Tribulation Period if they were believers during the Old Testament time and if they became believers during the Tribulation and were able to overcome.

Revelation 20:11-12 ¹¹Then I saw a great white throne and Him who sat on it, from whose face the earth and the heaven fled away. And there was found no place for them. ¹²And I saw the dead, small and great, standing before God, and books were opened. And another book was opened, which is *the Book* of Life. And the dead were judged according to their works, by the things which were written in the books.

Satan is Continuously Outwitted

More Details of the Last Half
of the Tribulation

[11]"And they overcame him by the blood of the Lamb and by the word of their testimony, and they did not love their lives to the death. [12]Therefore rejoice, O heavens, and you who dwell in them! Woe to the inhabitants of the earth and the sea! For the devil has come down to you, having great wrath, because he knows that he has a short time." [13]Now when the dragon saw that he had been cast to the earth, he persecuted the woman [nation of Israel] who gave birth to the male *Child*.

12:11-13

The reason for the cheering is because the accuser (Satan) of the brothers and sisters in Christ has just been evicted from among them! They overcame the Devil and his world! Their victory was based upon the shed **blood of the Lamb** and His death. This testimony gives the value of His death out of the unconditional love He has for all. Also their testimony is sealed by their faithfulness to shed their own blood. They **did not love their** own **lives**, even all the way **to death**. They were Christian martyrs who obviously believed in the resurrection (Revelation 2:10).

The last half of the Tribulation will be a time of terrible trouble on earth (Jeremiah 30:7; Daniel 9:27; Daniel 12:1; Zephaniah 1:15; Matthew 24:15-22). In verse 12 Satan's **wrath** is **great** because he had been prince of the world, and he knows his time is running out. The **short time** becomes one day in Revelation 18:8, and one hour in 18:10 and 18:17. **It will be Satan's final attempt in his awareness of a **short time** to prevent the return and the reign of Christ.**

Therefore, in Revelation verses 12:13-17, we learn Satan intensified his persecution of Israel, God's chosen nation when he had been cast to the earth. Confirming the blessed hope for believers that they will not suffer any of God's wrath nor Satan's **wrath**, let alone his **great wrath**, is given in three beautiful verses telling us we are not appointed to wrath, but to salvation: Romans 5:9; 1 Thessalonians 5:9; 1 Thessalonians 1:10. We are saved from wrath through the shed blood of the Lamb. The confirmation is also evidenced in Revelation 5:9-11 as we will already be in heaven praising Him.

In Chapters 13 to 17 Satan sets up his own counterfeit kingdom through the Beast, the false messiah (Revelation 13:1-17).

Vv. 11-13

Jeremiah 30:7 Alas! For the day *is* great, so that none *is* like it; and it *is* the time of Jacob's trouble, but he shall be saved out of it.

Daniel 9:27 Then he [Antichrist] shall confirm a covenant [treaty] with many for one week [seven years]; but in the middle of the week [three-and-a-half years] he shall bring an end to sacrifice and offering. And on the wing of abominations shall be one who makes desolate, even until the consummation, which is determined, is poured out on the desolate [or desolator].

Zephaniah 1:15 That day *is* a day of trouble and distress, a day of devastation and desolation, a day of darkness and gloominess, a day of clouds and thick darkness.

Matthew 24:15-22 [15] "Therefore when you see the 'abomination of desolation,' spoken of by Daniel the prophet, standing in the holy place" (whoever reads, let him understand), [16] then let those who are in Judea flee to the mountains. [17] Let him who is on the housetop not go down to take anything out of his house. [18] And let him who is in the field not go back to get his clothes. [19] But woe to those who are pregnant and to those who are nursing babies in those days! [20] And pray that your flight may not be in winter or on the Sabbath. [21] For then there will be great tribulation, such as has not been since the beginning of the world until this time, no, nor ever shall be. [22] And unless those days were shortened, no flesh would be saved; but for the elect's [chosen ones] sake those days will be shortened."

Vv. 11-13

Jeremiah 30:7: Even through the desolation, fear, darkness, gloom, earthly and celestial phenomena, devastation and destruction, wrath and death, of the Great Tribulation—**Jacob's trouble**—or *Israel's sufferings* will be ended and their future promised blessing will come about.

Daniel 9:27: The Antichrist will, during the first three-and-a-half years, deceive people into believing he is the great peace maker, but he will show his true colors during the last three-and-a-half years. The seventieth week will end in the Antichrist's defeat when Christ returns to establish His kingdom. Daniel 12:1: "*At that time Michael shall stand up, the great prince who stands watch over the sons of your people; and there shall be a time of trouble* [Tribulation], *such as never was since there was a nation, even to that time.*"

Zephaniah 1:15: *The **day of** God's wrath is pictured because of the wickedness, especially the wickedness of the men of Judah.*

Matthew 24:15-22: The words of the Lord Jesus are confirmation of Daniel's prophecy in Daniel 9:27 that, as Jesus states in Matthew 24:21: **"For then there will be great tribulation, such as has not been since the beginning of the world until this time, no, nor ever shall be."**

¹⁴But the woman was given <u>two wings of a great eagle</u>, that she might fly into the <u>wilderness</u> to her place, where she is nourished <u>for a time and times and half a time</u> [three-and-a-half years; verse 6], from the presence of the serpent.

12:14

Revelation 12:14 here tells us much: The believers in heaven can rejoice over the dragon's departure, but it is bad news for the earth and the sea! But *the faithful Jewish remnant on earth is given **two wings of a great eagle**, enabling them to quickly escape to a **wilderness** hideout* (Matthew 24:16-21: ¹⁶ then let those who are in Judea flee to the mountains. ¹⁷ Let him who is on the housetop not go down to take anything out of his house. ¹⁸ And let him who is in the field not go back to get his clothes. ¹⁹ But woe to those who are pregnant and to those who are nursing babies in those days! ²⁰ And pray that your flight may not be in winter or on the Sabbath. ²¹ For then <u>there will be great tribulation</u>, such as has not been since the beginning of the world until this time, no, nor ever shall be.). *(Some have *supposed* that these **wings** speak of a great Air Force.) The Jewish remnant is cared for and protected* until the end of the Tribulation (<u>Matthew 24:31</u>) by angels who are <u>possibly</u> Gentile believers on earth *from the serpent's attacks in this **wilderness** for three-and-a-half years* {**for a time and times and half a time** (<u>Daniel 7:25</u>; <u>Daniel 12:7</u>)} the time of "great tribulation" (Matthew 24:21). According to <u>Zechariah 13:7-9</u>, however, two thirds of the Jews will die.

¹⁵So <u>the serpent</u> spewed water out of his mouth like a flood after the woman, that he might cause her to be carried away by the <u>flood</u>. ¹⁶But the earth helped the woman, and the earth opened its mouth and swallowed up the flood which the dragon had spewed out of his mouth.

12:15-16

*In an effort to foil Israel's escape, **the serpent** causes a great **flood** to follow the people, but an apparent earthquake swallows the water and the devil is outwitted.*

¹⁷And the dragon was enraged with the woman, and he went to make war with the rest of her offspring, who keep <u>the commandments of God and have the testimony of Jesus Christ</u>.

12:17

*Furious over this humiliation, the Devil seeks to wreak vengeance on Jews who had not escaped—Jews who showed the reality of their faith by keeping **the commandments of God and have the testimony of Jesus Christ.***

Chapter 13 verses 1-18 begin describing a *one-world-government*.

V. 14

Matthew 24:31 "And <u>He will send His angels</u> with a great sound of a trumpet, and they will <u>gather together His elect</u> from the four winds, from one end of heaven to the other."

V. 14

<u>Matthew 24:31</u>: At the end of the Tribulation, *when the Savior descends, **He will send His angels** throughout the earth to **gather together His elect** people—the newly converted believing Jews, to the land of Palestine. From all the earth they will gather to greet their Messiah and to enjoy His glorious* reign.

Daniel 7:25 He [Antichrist] shall speak *pompous words* against the Most High, shall persecute [wear out] the saints of the Most High, and shall intend to change times [history] and law [abortion, drugs]. Then *the saints* shall be given into his hand for <u>a time and times and half a time</u> [three-and-a-half years].

Daniel 12:7 Then I heard the man clothed in linen, who *was* above the waters of the river, when he held up his right hand and his left hand to heaven, and swore by Him who lives forever, that *it shall be* for <u>a time, times, and half *a time*</u>; and when the power of the holy people has been completely shattered, all these *things* shall be finished.

<u>Daniel 7:25 and Daniel 12:7</u>: ****A time, times, and half *a time*** is an expression used in Daniel and in Revelation to refer to three-and-a-half years, or 1,260 days, or 42 months.** *Pompous* words in 7:25 are showy words with grandeur, splendid, magnificent—but deceiving—promise. **The first half of the Tribulation will be a time of relative peace for Israel because of the covenant with the Antichrist. However, in <u>Daniel 12:7</u>, the Antichrist will break the covenant, and there will be three-and-a-half years of tremendous persecution and wars.**

Zechariah 13:7-9 7"<u>Awake, O sword</u>, against My <u>Shepherd</u>, against the Man who is My Companion," says the LORD of hosts. "Strike the <u>Shepherd</u>, and <u>the sheep</u> will be <u>scattered</u>; then I will turn My hand against the little ones. 8And it shall come to pass in all the land," says the LORD, "that two-thirds in it shall be cut off *and* die, but *one*-third shall be left in it: 9I will bring the *one*-third through the fire, will refine them as silver is refined, and test them as gold is tested. They will call on My name, and I will answer them. I will say, 'This is My people'; and each one will say, 'The LORD *is* my God.'"

In <u>Zechariah 13:7-9</u> **the **sword** is the symbol of judicial power (Romans 13:4) and indicates the power that God has entrusted to human government.** Here in Zechariah, *Father God is quoted as He orders His **sword** to **awake** ... against His only begotten Son, the Lord Jesus. The **Shepherd** was struck at Calvary by crucifixion on the cross, and **the** Jewish **sheep** have been **scattered** ever since.*

Chapters 6-12 formed previews of the entire Seven-year Tribulation warnings. Chapter 13 focuses on the first half of the Tribulation Period. We will see that people will suffer the wrath of the false trinity by being forced to worship Satan, the Antichrist, and the False Prophet or else have no means to survive.

The Two Beasts from the Sea and the Land

The First Beast is the Antichrist;
(The Second Beast is the False Prophet v. 11)

**REVELATION 13:1-18
VERSES, COMMENTARY, REFERENCES
AND REFERENCES COMMENTARY
CAN BE FOUND ON THE
FOLLOWING SETS OF PAGES.**

INTRODUCTION

Chapter 13 introduces us to how Satan (the **dragon**) blasphemously sets up his own false "trinity". Satan acts as the Father, the Antichrist as the Son, and the False Prophet as the Spirit who attempts to bring glory to the Antichrist. Satan appoints two great beasts (men): the first **beast rising up out of the sea**—the Antichrist and his empire—and the second beast out of the earth or land—the False Prophet—possibly a Jew. The land could be the literal earth, or, possibly, the land of Israel. *These beasts symbolize men who will play prominent roles during the Tribulation Period. They combine the features of the four beasts of Daniel 7:3*-9.

ReferencesDaniel 7:3-9 ³"And the <u>four great beasts</u> came up from the sea, each different from the other. ⁴The first [Babylon] *was* like a <u>lion</u>, and had <u>eagle's wings</u>. I watched till its <u>wings</u> were <u>plucked off</u>; and it was lifted up from the earth and made to stand on two feet like a man, and a man's heart was given to it [Daniel 4:16, 4:34: Nebuchadnezzar's restoration]. ⁵And suddenly another beast, a second [Medo-Persia], like a <u>bear</u>. It was raised up on one side, and *had* <u>three ribs</u> [North, Lydia; East, Babylon; South, Egypt] <u>in its mouth </u>between its teeth. And they said thus to it: 'Arise, devour much flesh!' ⁶After this I looked, and there was another [Alexander of Greece], like a <u>leopard</u>, which had on its back four wings of a bird. The beast also had <u>four heads</u> [generals], and dominion was given to it. ⁷After this I saw in the night visions, and behold, a <u>fourth beast</u> [Roman Empire], <u>dreadful and terrible, exceedingly strong</u>. It had <u>huge iron teeth</u>; it was devouring, breaking in pieces, and trampling the residue with its feet. It *was* different from all the beasts that *were* before it, and it had <u>ten horns</u> [kings]. ⁸I was considering the horns, and there was another <u>horn</u>, a <u>little</u> one [the future Antichrist], coming up among them, before whom three of the first horns were plucked out by the roots [leaving seven kings]. And there, in this horn [the little horn], *were* eyes like the eyes of a <u>man</u>, and a mouth speaking <u>pompous</u> words. ⁹I watched till thrones were put in place, and the <u>Ancient of Days</u> was seated; His garment *was white as snow, and the hair of His head was* like pure wool. His throne was a fiery flame, its wheels a burning fire;"

Daniel 7:3-9: *The **four great beasts**—all rising up from the sea, just like the Antichrist will rise from the sea (Revelation 13:1)—represent the four world empires: Babylonian, Medo-Persian, Greek, and Roman; none of which honored God's chosen people. The **lion** stands for *Babylon*. The **eagle's wings** suggest swiftness of conquest. **The wings... plucked** may refer to Nebuchadnezzar's insanity, and the rest of verse 4 to his recovery and his becoming a believer in God. The **bear** pictures *Medo-Persia*. The **three ribs** which it held **in its mouth** perhaps represent the three previous sections of the Babylonian Empire which were overtaken by the Medes and Persians under King Cyrus—Babylon in the east; Egypt in the south; and the Lydian kingdom in NW Asia Minor* (today's western Turkey). *The **leopard** symbolizes *the Greek Empire* with rapid expansion by Alexander the Great. The **four heads** apparently are Alexander's generals after his death. The **fourth beast, dreadful and terrible, exceedingly strong,** with **huge iron teeth**, speaks of the *Roman Empire* which followed the Greek Empire. In verse 8 a CONSIDERABLE SPACE OF TIME takes place (this is the *Church Age* of which we are in right now) before the Roman Empire may be <u>revived</u>. Still future, it will have **ten horns**, that is ten kings, and a **little** [obscure] **horn**: the future head of the Roman Empire—the Antichrist. In verse 9 Daniel pictures the fifth and final world empire—the glorious kingdom of the <u>Lord Jesus Christ*</u>—**the Ancient of Days** (as described much like Him in Revelation 1:11-16). In Daniel 7:13 we will see **Ancient of Days** again, but perhaps it is best to think of Him being God the Father in that verse.

¹Then I stood on the sand of the sea. And I saw a <u>beast</u> [the Antichrist] <u>rising up out of the sea</u>, having <u>seven heads</u> and <u>ten horns</u>, and <u>on his horns ten crowns</u>, and on his heads a blasphemous name. ²Now the <u>beast</u> which I saw was like a <u>leopard</u>, his feet were like *the feet of* a <u>bear</u>, and his mouth like the mouth of a <u>lion</u>. The <u>dragon</u> [Satan] gave him his power, his <u>throne</u>, and <u>great</u> <u>authority</u>.

13:1-2

The first **beast**, the <u>Antichrist</u>, who, although not known yet, will already be *among* the church before the Rapture (<u>1 John 4:3</u>; <u>2 Thessalonians 2:3-4</u>). *He is the Gentile head of <u>the revived Roman Empire</u>, which will exist in a **ten**-kingdom form.* **The **sea** here represents the Gentile nations of the world, from one of which the <u>Antichrist</u> comes.** *The **seven heads** are said in Revelation 17:9-10 to be seven kings, or rulers, or seven different stages of the empire.* The Antichrist will deceive many into thinking he is the messiah in <u>2 Thessalonians 2:3-4</u> and <u>Daniel 11:36-37</u>. But the Antichrist will not be revealed until after a falling away of faith <u>and</u> until after the Holy Spirit indwelled Church is raptured (<u>2 Thessalonians 2:7-8</u>). The **ten horns** were predicted by <u>Daniel 7:24</u> to be a ten-kingdom form. *The **ten crowns on his horns** speak of the power to rule from a **throne** with **great authority**, which was given to him by the **dragon**.* **Satan is attempting to duplicate how God the Father gives all authority to the Son. The first **beast**—the Antichrist—will rule over the previous people and cultures of the three previous empires to the ancient Roman Empire of which Daniel's prophesies were fulfilled: Babylonian—**lion**; Medo-Persian—**bear**; Greek—**leopard**; all an outgrowth of the **iron toothed** Roman Empire.** *In short, the revived Roman Empire combines all the evil features of the preceding world empires. The empire and its ruler receive supernatural strength from Satan.*

Vv. 1-2

1 John 4:3 and every spirit that does not confess that Jesus Christ has come in the flesh is not of God. And this is the *spirit* of the Antichrist, which you have heard was coming, and is now already in the world.

2 Thessalonians 2:3-4 ³Let no one deceive you by any means; *for that Day will not come* unless the falling away comes first, and the man of sin is revealed, the son of perdition, ⁴who opposes and exalts himself above all that is called God or is worshiped, so that he [Antichrist] sits as God in the temple of God, showing himself that he is God.

Daniel 11:36-37 ³⁶Then the king [Antichrist] shall do according to his own will: he shall exalt and magnify himself above every god, shall speak blasphemies against the God of gods, and shall prosper till the wrath has been accomplished; for what has been determined shall be done. ³⁷He shall regard neither the God of his fathers nor the desire of women, nor regard any god; for he shall exalt himself above *them* all.

2 Thessalonians 2:7-8 ⁷For the mystery of the lawlessness is already at work; only He who now restrains *will* do so until He is taken out of the way [by way of the Rapture]. ⁸And then the lawless one [the Antichrist] will be revealed, whom the Lord will consume with the breath of His mouth and destroy with the brightness of His coming.

Daniel 7:24 The ten horns *are* ten kings *who* shall arise from this kingdom. And another shall rise after them; he shall be different from the first *ones*, and shall subdue three kings.

Vv. 1-2

In 1 John 4:3 the **spirit of the Antichrist** which **is now already in the world** is a solid fact. *There are many today who are willing to say good things about Jesus, but not to confess Him as God incarnate. They say that Christ is "divine," but not that He is *God*.*

2 Thessalonians 2:3-4: Christ will come to the air and rapture believers before the Day of the Lord begins the Tribulation period (1 Thessalonians 4:13-18; 1 Thessalonians 5:1-4; 2 Thessalonians 1:6-7; Revelation 4:1). *During the Tribulation those who refuse to worship the Antichrist will be persecuted and many will be martyred* (Revelation 20:4).

Daniel 11:36-37 is not only in complete agreement with 2 Thessalonians 2:4 but also reveals an even more startling description of the Antichrist.

2 Thessalonians 2:7-8 combines with 2 Thessalonians 2:3 to reveal the two things which must happen before the Antichrist will be revealed: In verse 3 we see where *that Day will not come* unless the falling away comes first, and in verses 7-8 the lawless Antichrist cannot be revealed until after the Holy Spirit indwelled believers of the Church are raptured off the earth. And then the Antichrist will be revealed. Comparing Scripture to Scripture we see that the Church is raptured before the Antichrist begins the Seven-year Tribulation Period. It is in total agreement with 1 Thessalonians 5:1-9, and agrees with the chronological order in Revelation Chapters 2, 3, 4, 5, and 6.

Daniel 7:24: The end of this verse tells us the Antichrist will **subdue three kings**. Therefore there will no longer be ten kings, but only seven.

³And I saw one of his heads as if it had been mortally wounded, and his <u>deadly wound was healed</u>. <u>And all the world marveled</u> and followed the <u>beast</u>. ⁴So they worshiped the <u>dragon</u> who gave <u>authority</u> to the <u>beast</u>; and they worshiped the <u>beast</u>, saying, "Who *is* like the <u>beast</u>? Who is able to make war with him? ⁵And he was given a mouth speaking great things and blasphemies, and he was given <u>authority</u> to continue for forty-two months [three-and-a-half years]. ⁶Then he opened his mouth in blasphemy against God, to blaspheme His name, His tabernacle, and those who dwell in heaven. ⁷It was granted to him to make war with the saints [the 144,000 who come to Christ during the Tribulation including the ones they minister to who will believe] and to overcome them. And <u>authority</u> was given him over every tribe, tongue, and nation [one world government—globalism]. ⁸<u>All who dwell on the earth will worship him,</u> <u>whose names have not been written in the Book of</u> <u>Life of the Lamb slain</u> from the foundation of the world. ⁹If anyone has an ear, let him hear.

13:3-9

One of the <u>Beast's</u> seven heads receives a **deadly wound**, and **all the world marveled** as the **wound was healed**. In John's vision the Antichrist was **wounded by the sword and lived** (<u>Revelation</u> <u>13:14</u>). Saying that *the **wound** is **healed** could possibly mean that the empire is revived—with an emperor—namely, the **beast***—the **Antichrist**. *They also worship the **dragon**.*

The beast's authority to make war lasts 42 months (three-and-a-half years). *The **beast** is **worshiped** by men. They are not only amazed at him; **they actually worship him** thinking he is God* **the Savior (2 Thessalonians 2:2; 2:11). The **beast** will persecute the saints of God, and **all whose names are not in the Book of Life of the Lamb will be deceived to worship Satan**** **and the Antichrist**. John writes of the Savior's plea, **"He who has an ear, let him hear what the Spirit says"**... (Revelation 2:7; 2:11; 2:17; 2:29; 3:6; 3:13; 3:22).

¹⁰He [the Antichrist] who leads into captivity <u>shall</u> <u>go into captivity</u>, he who kills with the sword [Antichrist's followers] must <u>be killed with the</u> <u>sword</u>. <u>Here is the patience and the faith of the</u> <u>saints</u>.

13:10

*The ones who have come to be true believers are assured that their persecutors **shall go into captivity** and **be killed with the sword**. This enables **the saints** [holy ones] to wait **patiently** with **faith*** (<u>Revelation 14:12</u>).

Vv. 3-9

Revelation 13:14 And he deceives those who dwell on the earth by those signs which he was granted to do in the sight of the beast, telling those who dwell on the earth to make an image to the beast who was wounded by the sword and lived.

Vv. 3-9

Revelation 13:14: *The Roman emperor [Antichrist by the will of Satan] gives unlimited authority to the False Prophet to act on his behalf. The purpose of his miracles (2 Thessalonians 2:9) is to deceive the people into worshiping a man (the Antichrist) as God.*

2 Thessalonians 2:2 not to be soon shaken in mind or troubled, either by spirit or by word or by letter, as if from us, as though the day of Christ had come.

2 Thessalonians 2:11 And for this reason God will send them strong delusion, that they should believe the lie...

2 Thessalonians 2:2 and 2:11: *The Thessalonians had mistakenly thought the Day of the Lord—the Tribulation—had already begun. The Rapture had to take place first* (2 Thessalonians 2:1-4). *The **lie**, of course is the Antichrist's claim to be God.*

V. 10

Revelation 14:12 Here is the patience of the saints; here *are* those who keep the commandments of God and the faith of Jesus.

V. 10

Revelation 14:12: The Tribulation period will require much patience, perseverance, and endurance. But the difference between temporary suffering and eternal life will be worth whatever one must go through.

The False Prophet Second Beast and the Mark of the Beast

¹¹Then I saw another <u>beast</u> [the false prophet] coming up out of the earth, and he had <u>two horns like a lamb</u> and spoke <u>like a dragon</u>. ¹²And he exercises all the authority of the first beast in his presence, and causes the earth and those who dwell in it to worship the first beast, whose deadly wound was healed. ¹³He performs great signs, so that he even makes <u>fire</u> come down <u>from heaven</u> on the earth in the sight of men. ¹⁴And he deceives those who dwell on the earth by those signs which he was granted to do in the sight of the beast, telling those who dwell on the earth to make an <u>image</u> to the beast who was <u>wounded</u> by the sword <u>and lived</u>.

13:11-14

The <u>second</u> **beast** is the False Prophet symbolizing the "Holy Spirit of God" in Satan's false "trinity". *He comes up out of the land. If the land is Israel, he is likely a Jew. He has **two horns like a lamb**, giving the appearance of gentleness and harmlessness* (<u>Matthew 7:15</u>), *but also suggesting that he speaks for the Lamb of God. He converses **like a dragon**, indicating that he is directly inspired and empowered by Satan. He works closely with the Antichrist first beast, even organizing an international campaign for the worship of the Antichrist, and makes an **image** [huge idol illustration]* of the Antichrist to show the Antichrist was **wounded—and lived**. The Antichrist is the political ruler and the False Prophet is the priestly religious leader who promotes global worship of the Antichrist. *The False Prophet has even been given supernatural power from Satan to cause **fire** to fall **from heaven**. The purpose of his miracles is to deceive the people into worshiping a man as though the man is God* (<u>Deuteronomy 13:1-3</u>). The second beast—false prophet—has now been introduced.

¹⁵He was granted *power* to give breath to the <u>image of the beast</u>, that the <u>image of the beast</u> should both speak and cause as many as <u>would not worship the image of the beast</u> to be killed.

13:15

Having been given power from Satan, the False Prophet gives a delusion to make the great **image** of the beast able to speak (<u>2 Thessalonians 2:4, 2:9-11</u>).The **image of the beast** not only appears able to speak, but also causes those who **would not worship the image** (idol) **to be killed**.

Vv. 11-14
Matthew 7:15 "<u>Beware of false prophets</u>, who come to you in sheep's clothing, but inwardly they are ravenous wolves."

Vv. 11-14
The Lord Jesus warned in <u>Matthew 7:15</u> to **beware of false prophets**, and the purpose of the Tribulation False Prophet's miracles is to deceive the people into worshiping a <u>man</u> as though the <u>man</u> is God.

Deuteronomy 13:1-3 [1]"If there arises among you a prophet or a dreamer of dreams, and he gives you a sign or a wonder, [2]and the sign or the wonder comes to pass, of which he spoke to you, saying, 'Let us go after other gods'—which you have not known—'and let us serve them,' [3]<u>you shall not listen to the words of that prophet</u> or that dreamer of dreams, for the LORD your God is testing you to know whether you love the LORD your God with all your heart and with all your soul."

Also, the LORD our God is quoted in <u>Deuteronomy 13:1-3</u> **not to listen to these kinds of deceivers**.

V. 15
2 Thessalonians 2:4 who opposes and exalts himself above all that is called God or that is worshiped, so that he sits as God in the temple of God, showing himself that he is God.
2 Thessalonians 2:9-11 [9]The coming of the lawless one is according to the working of Satan, with all power, signs, and lying wonders, [10]and with all unrighteous <u>deception</u> among those who perish, because <u>they did not receive the love of the truth, that they might be saved</u>. [11]And for this reason God will send them strong delusion, that they should <u>believe the lie</u>.

V. 15
In <u>2 Thessalonians 2:4 and 2:9-11</u> we learn that those who fall for all this unrighteous **deception** (and **believe the lie**) are led to perishing (into the eternal lake of fire), because God sends them a strong delusion, since **they did not receive the love of the truth, that they might be saved** (Revelation 19:20-21).

¹⁶He causes all, <u>both small and great, rich and poor,</u> <u>free and slave</u>, to <u>receive</u> a <u>mark on their right hand</u> <u>or on their foreheads</u>, ¹⁷and that no one may <u>buy</u> <u>or sell</u> except one who has the mark or the name of the beast, or <u>the number of his name</u> ["one world government" dictating to everyone in the world].

13:16-17

By mocking God's Word such as <u>Romans 2:11</u> (and <u>Galatians 3:28</u>—one of Satan's most misused and abused verses in Scripture) by saying, "**both small and great, rich and poor, free and slave,**" the False Prophet requires <u>all</u> people **to receive** the **mark or name of the beast** (the Antichrist, possibly Roman Emperor) **or the number of his name...on their right hand or on their foreheads**. **Only the <u>un</u>believers will comply. In not submitting to the political and religious system of the Antichrist Beast, the believers will <u>not</u> be able to **buy or sell**. This will be a severe economic test, but true believers will prefer death to renouncing their Savior.

Vv. 16-17
Romans 2:11 For there is no partiality with God.

Vv. 16-17
Romans 2:11 tells us plainly that *there is no partiality with God* to be saved. Some have been deceived into believing that this verse means there is no partiality for performing the responsibilities which God has prescribed in His Word for His way to conduct the assembly meeting. However, when comparing Scripture to Scripture, this verse is speaking plainly about salvation and salvation only.

Galatians 3:28 There is neither Jew nor Greek, there is neither slave nor free, there is neither male nor female; for you are all one in Christ Jesus.

Galatians 3:28: We all need to be careful, to watch out not to be deceived. This verse can so easily be "misinterpreted" to contradict God's Word to say "it is really okay for women to be senior leaders in the church," although 1 Corinthians 14:34-35 and 1 Timothy 2:11-12; 1 Timothy 3:2; and 1 Timothy 3:12 would then be contradicted. This would even further contradict God's pure, flawless Word (Proverbs 30:5; Psalm 12:6), that God's Word endures forever (Isaiah 40:8; 1 Peter 1:23; 1 Peter 1:25), that God does not change (Malachi 3:6), and that His Word is alive (Hebrews 4:12).
Some might believe we've been given *liberty* to have God's Word tell us what would seem to be more convenient and have it say what we want it to mean instead of His original intent:
2 Corinthians 3:17 says, *Now the Lord is the Spirit, and where the Spirit of the Lord is, there is* liberty, *that is, freedom from the bondage of the law, freedom from obscurity in reading the Scriptures, and freedom to gaze upon His face without a veil between,* We want to be cautious not to violate God's way. Some might be misinformed and mean well, but when the truth is revealed; we should **"hear what the Spirit says to the churches."**

[18]Here is wisdom. Let him who has understanding calculate the <u>number of the beast</u>, for it is the <u>number of a man</u>: His number is <u>666</u>.

13:18

The number of the Beast is **666**—trinity of evil; (777 represents "Holy Trinity.") **The number of his name,** of *mankind* is **666**.** Applying wisdom, we see that the Antichrist is *not* <u>God</u>, but rather *a man* (<u>Psalm 118:8</u>). Those who take the **number** or the **image** will receive the wrath of God (<u>Revelation 14:9-11</u>; <u>16:2</u>; 16:19; 18:6; <u>19:20</u>-21♦; 20:10♦; 2 Thessalonians 1:6♦). Those who resist the mark and image will win victory over the number of his name and will sing the song of the Lamb to <u>praise God</u> (Revelation 15:2-3; Revelation <u>20:4b</u>).

♦Verses also have to do with the subject of the mark of the beast

V. 18

Psalm 118:8 It is better to trust in the LORD than to put confidence in man.

V. 18

Psalm 118:8: If anyone takes the mark of man it then becomes a sign of permanent rejection of the Lord God and Savior. The mark of the beast spells eternal doom and suffering for those who accept the beast over Jesus Christ.

Revelation 14:9-11 ⁹Then a third angel followed them, saying with a loud voice, "If anyone worships the beast and his image, and receives *his* mark on his forehead or on his hand, ¹⁰he himself shall also drink of the wine of the wrath of God, which is poured out full strength into the cup of His indignation. He shall be tormented with fire and brimstone in the presence of the holy angels and in the presence of the Lamb. ¹¹And the smoke of their torment ascends forever and ever; and they have no rest day or night, who worship the beast and his image, and whoever receives the mark of his name."

By mocking God's Word, God will turn minds over to trusting in false teaching so sincerely that many will take the **mark** of the beast and will be **tormented** from then on **forever and ever** as told in Revelation 14:9-11.

Revelation 16:2 So the first went and poured out his bowl upon the earth, and a foul and loathsome sore came upon the men who had the mark of the beast and those who worshiped his image.

Revelation 16:2 informs us that a **foul and loathsome sore** will come **upon the men who** will take **the mark of the beast and those who** worship **his image**.

Revelation 19:20 Then the beast [Antichrist] was captured, and with him the False Prophet who worked signs in his presence, by which he deceived those who received the mark of the beast and those who worshiped his image.

Revelation 19:20 reminds all who read and understand this prophecy not to be **deceived** by the **signs** of a false prophet.

Revelation 20:4b Then I *saw* the souls of those who had been beheaded for their witness to Jesus and for the word of God, who had not worshiped the beast or his image, and had not received *his* mark on their foreheads or on their hands. And they lived and reigned with Christ for a thousand years.

Revelation 20:4b reminds us that **those** who exercise much patience, perseverance, and endurance, who **had not received** *the deceiver's* **mark on their foreheads or on their hands,** will not perish to the lake of fire, but will live **and** reign **with Christ for a thousand years**. For the unbeliever an opposite destination is revealed in Revelation 20:10: *The devil, who deceived them, was cast into the lake of fire and brimstone where the beast and the false prophet are. And they will be tormented day and night forever and ever.* Then those who rejected Christ who will be judged by the Son of God at the great white throne (Revelation 20:11) will join them: Revelation 20:15: *And anyone not found written in the Book of Life was cast into the lake of fire.*

The Messages of Six Angels

¹Then I looked, and behold, a <u>Lamb</u> standing on <u>Mount Zion</u>, and with Him <u>one hundred *and* forty-four thousand</u>, having His Father's name written on their foreheads.

14:1

The **Lamb is Christ. **Mount Zion** is Jerusalem. This verse is looking forward to Christ's Second Coming for His Millennial reign.** The **144,000** who will be in Jerusalem when He arrives are the same as the ones in Revelation 7:1-8.

²And I heard a voice from heaven, like <u>the voice of many waters</u>, and <u>like the voice of loud thunder</u>. And I heard the sound of harpists playing their harps. ³They sang as it were a new song before the throne, before the <u>four</u> living <u>creatures</u>, and the <u>elders</u>; and no one could learn that song except the hundred *and* forty-four thousand who were redeemed from the earth. ⁴These are the ones who were <u>not defiled with women</u>, for they are <u>virgins</u>. These are the ones who follow the Lamb wherever He goes. These were <u>redeemed</u> from *among* men, *being* <u>first-fruits</u> to God and to the Lamb. ⁵And in their mouth was found no deceit, for <u>they are without fault</u> before the throne of God.

14:2-5

The voice of many waters like the voice of loud thunder represents God's authority and power. **The **four creatures** and **elders** are the angels and elders of Revelation 4:4-8. That the 144,000 are **virgins** and **not defiled with women** may indicate either (literally) celibacy and sexual purity or (figuratively) moral and religious purity (refusal to submit to the False Prophet's system). The 144,000 are the **first fruits** of the **redeemed**—the first to be saved—<u>during the Tribulation period</u> (following the Rapture of the Church). That **they are without fault** means that they are ethically blameless (<u>Ephesians 1:4;</u> Ephesians 5:27; <u>Philippians 2:15;</u> <u>Colossians 1:22;</u> <u>1 Peter 1:19;</u> <u>Jude 24</u>).**

The voice of loud thunder is a representation of God's audible power (<u>Psalm 77:18</u>).

Vv. 2-5

Ephesians 1:4 just as He chose us in Him before the foundation of the world, that we should be holy and without blame before Him in love,

Vv. 2-5

In Ephesians 1:4 we read of God's omniscience to know everything there is to know past present and future (Psalm 139:1-6). He even knew who would love Him and believe in Him to receive the holy righteousness of God through the Lord Jesus Christ (Romans 3:22-23.).

Philippians 2:15 that you may become blameless and harmless, children of God without fault in the midst of a crooked and perverse generation, among whom you shine as lights in the world,
Colossians 1:22 in the body of His flesh through death, to present you holy, and blameless, and above reproach in His sight—
1 Peter 1:19 but with the precious blood of Christ, as of a lamb without blemish and without spot.
Jude 24 Now to Him who is able to keep you from stumbling, and to present you faultless before the presence of His glory with exceeding joy,

Philippians 2:15, Colossians 1:22, 1 Peter 1:19, and Jude 24 give the wonderful truth and promise that being believers, we and the 144,000 will all be seen as **holy, and blameless...without blemish and without spot**, children of God without fault in the midst of a crooked and perverse generation, among whom we shine as lights in the world.

Psalm 77:18 The voice of Your thunder *was* in a whirlwind; the lightnings lit up the world; the earth trembled and shook,

Psalm 77:18 provides an electrifying example of our Almighty God's awesome power with which we can all simultaneously, physically and spiritually feel and sense. But when we hear God speaking to us individually, His indwelling Spirit is reminding us in our consciences of what we've heard or read in His guiding and saving Word.

⁶Then I saw another angel flying in the midst of heaven, having the everlasting gospel to preach to those who dwell on the earth—to every nation, tribe, tongue, and people— ⁷saying with a loud voice, "Fear God and give glory to Him, for the hour of His judgment has come; and worship Him who made heaven and earth, the sea and springs of water." ⁸And another angel followed, saying, "Babylon is fallen, that great city [♦], because she has made all nations drink of the wine of the wrath of her fornication."

14:6-8

The announcement by the first two angels is the anticipation of coming events. **The **everlasting gospel** (Matthew 24:14) is that the "Good News" is not only of salvation through faith in Christ, but added here, that Christ will win and the Beast will be judged. The **everlasting gospel** definitely focuses on people being redeemed back to God through Christ and the coming of His eternal kingdom. For unbelievers there are three negative parts of this "News": **the hour of... judgment has come** (Revelation 14:7); **Babylon♦ is fallen** (Revelation 14:8); and those who **worship the beast**" will be tormented **forever and ever** (Revelation 14:9-11). **All nations**—the whole world—are commanded to **fear God** and **give glory to Him** instead of the Beast** (Revelation 14:6-7).

[**Jeremiah 51:7** *Babylon was a golden cup in the LORD'S hand, that made all the earth drunk. The nations drank her wine; therefore the nations are deranged.*]

♦[Exactly what city this is, we do not know for sure; some believe it to be Rome, some Dubai with its claim to the world's tallest building, yet others think it could be New York City or Jerusalem. On the other hand, from what we know so far, it could even refer to the entire worldwide political, economical, and religious kingdom of the Antichrist that is prophesied in Isaiah Chapter 24: the coming judgment on the earth.]

Vv. 6-8

Matthew 24:14 "And this gospel of the kingdom will be preached in all the world as a witness to all the nations, _and then the end will come_."

Vv. 6-8

Matthew 24:14 is the end of the world; not the same as Romans 11:25 in which the last member will be added to the church, completing the Body of Christ. That is when He will rapture His Church home to heaven. **The end** that **will come** at the Rapture will be **the end** of the Church Age. But the context of Matthew 24 is about the Tribulation which occurs after the Rapture.

⁹Then a third angel followed them, saying with a loud voice, "If anyone worships the beast [the Antichrist] and his image, and receives *his* mark on his forehead or on his hand, ¹⁰he himself shall also drink of the wine of the wrath of God, which is poured out full strength into the cup of His indignation. He shall be tormented with fire and brimstone in the presence of the holy angels and in the presence of the Lamb.

14:9-10

A third angel informs us that unbelievers, beginning at mid-Tribulation (which is the same of the beginning of the Great Tribulation) who have received the **mark** of the **beast** and **worshiped** him will all eventually receive God's eternal punishment in the lake of **fire** (Matthew 25:41; Revelation 20:15). **The wine of the wrath of God** will make **all nations** drunk (v. 8). God's righteous anger (Job 21:20; Psalm 75:8; Isaiah 51:17; Jeremiah 25:15-16♦) is **poured out** in full strength on those who reject Him. **The cup of His indignation** *symbolizes* the place of God's punishment of sinners...all taking place **in the presence of** Christ and His **angels** making the punishment even more intense and shameful.** This will only be a *foretaste* of the pangs of eternal hell. And the Savior, who died for us, took this wrath of God for each one of us! Later, at the Great White Throne Judgment (Revelation 20:11-15) the unbelievers will pay that *eternal* price of having chosen Satan and evil over God's truth, love, and righteousness.

♦Jeremiah 25:15-38 details the wrath of the Lord from on high.

Vv. 9-10

Matthew 25:41 "Then He will also say to those on the left hand, 'Depart from Me, you cursed, into the everlasting fire prepared for the devil and his angels:'"

Vv. 9-10

Matthew 25:41 quotes the Lord Jesus as He refers back to 25:33 so that we can understand whom those are that are on **the left hand**: He sets His true followers—the sheep—on His right, but the **cursed**—the goats—on **the left**. Furthermore, here in verse 41 He promises the unbelievers an eternal future **into the everlasting fire prepared for the devil and his angels**.

Job 21:20 Let his eyes see his destruction, and let him drink of the wrath of the Almighty.

Psalm 75:8 For in the hand of the LORD *there is* a cup, and the wine is red; it is fully mixed, and he pours it out; surely its dregs shall all the wicked of the earth drain *and* drink down.

Isaiah 51:17 Awake, awake! Stand up, O Jerusalem, you who have drunk at the hand of the LORD the cup of His fury; you have drunk the dregs of the cup of trembling, *and* drained it out.

Jeremiah 25:15-16 ¹⁵For thus says the LORD God of Israel to me: "Take this wine cup of fury from My hand, and cause all the nations, to whom I send you, to drink it. ¹⁶And they will drink and stagger and go mad because of the sword that I will send among them."

Job 21:20, Psalm 75:8, Isaiah 51:17, and Jeremiah 25:15-16 all speak of the **drink of the wrath of the Almighty**, or the **wine cup of His fury**. The **cup** *here* portrays the totality of God's divine judgment on the wicked (also in Psalm 75:8; Isaiah 51:17, Isaiah 51:22; Jeremiah 25:15-16; Jeremiah 49:12; Jeremiah 51:7; Ezekiel 23:31-34; Revelation 16:19; Revelation 17:4; *and here in* Revelation 14:10). The cup can also represent blessings or salvation for a righteous person. (Psalm 16:5; Psalm 23:5; Psalm 116:13). Jesus voluntarily drank the cup of suffering (Matthew 20:22; Matthew 26:39; Matthew 26:42; Mark 10:38; Mark 14:36; Luke 22:20; John 18:11).

Revelation 20:11-15 ¹¹Then I saw a great white throne and Him who sat on it, from whose face the earth and the heaven fled away. And there was found no place for them. ¹²And I saw the dead, small and great, standing before God, and books were opened. And another book was opened, which is *the Book* of Life. And the dead were judged according to their works, by the things which were written in the books. ¹³The sea gave up the dead who were in it, and Death and Hādēs delivered up the dead who were in them. And they were judged, each one according to his works. ¹⁴Then Death and Hādēs were cast into the lake of fire. This is the second death. ¹⁵And anyone not found written in the Book of Life was cast into the lake of fire.

In Revelation 20:11-15 **the great white throne** depicts divine judgment as well as divine government. The judgment will take place neither on **earth** nor in its atmospheric **heaven** (Revelation 20:11-21:1; Matthew 25:31-46), since the present universe will be dissolved (Isaiah 51:6; Matthew 24:35; 2 Peter 3:10-12). The **dead** are the unbelieving **dead** of all past ages—that is, the *rest of the dead* mentioned in Revelation 20:5a. They are **judged** from two sets of **books** containing the record of every unsaved person's life. Each person is judged in accordance with his **works** (Romans 2:6, Romans 2:16; Romans 3:23; Romans 6:23). The **Book of Life** contains the name of every person who has received eternal life through faith in the Lord Jesus Christ. **Death and Hādēs** are the temporary holding places of unsaved bodies and souls (Luke 16:19-31). The **second death** is eternal punishment in the **lake of fire**.**

[11]And the smoke of their torment ascends forever and ever; and they have no rest day or night, who worship the beast and his image, and whoever receives the mark of his name."

14:11

Verse 11 reminds us that hell consists of eternal and conscious punishment. The **smoke of their torment ascends** perpetually—**no** relief **day or night**. Daniel 12:2; John 5:29 give consequences for both the saved and unsaved.

[12]Here is the patience of the saints; here *are* those who keep the commandments of God and the faith of Jesus. [13]Then I heard a voice from heaven saying to me, "Write: 'Blessed *are* the dead who die in the Lord from now on.'" "Yes," says the Spirit, "that they may rest from their labors, and their works follow them."

14:12-13

The Church—the Body of Christ—His Bride—will have already been raptured before the Tribulation period (Revelation 4:1; 5:11). The ones who die **in the Lord** from here on are Tribulation martyrs. Coming to Christ in the Tribulation Period, they will endure extreme persecution including death (Revelation 7:9-14). During their suffering, **patience** will certainly be required. These saints will surely be leaning on the Lord Jesus Christ for His comfort. They will be called to endure the savagery of the beast and to obey **God** by refusing to worship man or idol, and to hold fast their confession of **faith in Jesus**. They will be **blessed** by being in the third and last part of the first resurrection and will reign with Christ and the other saints during the Millennium.

V. 11

Daniel 12:2 And many of those who sleep in the dust of the earth shall awake, some to everlasting life, some to shame *and* everlasting contempt.

John 5:29 "and come forth—those who have done good, to the resurrection of life, and those who have done evil, to the resurrection of condemnation."

V. 11

Eternal separation is now made between those who have **life and those who have **death** (Daniel 12:2; John 5:28-29).**

¹⁴Then I looked, and behold, a white cloud, and on the cloud sat *One* like the Son of Man, having on His head a golden crown, and in His hand a sharp sickle.

14:14

The **Son of Man is Christ, the Messiah (Revelation 1:13; Daniel 7:13; Matthew 26:63-64). The **cloud** relates to Christ's soon Second Coming (Matthew 24:30; Acts 1:9-11). The **crown** pictures Him as the ruler of the earth, and the **sickle** symbolizes **judgment** as an instrument of the harvest

(John 5:27** *"and* [the Father] *has given Him authority to execute judgment also, because He is the Son of Man."*).

V. 14

Revelation 1:13 and in the midst of the seven lampstands *One* like the <u>Son of Man</u>, clothed with a garment down to the feet and girded about the chest with a golden band.

Daniel 7:13 "I was watching in the night visions, and behold, *One* like the <u>Son of Man</u>, coming with the clouds of heaven! He came to the Ancient of Days, and they brought Him near before Him.

Matthew 26:63-64 ⁶³But Jesus kept silent. And the high priest answered and said to Him, "I will <u>put</u> You <u>under oath by the living God</u>: Tell us if You are <u>the Christ</u>, <u>the Son of God</u>!" ⁶⁴Jesus said to him, "It is as you said. Nevertheless, I say to you, hereafter you will see the <u>Son of Man</u> sitting at the right hand of the Power, and coming on the <u>clouds</u> of heaven."

Matthew 24:30 "Then the <u>sign</u> of the <u>Son of Man</u> will appear in heaven, and <u>then all the tribes of the earth will mourn</u>, and they will see the <u>Son of Man</u> coming on the <u>clouds</u> of heaven with power and great glory."

Acts 1:9-11 ⁹Now when He had spoken these things, while they watched, He was taken up, and <u>a cloud received Him</u> out of their sight. ¹⁰And while they looked steadfastly toward heaven as He went up, behold, two men stood by them in white apparel, ¹¹who also said, "Men of Galilee, why do you stand gazing up into heaven? <u>This *same* Jesus, who was taken up from you into heaven, will so come in like manner as you saw Him go into heaven."</u>

V. 14

<u>Revelation 1:13</u> describes John's vision of how **the Son of Man**—the Messiah—appeared when John saw Him in the vision of the prophecy.

In <u>Daniel 7:13</u> **The Son of Man** in Daniel's prophecy also describes who Daniel saw in the vision—the Son of God approaching God the Father. Jesus took to referring to Himself as the Son of Man from Daniel's writings.

In <u>Matthew 26:63-64</u> Jesus no longer remained silent <u>as He did</u> when the high priest had previously been questioning Him. He only answered now because the high priest **put** Him **under oath by the living God**. Jesus, being compelled to answer (since He is also God Himself), admits that He is **the Christ** (the Messiah—the Savior), **the Son of God**. This is in no way boasting. It is merely the *truth*. The rest of His answer refers to His Second Coming at the end of the Great Tribulation.

In <u>Matthew 24:30</u> Jesus is again referring to His Second Coming at the end of the Seven-year Tribulation period. He mentions the word **sign** of <u>Himself</u>, and "**then all the tribes of the earth will mourn**." We believers have no way of knowing when He will come to rapture us (Matthew 24:36; Matthew 25:13; Mark 13:32). But as we read, we learn He will come in the air to take us up in the clouds <u>before</u> the Tribulation. We need to live each day in expectation of Christ's imminent return.

The last sentence in <u>Acts 1:9-11</u> says, **"This *same* Jesus, who was taken up from you into heaven, will so come in like manner as you saw Him go into heaven."** 1 Thessalonians 4:17 is in agreement as it tells us *we ...shall be caught up together...<u>in</u> <u>the clouds</u>—<u>not</u>* here on earth.—*And thus we shall always be with the Lord.*

[15]And another angel came out of the temple, crying with a loud voice to Him who sat on the cloud, "Thrust in Your sickle and reap, for the time has come for You to reap for the harvest of the earth is ripe." [16]So He who sat on the cloud thrust in His sickle on the earth, and the earth was reaped.

14:15-16
The fourth angel came out of the temple saying that **the time is come** to finish the judgment of the **earth**. The Second Coming of Christ includes more judgment. **The harvest of the earth is ripe** means it is time for God's judgment of the earth right now! To **reap** and harvest **the earth** means to judge and punish its people (Hosea 6:11; Matthew 13:30; Matthew 13:40-42).**

[17]Then another angel came out of the temple which is in heaven, he also having a sharp sickle. [18]And another angel came out from the altar, who had power over fire, and he cried with a loud cry to him who had the sharp sickle, saying, "Thrust in your sharp sickle and gather the clusters of the vine of the earth, for her grapes are fully ripe." [19]So the angel thrust his sickle into the earth and gathered the vine of the earth, and threw *it* into the great winepress of the wrath of God. [20]And the winepress was trampled outside the city, and blood came out of the winepress, up to the horses' bridles, for one thousand six hundred furlongs [184 miles].

14:17-20
These next verses represent God's wrath. The fifth **angel came out of the temple also having a sharp sickle.** The sixth **angel came out from the altar, who had power over fire** *which symbolizes even more judgment to follow. The mature grapes are gathered and thrown **into the great winepress of the wrath of God.** The trampling of grapes in the process of making wine is used here as a picture of *crushing* judgment.* The **winepress was trampled outside the city** of Jerusalem, **and blood came out of the winepress** for **one thousand six hundred furlongs.** One furlong equals 8.7 miles, so 1,600 furlongs equals 184 miles! This would reach **the full length of Palestine.** In short, the wrath of God—for the unbelievers rejecting Him and doing evil and worshiping an idol—is absolutely enormous! **The amount of blood that results from the **winepress** emphasizes the *severity* of the judgment.** The **great winepress of the wrath of God** pictures the violence and intensity of God's coming judgment on the earth and the unbelievers (Revelation 19:15; Lamentations 1:15a, c; Joel 3:12-14; Isaiah 63:2-3a). Perhaps the reference is to the coming Battle of Armageddon (Revelation 16:14-16).

Chapter 14 Verses 15-20
References

Vv. 15-16

Hosea 6:11 Also, O Judah, a harvest is appointed for you, when I return the captives of My people.

Matthew 13:40-42 [40] "Therefore as the tares are gathered and burned in the fire, so it will be at the end of this age. [41] The Son of man will send out His angels, and they will gather out of His kingdom all things that offend, and those who practice lawlessness, [42] and will <u>cast them into the furnace of fire.</u> There will be wailing and gnashing of teeth."

Vv. 17-20

Revelation 19:15 Now out of His mouth goes a sharp sword, that with it He should strike the nations. And He Himself will rule them with a rod of iron. He Himself treads <u>the winepress of the fierceness and wrath of Almighty God.</u>

Lamentations 1:15a [15a]"The Lord has trampled underfoot all my mighty *men* in my midst ...

Lamentations 1:15c [15c]The Lord trampled *as* in a winepress the virgin daughter of Judah.

Joel 3:12-14 [12]"Let the nations be wakened, and come u to the Valley of Jehoshaphat; For there I will sit to judge all the surrounding nations. [13]Put in the sickle, for the harvest is ripe. Come, go down; for the winepress is full, the vats overflow—for <u>their wickedness *is* great</u>." [14]Multitudes, multitudes in the valley of decision! For the day of the LORD *is* near in the valley of decision.

Isaiah 63:2-3a [2]Why *is* Your apparel red, and Your garments like one who treads in the winepress? [3a]"I have trodden the winepress alone, and from the peoples no one *was* with Me, for I have trodden them in My anger, and trampled them in My fury;"

Chapter 14 Verses 15-20
References Commentary

Vv. 15-16

In <u>Hosea 6:11</u> **The southern kingdom would fare no better than Ephraim, but some 130 years later for the <u>same reasons</u> of idolatry, but by a different God-sent agent, **Babylon**.**

Matthew 13:30 and <u>Matthew 13:40-42</u> tell us if we pull up tare weeds the roots are tangled with wheat roots and it is virtually impossible to pull up one without also pulling up the other. So is God's plan for allowing unbelievers to be together with new Tribulation Period believers. *The reapers are angels who, at the Second Advent (Second Coming) will round up all evildoers and throw **them into the furnace of fire,** where they will weep and gnash their teeth.*

Vv. 17-20

The three passages of <u>Revelation 19:15,</u> <u>Lamentations 1:15a, c</u> and <u>Joel 3:12-14</u> all speak of **the winepress of the fierceness and wrath of Almighty God,** because **their** [the unbelievers] **wickedness is great.**

<u>Isaiah 63:2-3a</u> describes how God's wrath will be felt by the unbelievers but the passage goes on to vs. 3b-6 telling that the reason for bringing an end to the age is because the year of His redeemed believers has come.

Preparation for the Seven Golden Bowls of God's Wrath

¹Then I saw another sign in heaven, great and marvelous: <u>seven</u> angels having the <u>seven last plagues</u>, for in them the <u>wrath of God</u> is <u>complete</u>.

15:1

*The **wrath of God began to be revealed in Chapter 6 with the seven seals, and will be finished with these **seven last plagues** which will be from the seven bowls.** *From this we know we are getting closer to the end of the Tribulation.*

²And I saw *something* like a <u>sea of glass</u> mingled with fire, and those who have the <u>victory over the beast</u>, over his <u>image</u> and over his <u>mark</u> *and* over the number of his name, standing on the sea of glass, having harps of God. ³They sing the <u>song of Moses</u>, the servant of God, <u>and the song of the Lamb</u>, saying: "Great and marvelous *are* Your works, Lord God <u>Almighty</u>! Just and true *are* your ways, O King of the saints! ⁴Who shall not fear You, O Lord, and glorify Your name? For *You* alone *are* holy. For <u>all nations</u> shall <u>come and worship</u> before You, for Your judgments have been manifested."

15:2-4

The **sea of glass was also seen before God's throne in <u>Revelation 4:6</u>. The **victory over the beast** is <u>won by faith in Christ</u> (<u>1 John 2:15-16</u>; <u>1 John 5:4-5</u>) which provides strength to refuse submitting to the Antichrist.** *Doubtless those who refused to take the **image** or **mark** will be martyred. But they will end up in heaven, singing **the song of Moses...and the song of the Lamb**, composed almost entirely of quotations from the Old Testament* **(<u>Exodus 15:1-3</u>; <u>Exodus 15:11</u>; <u>Exodus 15:18</u> or <u>Deuteronomy 32:3-4</u>).** *The **song of Moses** is about God's bringing His people out from slavery in Egypt. **The song of the Lamb** celebrates the final deliverance from Satan and all foes of spiritual life having belief in the One True Godhead.* ****All nations** will **come and worship** God in His Millennial kingdom.** The Son of God is for the fourth time (Revelation 1:8) referred to as **Almighty** reminding us of His equality with God the Father.

Vv. 2-4

Revelation 4:6 Before the throne *there was* a sea of glass, like crystal. And in the midst of the throne, and around the throne, *were* four living creatures full of eyes in front and in back.

1 John 2:15-16 ¹⁵Do not love the world or the things in the world. If anyone loves the world, the love of the Father is not in him. ¹⁶For all that is in the world—the lust of the flesh, the lust of the eyes, and the pride of life—is not of the Father but is of the world.

1 John 5:4-5 ⁴For whatever is born of God overcomes the world. And this is the victory that has overcome the world—our faith. ⁵Who is he who overcomes the world, but he who believes that Jesus is the Son of God?

Exodus 15:1-3 ¹Then Moses and the children of Israel sang this song to the LORD, and spoke, saying: "I will sing to the LORD, for He has triumphed gloriously! The horse and its rider He has thrown into the sea! ²The LORD *is* my strength and song, and He has become my salvation; He *is* my God, and I will praise Him; my father's God, and I will exalt Him. ³The LORD is a man of war; the LORD *is* His name." ...
Exodus 15:11 "Who *is* like You, O LORD, among the gods? Who *is* like You, glorious in holiness, fearful in praises, doing wonders? ...
Exodus 15:18 The LORD shall reign forever and ever."

Deuteronomy 32:3-4 ³"For I proclaim the name of the LORD: ascribe greatness to our God. ⁴*He is* the Rock, His work *is* perfect; for all His ways *are* justice, a God of truth and without injustice; righteous and upright *is* He."

Vv. 2-4

Revelation 4:6: *The **sea of glass like crystal** tells us that the throne is located in a place that is undisturbed by the restless, wild tossings of this world, or by the opposition of the wicked, who are like a *troubled* sea.* The **four living creatures** are probably cherubim.

1 John 2:15-16, much like Genesis 3:6, which says *the woman saw the tree was good for food, that it was pleasant to the eyes, and a tree desirable to make one wise, she took of its fruit and ate.* This indirectly points out that the world is being overrun with so many temptations such as drugs, alcohol, pornography, huge amounts of money, and attractive false teachings. These things are all temporary, and people have become victims of such passing things.

1 John 5:4-5: *Only the man who **is born of God** really **overcomes the world**, because by **faith** he is able to rise above the perishing things of this world and to see things in their true, eternal perspective.* The simple believer who realizes that the things which are seen are temporary and the things which are not seen are eternal. Nothing could be more important than our loved ones' eternal futures.

Exodus 15:1-3, Exodus 15:11 and Exodus 15:18 is described by Matthew Henry: *"It is the most ancient song we know of; it is a holy song, consecrated to the honor of God, and intended to exalt His name and celebrate His praise, and His name only: It is a typical song {depicting} the triumphs of the gospel church, in the downfall of its enemies; and put together with this song of the Lamb here in Revelation 15:2-3, they are said to be sung upon a **sea of glass**,* as this in Exodus 15 *was upon the Red Sea."*

In Deuteronomy 32:3-4 *Moses speaks of attributing **greatness to God**. The song reveals God's **greatness** in the context of His historical dealings with His people.*

⁵After these things I looked, and behold, the <u>temple of the tabernacle</u> of the testimony in heaven was <u>opened</u>. ⁶And out of the temple came the <u>seven angels</u> having the <u>seven plagues</u>, clothed in pure bright linen, and having their <u>chests</u> girded with <u>golden bands</u>. ⁷Then one of the four living creatures gave to the seven angels <u>seven golden bowls</u> <u>full of the wrath of God who lives forever and ever</u>. ⁸The temple was filled with <u>smoke</u> <u>from the glory of God and from His power</u>, and <u>no one</u> was <u>able to enter the temple</u> till the <u>seven</u> plagues of the <u>seven</u> angels were completed.

15:5-8

Next John saw the Most Holy place in **the temple of the tabernacle opened** (**the temple represents the presence of God Himself**) and **out came** *the bright, pure, linen clothed **seven angels** who have the last **seven plagues**. The **golden bands** around their **chests** declare they are equipped to execute righteous judgment by which God will be glorified.* The **seven golden bowls** are bowls (also called *vials* in the KJV) and they are **full of the wrath of God who lives forever and ever**. The **smoke** is **from the glory of God and from His power**. The immediate verse that follows Moses' relaying that God Himself would *come down upon Mount Sinai in the sight of all the people* (Exodus 19:11-15) made the people tremble (<u>Exodus 19:16</u>), and the cloud of smoke covered their meeting place (<u>Exodus 19:18</u>; <u>Exodus 40:34</u>). (The next Chapter of Exodus, Chapter 20, is where God gives the Ten Commandments on Mount Sinai.) **Until the seven plagues** are finished, no one is **able to enter the temple**. The time for any priestly intercession is past; God's judgment will now be completed.** Intercession is the act of intervening or mediating between differing parties, particularly the act of praying to God on behalf of another person. Since **no one** is **able to enter the temple** to pray to God, there is absolutely no hope left for any unbeliever left on the earth. However, the Tribulation-period-newly-converted <u>believers</u> will be blessed during the battle of Armageddon by the Lord Jesus as we will see in Revelation 16:15-16.

Vv. 5-8

Exodus 19:16 Then it came to pass on the third day, in the morning, that there were thunderings and lightnings, and <u>a thick cloud on the mountain</u>; and the sound of the <u>trumpet</u> was very <u>loud</u>, so that all the people who were in the camp trembled.

Exodus 19:18 Now Mount Sinai *was* completely in <u>smoke</u>, because the LORD descended upon it in fire. Its <u>smoke</u> ascended like the <u>smoke</u> of a furnace, and <u>the whole mountain quaked greatly</u>. ...

Exodus 40:34 Then the <u>cloud covered the tabernacle of meeting</u> because the cloud rested above it, and the glory of the LORD filled the tabernacle.

Vv. 5-8

All the things spoken of in <u>Exodus 19:16, Exodus 19:18 and Exodus 40:34</u>—**thunderings and lightnings**, **a thick cloud on the mountain**; the **loud trumpet**, seeing each other trembling; a cloud of **smoke covered the tabernacle of meeting, in fire** and **smoke, because the LORD** was coming down to meet with the people; **the whole mountain quaking greatly**—*the Israelites probably spoke among themselves of the terrors of meeting God, especially on the basis of law-keeping. They all had been taught that Mount Sinai was a forbidden place. Only Moses and Aaron were allowed to ascend the **mountain**. Neither mankind nor animal were to touch it on penalty of death* (Exodus 19:13). No wonder they trembled.

The Seven Bowl Judgments of God's Wrath

¹Then I heard a loud voice from the temple saying to <u>the seven angels</u>, "Go and pour out the <u>bowls of the wrath of God on the earth</u>."

16:1

Then John heard a loud voice telling **the seven angels** to <u>complete</u> God's **wrath on the earth**. **The **bowls of the wrath of God** represent the climax of God's punishment of sinners during the Tribulation period.** There is no more offer to allow for repentance. The seven bowls are emptied rapidly in a short period of time. **The judgments are somewhat parallel to the ten plagues on Egypt (<u>Exodus</u> 7-12; <u>7:17-18</u>; <u>8:4</u>, <u>8:17</u>, <u>8:24</u>; <u>9:3</u>, <u>9:6a</u>) and to the trumpets (Revelation Chapters 8-9). The bowls are more total and universal in their effects than were the trumpets, and generally affect people more directly.**

V. 1 Exodus Ten Plagues:

Exodus 7:17-18 ¹⁷"Thus says the LORD: "By this you shall know that I *am* the LORD. Behold, I will strike the waters which *are* in the river with the rod that *is* in my hand, and they shall be turned to blood. ¹⁸And the fish that *are* in the river shall die, the river shall stink, and the Egyptians will loathe to drink the water of the river.""

Exodus 8:4 "And the frogs shall come up on you, on your people, and on all your servants.""

V. 1

Exodus 7:17-18: The effects of this first plague (the **fish** died and the **river** stank, and it was not drinkable in verse 21) **seem to prove that the **blood** was real, as it shall be also under the second trumpet of Revelation 8:8-9 and the second and third bowls of Revelation 16:3-4.**

Exodus 8:4: In verse 7 *the magicians were able to produce **frogs** also—as if there were not enough already! They probably did this by demonic power, but they dared not destroy the **frogs** because the frog was worshiped as the god of fertility!* (**The goddess Heket, the spouse of the ram-god Khnum, was depicted in the form of a woman with a frog's head.** Our true God used the situation to show what He thinks of other gods before Himself.) *When the **frogs** died the next day, there was a tremendous stench from their dead bodies, but **Pharaoh** once again **hardened his heart**.*

Exodus 8:17 And they did so. For Aaron stretched out his hand with his rod and struck the dust of the earth, and it became lice on man and beast. All the dust of the land became lice throughout all the land of Egypt.

In Exodus 8:17 the third plague, like the sixth and ninth ending cycles, concludes a cycle and comes unannounced as a special judgment: **the dust of the earth** turned into **lice**. *This time the magicians, unable to produce **lice**, warned Pharaoh that a power greater than theirs* (**the finger of God** *verse 19) was at work, but the king was inflexible. The more he hardened his own **heart**, the more God hardened it.*

Exodus 8:24 And the LORD did so. Thick swarms *of flies* came into the house of Pharaoh, *into* his servants' houses, and into all the land of Egypt. The land was corrupted because of the swarms *of flies*.

Exodus 8:24: **Each of the plagues in a new cycle (the first, fourth, and seventh) proceeds with a warning from Moses to Pharaoh.** *In the NKJV the italicized *flies* may in Hebrew probably, literally, mean **swarms** of a mixture of many species. Since most or all of the plagues were aimed at the false gods of Egypt (the "sacred" Nile, and virtually every creature was a deity in Egypt) this could have been an attack by God against Khepri, the god of the sacred beetle.*

Exodus 9:3 "behold, the hand of the LORD will be on your cattle in the field, on the horses, on the donkeys, on the camels, on the oxen, and on the sheep—a very severe pestilence.

Exodus 9:6a So the LORD did this thing on the next day, and all the livestock of Egypt died:

Exodus 9:3, Exodus 9:6a: *The discriminating judgment by God to **kill the Egyptian livestock**, but not the Israelites' animals cannot be explained by natural phenomena. The Egyptians worshiped various animals such as the bull-gods Apis and Mnevis, the cow-god Hathor, and the ram-god Khnum.* (See also Deuteronomy 28:18)

²So the <u>first</u> went and poured out his <u>bowl</u> upon the earth, and a <u>foul and loathsome sore</u> came upon the men who had <u>the mark of the beast</u> <u>and</u> those who <u>worshiped his image.</u>

16:2

The **first bowl** causes a **foul and loathsome sore** to break out on **those who worshiped the mark of the beast and his image**. (****Parallels Egypt's sixth plague; <u>Exodus 9:9-10;**</u>** the seventh to tenth plagues are listed in Exodus respectively; <u>Exodus 9:24</u>; <u>Exodus 10:4</u>; <u>Exodus 10:22</u>; <u>Exodus 12:29</u>; <u>Romans 9:17</u>)

³Then the <u>second</u> angel poured out his <u>bowl</u> on the <u>sea</u>, and it became <u>blood</u> as of a dead *man*; and <u>every living</u> creature <u>in the sea died</u>. ⁴Then the <u>third</u> angel poured out his <u>bowl</u> on the <u>rivers and springs</u> of water, and they became <u>blood</u>. ⁵And I heard <u>the angel of the waters</u> saying; "You are righteous, O Lord, the One who is and <u>who was</u> and <u>who is to be</u>, because You have judged these things. ⁶For they have <u>shed</u> the <u>blood</u> of saints and prophets, and You have given them <u>blood to drink</u>. For <u>it is their just due</u>. ⁷And I heard another from the altar saying, "Even so, <u>Lord God</u> <u>Almighty</u>, true and righteous *are* Your <u>judgments.</u>"

16:3-7

The **second bowl** turns the entire **sea** to **blood** and kills **every living** soul **in the sea**. The **third bowl** turns all the **rivers and springs** to **blood**. *At this point **the angel of the waters** defends the justice of God's judgments. Men who had **shed blood** in large quantities are rewarded with **blood to drink** instead of water.* **It is their just due**. The Lord Jesus is for the fifth time referred to as **Lord God Almighty**.

⁸Then the <u>fourth</u> angel poured out his <u>bowl</u> on the sun, and power was given to him to scorch men with fire. ⁹And men were scorched with great heat, and they blasphemed the name of God who has power over these plagues; and <u>they did not repent</u> and give Him glory.

16:8-9

*The **fourth bowl** causes men to suffer severe sunburn or solar radiation. This does **not**, however, cause them to **repent**. Instead, they curse God for this scorching heat on them.*

V. 2

Exodus 9:9-10 ⁹"And it will become fine dust in all the land of Egypt, and it will cause <u>boils</u> that <u>break out in sores on man and beast</u> throughout all the land of Egypt." ¹⁰Then they took ashes from the furnace and stood before Pharaoh, and Moses scattered *them* toward heaven. And *they* caused <u>boils</u> that break out in sores on man and beast.

V. 2

In <u>Exodus 9:9-10</u> *even the magicians were affected by the **boils**.* (See also Deuteronomy 28:24, 27)

Exodus 9:24 So there was <u>hail</u>, and <u>fire mingled with the hail</u>, so very heavy that there was none like it in all the land of Egypt since it became a nation.

We saw **hail** in <u>Exodus 9:24,</u> in Revelation 8:7, Revelation 11:19 and we will see it again in Revelation 16:21.

Exodus 10:4 'Or else, if you refuse to let My people go, behold, tomorrow I will bring <u>locusts</u> into your territory.'

In <u>Exodus 10:4</u> *the Egyptian god Serapis was powerless to protect from **locusts**.* The locusts were previewed at the sound of the fifth trumpet in Revelation 9:1-3.

Exodus 10:22 So Moses stretched out his hand toward heaven, and there was <u>thick darkness</u> in all the land of Egypt three days.

In <u>Exodus 10:22</u> *the **darkness** humbled one of the greatest Egyptian gods, the sun god Ra.* (See also Deuteronomy 28:29)

Exodus 12:29 And it came to pass at midnight that <u>the LORD struck all the firstborn</u> in the land of Egypt, from the firstborn of Pharaoh who sat on his throne to the firstborn of the captive who *was* in the dungeon, and all the firstborn of livestock.

In <u>Exodus 12:29</u> *the Israelites were at last permitted to leave Egypt.*

Romans 9:17 For the Scripture says to the Pharaoh, *"For this very purpose I have raised you up, that I may show My power in you, and that My name may be declared in all the earth."*

Paul quotes Exodus 9:16 in <u>Romans 9:17</u> as God gives His purpose for using **Pharaoh** for this kind of judgment.

¹⁰Then the <u>fifth</u> angel poured out his <u>bowl</u> on the throne of the beast [the Antichrist], and his <u>kingdom</u> became full of <u>darkness</u>; and they gnawed their tongues because of the <u>pain</u>. ¹¹They blasphemed the God of heaven because of their pains and their sores, and <u>did not repent</u> of their deeds.

¹²Then the <u>sixth</u> angel poured out his <u>bowl</u> on the great river <u>Eūphrātēs</u>, and its water was dried up, so that the way of the kings <u>from the east</u> might be prepared. ¹³And I saw <u>three</u> unclean <u>spirits</u> like <u>frogs</u> *coming* out of the mouth of the <u>dragon</u> [Satan], out of the mouth of <u>the beast</u> [Antichrist], <u>and</u> out of the mouth of <u>the false prophet</u>. ¹⁴For they are <u>spirits of demons</u>, <u>performing</u> signs, *which go* out to the kings of the earth and of the whole world, to gather them to the <u>battle</u> [Armageddon] of that great day of God Almighty. ¹⁵<u>*"Behold, I am coming as a thief. Blessed is he who watches, and keeps his garments, lest he walk naked and they see his shame."*</u>

16:10-11

The **fifth bowl** causes **darkness** on the **kingdom** of **the beast**. His followers suffer **pain**, *but it does not soften their hearts. They only become more settled in their hatred of God.*

16:12-15

The **sixth bowl** dries up the river **Eūphrātēs** allowing armies **from the east** to come toward Israel. *Then John sees **three frog**-like **spirits** issuing from **the mouth of the dragon** (Satan), **the beast** (Antichrist), **and the mouth of the false prophet**—the **spirits are of demons, performing** miracles to deceive the world's rulers, and to lure them to a climactic **battle** on the **great day of God Almighty.** <u>Immediately prior</u> to the battle of **Armageddon**, the Lord Jesus Christ is quoted, **"Behold, I am coming as a thief. Blessed *is* he who watches; and keeps his garments, lest he walk naked and they see his shame."** *This is His special blessing on the tribulation saints, those who are watching for His Return—His Second Coming, and have kept themselves pure from the idolatrous worship of that day. He will come to the <u>unsaved</u> as a **thief**.* He is also coming as a thief in the night to rapture the Church and save them from wrath (<u>1 Thessalonians 5:1-4</u>, <u>1 Thessalonians 5:9</u>). Verse 14 refers to the Lord Jesus Christ as God Almighty for the sixth time.

¹⁶And they <u>gathered</u> them together <u>to the place</u> called <u>in Hebrew, Armageddon</u>.

16:16

So the warriors were **gathered to the place in Hebrew, Armageddon**. In Hebrew, *Har Megiddon*, or Mount Megiddō in Northern Israel—about 10 km SW of Nazareth, 35 km SW of the Sea of Galilee, and 25 km east of the Mediterranean coast (the sight of battles in <u>Judges 5:19</u>; <u>2 Kings 23:29</u>).

Vv. 12-15

1 Thessalonians 5:1-4 ¹But concerning the times and the seasons, brethren, you have no need that I should write to you. ²For you yourselves know perfectly that the day of the Lord so comes as a thief in the night. ³For when they [the unsuspecting, unbelievers] say, "Peace and safety!" then sudden destruction [Tribulation] comes upon them, as labor pains upon a pregnant woman. And they shall not escape. ⁴But you, brethren, are not in darkness, so that this Day should overtake you as a thief.

1 Thessalonians 5:9 For God did not appoint us to wrath, but to obtain salvation through our Lord Jesus Christ.

Vv. 12-15

1 Thessalonians 5:1-4 and 5:9 flows like there should be no chapter break from the Rapture passage in the previous chapter of 1 Thessalonians 4:13-18. Then in 2 Thessalonians 2:1, 2:2a, 2:2c, 2:3a, 2:6-8a Paul the Apostle writes again to remind them that the Rapture has not yet happened: ¹*Now, brethren, concerning the coming of our Lord Jesus Christ and our gathering together to Him, we ask you,* ²ᵃ*not to be soon shaken in mind or troubled,* ²ᶜ*as though the day of Christ* [the "day of Christ is any judgment day He judges not only for punishment, but in this case for Rapture and for rewards in heaven] *had come.* ³ᵃ*Let no one deceive you by any means; for that Day will not come unless the falling away comes first, and the man of sin* [the Antichrist] *is revealed,* [But when we continue reading, not only must the falling away of faith by those in apostate churches happen, but we also see in verses 7-8a that the evangelizing Church led by the Holy Spirit must also be taken out of the world before the Antichrist can be revealed:] ⁶*And now you know what is restraining, that he may be revealed in his own time.* ⁷*For the mystery of the lawlessness is already at work; only He who now restrains will do so until He is taken out of the way* [taken up by Rapture]. ⁸ᵃ*And then the lawless one* [the Antichrist] *will be revealed...* [Christ will come back again like a thief seven years later for His Second Coming to earth.]

V. 16

Judges 5:19 "The kings came *and* fought, then the kings of Cānaan fought in Tāanach, by the waters of Megiddō; they took no spoils of silver.

2 Kings 23:29 In his days Pharaoh Nēcho king of Egypt went to the aid of the king of Assyria, to the River Eūphrātēs; and King Jōsīah went against him. And *Pharaoh Nēcho* killed him at Megiddō when he confronted him.

V. 16

Judges 5:19: **Soggy ground and God's well-timed cloudburst immobilized Sisera's military chariots.**

2 Kings 23:29: Judah's King Jōsīah was killed at the battle of Megiddō. But the Egyptians were defeated by the Babylonians at the Eūphrātēs River (2 Kings 24:7). It is interesting to note that Megiddō is near the battle ground of Armageddon.

Battle of Armageddon
The Seventh and Final Bowl of
Wrath Finishes the Tribulation

16:17-18

¹⁷Then the <u>seventh angel</u> poured out his <u>bowl</u> into the air, and a loud voice came out of the temple of heaven, from the throne, saying, "<u>It is done!</u>" ¹⁸And <u>there were noises</u> <u>and thunderings and lightnings;</u> <u>and there was a great earthquake</u>, such a mighty and great earthquake as had not occurred <u>since</u> men were on the earth.

That this is the final bowl, judgment is given by **a loud voice from the throne: "It is done!"** **With this **seventh bowl** and the <u>return</u> of Christ Himself, the judgments of the Tribulation Period are now finished.** *The wrath of God is <u>over</u> as far as the <u>Tribulation Period</u> is concerned.* <u>The unbelievers</u> <u>who have taken the mark have no further</u> <u>opportunity for repentance</u> (Revelation 14:9-10). When the **seventh angel** poured out his bowl into the air, **there were noises and thunderings and lightnings; and there was a great earthquake** bigger than any **earthquake** that had ever occurred **since** the beginning of mankind (<u>Ezekiel 38:18-22</u>).

16:19

¹⁹Now the <u>great city</u> was divided into three parts, and the <u>cities of the nations</u> fell. And <u>great Babylon</u> was remembered before <u>God</u>, to give her <u>the cup</u> of the wine of the fierceness of His wrath. [**Jeremiah 51:7** *Babylon was a golden cup in the LORD'S hand, that made all the earth drunk. The nations drank her wine; therefore the nations are deranged.*]

****The great city** of **Babylon, divided into three parts** by the huge earthquake, drinks **the cup** which symbolizes God's wrath (Revelation 14:10),** God's anger and fury. *He has not forgotten her unremorseful idolatry, cruelty, and religious confusion. The **cities of the nations** are laid flat.* **The great city, Babylon** is further described and identified in Chapters 17 and 18 as possibly Rome or perhaps all of the Antichrist's evil world.

16:20

²⁰Then <u>every island</u> fled away, and <u>the mountains</u> were not found.

***Every island** and **the mountains** disappear as God's earthquake flattens the earth.* Ezekiel also quotes God on this in Ezekiel 38:20b.

Vv. 17-18

Revelation 14:9-10 ⁹Then a third angel followed them, saying with a loud voice, "If anyone worships the beast and his image, and receives his mark on his forehead or on his hand, ¹⁰"he himself [the unbeliever who's taken the mark] shall also drink of the <u>wine of the wrath of God</u>, which is <u>poured out</u> <u>full strength</u> into the cup of His indignation."

Vv. 17-18

<u>Revelation 14:9-10</u>: The **wine of the wrath of God** will make **all nations** drunk. God's righteous anger (Job 21:20; Psalm 75:8; Isaiah 51:17; Jeremiah 25:15-38) is **poured out** in full strength on those who reject Him. **The **cup of His indignation** *symbolizes* the place of God's punishment of sinners...all taking place **in the presence of** Christ and His **angels** making the punishment even more intense and shameful.** This will only be a *foretaste* of the pangs of the eternal Lake of Fire. And the Savior, who died for us, took more than this wrath of God for each one of us! Later, at the Great White Throne Judgment (Revelation 20:11-15) **the unbelievers will pay that *eternal* price of having chosen Satan and evil over God and righteousness.**

Ezekiel 38:18-22 ¹⁸"And it will come to pass at the same time, when <u>Gog</u> comes against the land of Israel," says the Lord GOD, "*that* My fury will show in My face. ¹⁹For in My <u>jealousy</u> *and* in the fire of My <u>wrath</u> I have spoken: 'Surely in that day there shall be <u>a great earthquake</u> in the <u>land</u> of Israel, ²⁰so that the fish of the sea, the birds of the heavens, the beasts of the field, all creeping things that creep on the earth, and all men who *are* on the face of the earth shall shake at My <u>presence</u>. <u>The mountains shall be thrown down</u>, the steep places shall fall, and every wall shall fall to the ground.' ²¹I will call for a sword against Gog throughout all My mountains," says the Lord GOD. "Every man's sword will be against his brother. ²²And I will bring him to judgment with <u>pestilence</u> and <u>bloodshed</u>; I will rain down on him, on his troops, and on the many peoples who *are* with him, <u>flooding rain</u>, great <u>hailstones</u>, fire, and <u>brimstone</u>.""

<u>Ezekiel 38:18-22</u>: *The forces of **Gog** will swarm over the land. But they will meet the blazing **wrath** and **jealousy** of God. The **land** will be terribly shaken by **a great earthquake**; Gog's men will be terrified by **pestilence**, **bloodshed**, **flooding rain**, **hailstones**, fire, and **brimstone**. The destruction of the enemies of God's people reminds us of the Lord's promise in Isaiah 54:17: "*No weapon formed against you shall prosper...This is the heritage of the servants of the LORD.*"* Also, in Joshua 10:11, the discriminating **hailstones** affected only the enemy—as here in Ezekiel, those against God are the ones being shaken and terrified.

²¹And great <u>hail</u> from heaven fell upon men, *each hailstone* about the weight of a <u>talent</u> [60-100 pounds!].

16:21

The *large* hail (a **talent** weighs about 60 to 100 pounds) may help to destroy the cities (<u>Joshua 10:11</u>; <u>Ezekiel 38:18-22</u>). But unbelieving mankind still blasphemes **God** and has no opportunity for repentance. Not only is the seventh <u>bowl</u> the last of the seven <u>plagues</u> (<u>Revelation 15:6-8</u>), but also it completes the previews of both the seventh <u>seal</u> (<u>Revelation 8:1</u>) and the seventh <u>trumpet</u> (<u>Revelation 11:15</u>).**

V. 21

Joshua 10:11 And it happened, as they fled before Israel *and* were on the descent of Beth Horon, that the LORD cast down large hail-stones from heaven on them as far as Azēkah, and they died. *There were* more who died from the hailstones than the children of Israel killed with the sword.

Ezekiel 38:18-22 [18]"And it will come to pass at the same time, when Gog comes against the land of Israel," says the Lord God, "that My fury will show in My face. [19]For in My jealousy and in the fire of My wrath I have spoken: 'Surely in that day there shall be a great [a]earthquake in the land of Israel, [20]so that the fish of the sea, the birds of the heavens, the beasts of the field, all creeping things that creep on the earth, and all men who are on the face of the earth shall shake at My presence. The mountains shall be thrown down, the steep places shall fall, and every wall shall fall to the ground.' [21]I will call for a sword against Gog throughout all My mountains," says the Lord God. "Every man's sword will be against his brother. [22]And I will bring him to judgment with pestilence and bloodshed; I will rain down on him, on his troops, and on the many peoples who are with him, flooding rain, great hailstones, fire, and brimstone.

Revelation 15:6-8 [6]And out of the temple came the seven angels having the seven plagues, clothed in pure bright linen, and having their chests girded with golden bands. [7]Then one of the four living creatures gave to the seven angels seven golden bowls full of the wrath of God who lives forever and ever. [8]The temple was filled with smoke from the glory of God and from His power, and no one was able to enter the temple till the seven plagues of the seven angels were completed.

Revelation 8:1 When He opened the seventh seal, there was silence in heaven for about half an hour.

Revelation 11:15

-CONTINUED ON NEXT PAGE UNDER REFERENCES!-

V. 21

In Joshua 10:11and Ezekiel 38:18-22 God used hailstones for judgment against His enemies; *note that the *discriminating* hail killed *only* the enemy.*

Revelation 15:6-8: ***Out came** the bright, pure, linen clothed **seven angels** who have the last **seven plagues**. The **golden bands** around their **chests** declare they are equipped to execute righteous judgment by which God will be glorified.* The **seven golden bowls** are called *vials* in the KJV, and they are **full of the wrath of God who lives forever and ever.** The **smoke** is **from the glory of God and from His power.** Since **no one** is **able to enter the temple** to pray to God, there is absolutely no hope left for any unbeliever left on the earth.

Revelation 8:1: **The **seventh seal** probably contains the **seven trumpets.**** The Lamb opens the seventh seal, and then silence is held for about half an hour to indicate the beginning of these further series of judgments. The first four trumpets were blasted in Chapter 8.

-CONTINUED ON NEXT PAGE UNDER REFERENCES COMMENTARY!-

**-VERSE 21 REPEATED
FROM PREVIOUS PAGE -**

**-COMMENTARY REPEATED
FROM PREVIOUS PAGE-**

16:21

²¹And great <u>hail</u> from heaven fell upon men, *each hailstone* about the weight of a <u>talent</u> [<u>60-100 pounds</u>!].

The *large* **hail (a **talent** weighs about 60 to 100 pounds) may help to destroy the cities (<u>Joshua 10:11</u>; <u>Ezekiel 38:18-22</u>). But unbelieving mankind still blasphemes **God** and has no opportunity for repentance. Not only is the seventh <u>bowl</u> the last of the seven <u>plagues</u> (<u>Revelation 15:6-8</u>), but also it completes both the seventh <u>seal</u> (<u>Revelation 8:1</u>) and the seventh <u>trumpet</u> (<u>Revelation 11:15</u>).**

-CONTINUED FROM PREVIOUS PAGE-

-CONTINUED FROM PREVIOUS PAGE-

V. 21

Revelation 11:15 Then the <u>seventh</u> angel sounded: And there were loud voices in heaven, saying, "The <u>kingdoms of this world</u> have become *the kingdoms* of our Lord and of His Christ, and he shall <u>reign forever and ever</u>!"

V. 21

<u>Revelation 11:15</u>: **<u>The **seventh** trumpet results in the millennial kingdom of Christ</u>. The seven vials or bowls (Revelation 16:1) are probably contained in the judgment of the seventh trumpet. They will occur in a very brief period of time at the end of the Great Tribulation. <u>The Second Coming of Christ</u>, while a great blessing for believers, <u>will be God's most severe judgment of the earth</u>. The **kingdoms of this world** will be completely overthrown by the coming kingdom of Christ (Revelation 19:11, Revelation 20-21; Daniel 2:34-35a, Daniel 2:44), who will **reign for ever and ever** (Daniel 7:13-14, Daniel 7:27).**

{**Chapters **17** and **18** picture the judgment of God on a system, empire, or city called Babylon the Great (Revelation 17:5)**; it is a more detailed description of the <u>Battle of Armageddon</u>. The great city is thought by many to be Rome. *Chapter 17 describes the *religious* Babylon and Chapter 18 the commercial aspect.* *Religious* Jerusalem certainly includes Islamic Muslim sects (<u>Ezekiel 8:15-16</u>) and apostate Christendom, both Protestant and Catholic. *According to MacDonald it may include the ecumenical (habitable world—"universal") so-called *church*.* Specifically concerning the Muslims or idol worship, Ezekiel 8:15-16 offers interesting insight to the practice of facing the east while praying. Revelation 17:5: *And on her forehead a name was written: MYSTERY, BABYLON THE GREAT, THE MOTHER OF HARLOTS AND OF THE ABOMINATIONS OF THE EARTH* is printed here only as an appetizing preview for the mystery of Babylon.}

The Fall and Doom of Babylon the Great
(Roman Empire) Predicted

¹Then <u>one of the seven angels</u> who had the seven bowls came and talked with me, saying to me, "Come, I will show you <u>the judgment of the great harlot</u> who <u>sits on many waters</u>, ²with whom <u>the kings of the earth committed fornication</u>, and <u>the inhabitants of the earth</u> were made <u>drunk with the wine of her fornication</u>." ³So he carried me away in the Spirit into the wilderness. And I saw a woman [possibly the risen Roman Empire] <u>sitting on a scarlet beast</u> *which was* <u>full of</u> <u>names</u> of blasphemy, having <u>seven heads and ten horns</u>.

17:1-3

One of the seven angels** invites John to witness **the judgment of the great harlot (whore in KJV). *The **harlot** "*church*" (called **harlot** because of not being faithful to Almighty God, but worshiping idols instead) **sits on many waters**, controlling great areas of the Gentile world.* **The **waters** represent the various peoples and nations of the earth (<u>Revelation 17:15</u>).** ***The kings of the earth** have **committed fornication** with her; she has seduced political leaders with her compromise and intrigue. **The inhabitants of the earth** have become **drunk with the wine of her fornication**; vast numbers have come under her evil influence and have been reduced to staggering wretchedness. The apostate, **harlot** *church* is seen **sitting on a scarlet beast**. As we have seen in <u>Revelation 13:1-2</u>; <u>Revelation 17:9-10</u>, this **beast** is probably <u>the revived Roman Empire</u>. The beast is **full of** blasphemous **names** and has **seven heads and ten horns**.*The **seven heads** are the seven kings, or rulers, *or* seven different stages of the empire (<u>Revelation 17:10</u>). The **ten horns** were predicted by <u>Daniel 7:24</u> to be a ten-kingdom form.

Vv. 1-3

Revelation 17:15 Then he said to me, "The waters which you saw, where the harlot sits, are peoples, multitudes, nations, and tongues.

Revelation 13:1-2 ¹Then I stood on the sand of the sea. And I saw a beast rising up out of the sea, having seven heads and ten horns, and on his horns ten crowns, and on his heads a blasphemous name. ²Now the beast which I saw was like a leopard, his feet were like *the feet* of a bear, and his mouth like the mouth of a lion. The dragon gave him his power, his throne, and great authority.

Revelation 17:9 "Here *is* the mind of which has wisdom: The seven heads are seven mountains on which the woman sits.

Revelation 17:10 "There are also seven kings. Five have fallen, one is, *and* the other has not yet come. And when he comes, he must continue a short time.

Daniel 7:24 "'The ten horns *are* ten kings *who* shall arise from this kingdom. Another shall rise after them; he [Antichrist] shall be different from the first *ones*, and shall subdue three kings.

Vv. 1-3

Revelation 17:15: ****The waters where the harlot sits, are peoples, multitudes, nations,** and **tongues** indicating the worldwide influence and authority of the harlot.**

Revelation 13:1-2: The first beast, Antichrist, who, although not known yet, will already be *among* the church before the Rapture (1 John 4:3; 2 Thessalonians 2:3-4). He is the Gentile head of a revived Roman Empire, which will be a ten-kingdom form. **The **sea** here is the Gentile nations of the world, from one of which the Antichrist comes.** *The **seven heads** are said in Revelation 17:9-10 to be seven kings, or rulers, or seven different stages of the empire.

Revelation 17:10: **The **seven kings** are likely the seven kingdoms or empires which throughout history have ruled over Israel and much of the back-then-known world:** **Five have fallen**: Egypt, Assyria, Babylon, Persia, Greece. Rome was the sixth, and will be revived as the seventh future Roman Empire (Daniel 2:41-44; Daniel 7:7, 20, 24).

The **ten horns** were predicted by Daniel 7:24 to be ten kingdoms. **Ten crowns on his horns** speak of the power to rule, from a **throne** with **great authority**, given to him by the **dragon**.* Satan is attempting to duplicate how the Father gives all authority to the Son. The first **beast**—Antichrist—will rule over the three previous **subdued** empires to the ancient Roman Empire of which Daniel's prophesies were fulfilled: Greek: **leopard**; Medo-Persia: **bear**; Babylon: **lion**. *In short, the revived empire combines all the evil features of the preceding world empires. The new empire and its ruler receive supernatural strength from Satan.* (All of Daniel's prophecies so far have been fulfilled.)

The Fall and Doom of Babylon the Great
(Roman Empire) Predicted

⁴The woman was arrayed in purple and scarlet, and adorned with gold and precious stones and pearls, having in her hand a golden cup full of abominations and the filthiness of her fornication. ⁵And on her forehead a name was written: MYSTERY, BABYLON THE GREAT, THE MOTHER OF HARLOTS AND OF THE ABOMINATIONS OF THE EARTH. ⁶I saw the woman, drunk with the blood of the saints and with the blood of the martyrs of Jesus. And when I saw her, I marveled with great amazement.

17:4-6

The elegant clothing and jewelry of the **woman show her wealth and attractiveness, but her activities** (such as probable emperor worship) **are filthy and abominable to God. Her mysterious, hidden truth name is **BABYLON THE GREAT**. The harlot will do what literal Babylon did in the past:

1) oppress God's people; and
2) propagate a false religious system

—much of the world's idolatry can be traced back to historical Babylon in Mesopotāmia (Genesis 11:7-9), including the mother-child cult of Sumerian-Tammūz (Jeremiah 44:18-19; Ezekiel 8:13-14), which entered other cultures as Ashtaroth-Bāal, Aphrodite-Eros, Venus-Cupid, and even Madonna-Child. As the fountainhead of idolatry, Babylon the harlot is the **MOTHER OF HARLOTS AND ABOMINATIONS OF THE EARTH**. The harlot has convinced terrorists to shed the blood of Christian martyrs down through the centuries, and will still be doing it here during the Tribulation Period.** *She is drunk with their blood.*

[This **MYSTERY of BABYLON THE GREAT, THE MOTHER OF HARLOTS AND OF THE ABOMINATIONS OF THE EARTH** has now been possibly revealed enough to be partially solved. We cannot say with absolute certainty, but we can conclude that the whore of Babylon is an evil world system, controlled by the Antichrist during the last days before the Savior's return to earth. The Antichrist beast is the center of attention in an ungodly, end-times, huge *religious* craze— and he is also called a beast. The Antichrist beast and his beast of an empire are together, possibly, BABYLON THE GREAT, THE MOTHER OF HARLOTS AND THE ABOMINATIONS OF THE EARTH. In Revelation 19:20 we will see the vindictive Antichrist, along with the false prophet, hurled into the lake of fire burning with brimstone.]

Vv. 4-6

Genesis 11:7-9 ⁷"Come, let Us go down and there confuse their language, that they may not understand one another's speech." ⁸So the LORD scattered them abroad from there over the face of <u>all the earth</u>, and they ceased building the city. ⁹Therefore its name is called Bābel, because there the LORD confused the language of <u>all the earth</u>; and from there the LORD scattered them abroad over the face of <u>all the earth</u>.

Jeremiah 44:18-19 ¹⁸"But since we stopped burning incense to the queen of heaven and pouring out drink offerings to her, we have lacked everything and have been consumed by the sword and by famine." ¹⁹*The women also said*, "And when we burned incense to the queen of heaven and poured out drink offerings to her, did we make cakes for her, to worship her, and pour out drink offerings to her without our husbands' *permission?*"

Ezekiel 8:13-14 ¹³And He said to me, "Turn again, *and* you will see greater abominations that they are doing." ¹⁴So He brought me to the door of the north gate of the LORD'S house; and to my dismay, women were sitting there weeping for Tammūz [a Sumerian fertility god similar to the Greek God Adonis].

Revelation 19:20 Then the <u>beast</u> was <u>captured</u>, and <u>with him the false prophet</u> who worked signs in his presence, by which he deceived those who received the mark of the beast and those who worshiped his image. <u>These two were cast alive into the lake of fire burning with brimstone.</u>

Vv. 4-6

<u>Genesis 11:7-9</u>: *Babel means *confusion*, the inevitable result if God is left out or if things aren't in accordance with—or—according to God.*

<u>Jeremiah 44:18-19</u>: *The people served the goddess queen of heaven.*

In <u>Ezekiel 8:13-14</u> **worship of Tammūz was one of many fertility cults of the Assyrian deity. Weeping for Tammūz was an act intended to bring *him* back from *"a lower world."***

<u>Revelation 19:20</u>: Both the Antichrist **beast and the false prophet** will be **captured** and hurled **alive into the lake of fire burning with brimstone.**

Reasoning for Babylon Possibly being the Revived Roman Empire:

17:7-8

⁷But the angel said to me, "Why did you marvel? I will tell you the mystery of the woman and of the beast [the Antichrist and his empire] that carries her, which has the seven heads and the ten horns. ⁸The beast [possibly the Roman Empire of the past] that you saw <u>was</u>, and <u>is not</u>, and <u>will ascend out of the bottomless pit</u> [will reappear in an extreme devilish form] and go to <u>perdition</u> [destruction]. And those who dwell on the earth will <u>marvel</u>, whose names are not written in the Book of Life from the foundation of the world, when they see the <u>beast</u> that <u>was</u>, and <u>is not</u>, and <u>yet is</u>."

**The beast as an empire goes through four stages:

<u>1ˢᵗ</u>: It **was**, that is, it existed in the form of the ancient Roman Empire at the time of Christ's crucifixion.

<u>2ⁿᵈ</u>: It **is not**, that is, it has not existed as an empire since the fifth century and will not exist again until the Antichrist appears during the Tribulation.

<u>3ʳᵈ</u>: Satan **will ascend out of the bottomless pit** and raise up the Antichrist as the emperor/false messiah (<u>Revelation 11:7</u>; <u>Revelation 13:3-4</u>).

<u>4ᵗʰ</u>: The Roman Empire will possibly be back to life (**yet is**), but not for long, as Revelation 19:21 tells us there is a reservation for **perdition**—immediate and then eternal suffering for her followers.

17:9

⁹"Here is <u>the mind which has wisdom</u>: <u>The seven heads are seven mountains on which the woman sits</u>. [Rome is said to be on seven <u>mountains</u> or hills.]

The mind which has wisdom will understand the mystery. **The seven heads are seven mountains on which the woman sits.** **The city of Rome, perhaps the location of the harlot's headquarters, was known throughout the ancient world as a city built on seven hills or **mountains**** from where the Vatican in Rome has given much worldwide influence—and is still doing so to this day.

Vv. 7-8

Revelation 11:7 When they [the two witnesses of Revelation 11:3: possibly <u>Moses and Elijah</u>] finish their testimony, the <u>beast</u> that ascends out of the bottomless pit will make war against them, overcome them, and <u>kill them</u>.

Vv. 7-8

<u>Revelation 11:7</u>: **The **beast** is the Antichrist (Revelation 13:1, Revelation 13:8) or false messiah under the control of Satan. At the end of three-and-a-half years of preaching, the witnesses will be **killed** by the **beast** in the great city (Jerusalem; *where also our Lord was crucified*** {just outside the wall of Jerusalem})

Revelation 13:3-4 ³And I saw <u>one of his heads</u> as if it had been <u>mortally wounded</u>, and his <u>deadly wound was healed</u>. And <u>all the world</u> <u>marveled</u> and followed the beast. ⁴So they worshiped the dragon who gave authority to the beast; and they worshiped the beast, saying, "Who *is* like the beast? Who is able to make war with him?"

<u>Revelation 13:3-4</u>: **One of the beast's seven heads** receives a **deadly wound**, and **all the world marveled** as the **wound was healed**. The Antichrist was possibly **wounded** and lived (Revelation 13:14). Or—the thing that ceased—or was deceased—was the imperial form of government. Saying that the **wound** is **healed** could mean the empire is revived—with an emperor—namely, the **beast**—the Antichrist.

[10]There are also <u>seven kings</u>. <u>Five have fallen</u>, one is, *and* the other has not yet come. And when he comes, he must continue a <u>short time</u>. [11]The <u>beast</u> [Antichrist] that <u>was</u>, and <u>is not</u>, <u>is himself</u> <u>also</u> the <u>eighth</u>, and <u>is of the seven</u> [of the seven means: the Antichrist is similar to the seven wicked, idolatrous kings ruling over ten nations from Revelation 12:3], <u>and is going to perdition</u> [destruction]. [**The beast,** the final world kingdom ruled by the Antichrist, is **the eighth** king or kingdom. He **is of the seven** in that he is the culmination of all the previous, pagan, idolatrous empires. But he will go **into perdition**, the lake of fire.**]

17:10-11

The **seven kings are likely the seven kingdoms or empires which throughout history have ruled over Israel and much of the back-then-known world: **Five have fallen**: <u>Egypt</u>, <u>Assyria</u>, <u>Babylon</u>, <u>Persia</u>, <u>Greece</u>; and Rome was the sixth, and the future revived Roman Empire would be the seventh (<u>Daniel 2:41-44</u>; <u>Daniel 7:7, 7:20, 7:24</u>). The rule will be for a **short** time.** The **eighth beast** that <u>was</u>, and <u>is not</u>—is the future world kingdom ruled by the Antichrist, and **is himself similar to the seven, and is going to perdition** (entire loss or ruin; utter destruction; can be applied to a *place* or a *soul*). Quoting J M Mason: "If we reject the truth, we seal our own perdition."

Vv. 10-11

Daniel 2:41-44 ⁴¹Whereas you saw the <u>feet</u> and toes, partly of potter's clay and partly of <u>iron</u>, the kingdom shall be divided; yet the strength of the iron shall be in it, just as you saw the iron mixed with <u>ceramic clay</u>. ⁴²And *as* the toes of the feet *were* partly of iron and partly of clay, *so* the kingdom shall be partly strong and partly fragile. ⁴³"As you saw <u>iron</u> mixed with <u>ceramic clay</u>, they will mingle with the seed of men; but they will not adhere to one another, just as <u>iron</u> does not mix with <u>clay</u>. ⁴⁴And in the days of these kings the God of heaven will set up a kingdom which shall never be destroyed; and the kingdom shall not be left to other people; it shall break in pieces and consume all these kingdoms, and it shall stand forever."

Vv. 10-11

<u>Daniel 2:41-44</u>: *The **feet** of **iron** and **ceramic clay** (baked clay) depict a weakened Roman Empire. (In Daniel 2:38 the **head of gold** is the absolute monarch of Babylon, Nebuchadnezzar. Persia was the **arms of silver**, one arm representing Media and the other Persia. Greece, the third kingdom, was the **belly and thighs of bronze*** {Daniel 2:32}.)

Daniel 7:7 "After this I saw in the night visions, and behold, a <u>fourth beast</u>, dreadful and terrible, exceedingly strong. It had huge iron teeth; it was devouring, breaking in pieces, and trampling the residue with its feet. It *was* different from all the beasts that *were* before it, and it had <u>ten horns</u>.

<u>Daniel 7:7</u>: *The **fourth beast** (Roman Empire), following the Grecian Empire, would cease, and then, after considerable time, would be revived. The **ten horns are ten kings** in the revived empire.* (In verse 8 the little horn is the Antichrist—head of the Revived Roman Empire.)

Daniel 7:20 And the <u>ten horns</u> that *were* on its head, and the other *horn* which came up, <u>before which three fell</u>, namely, that horn [the Antichrist] which had eyes and a mouth which spoke <u>pompous</u> words, whose appearance *was* greater than his fellows.
Daniel 7:24 The <u>ten horns *are* ten kings</u> *who* shall arise from this kingdom. And another shall rise after them; he shall be different from the first *ones*, and <u>shall subdue three kings</u>."

<u>Daniel 7:20, Daniel 7:24</u>: *Daniel saw the little horn…making war with the saints* (Daniel 7:21) *of the Tribulation Period until the Ancient of Days came, ended their sufferings, and gave them the kingdom (Daniel 7:22). The future **pompous** little horn (Antichrist) will blaspheme the Most High, persecute the saints, and intend to change the Jewish calendar for three-and-a-half years* (Daniel 7:25). (This is the Great Tribulation referred to by the Lord Jesus in Matthew 24:21.) *But the Antichrist will be stripped of his power and the glorious, everlasting kingdom of our Lord will begin* (Daniel 7:27).

[12]The ten horns which you saw are ten kings who have received no kingdom as yet, but they receive authority for one hour as kings with the beast. [13]These are of one mind, and they will give their power and authority to the beast. [14]These will make war with the Lamb, and the Lamb will overcome them, for He is Lord of lords and King of kings; and those *who are* with Him *are* called, chosen, and faithful."

17:12-14

*Sure enough, **the ten horns** symbolizing the future **kings** who will serve under the Roman **beast**, will rule for only **one hour** (**short time**, Revelation 17:10; 18:10, 18:17, 18:19). The ten kings unanimously yield **their power and authority** to the Roman **beast** for him to have worldwide control (one government). This ten-kingdom empire goes to war against the Lord Jesus when He returns for His **Second Coming** at the **end of the Tribulation*** (**Revelation 16:14; 19:19**). *They will meet their demise in this *battle of Armageddon*, because the **Lamb** is **Lord of lords and King of kings**.* **Those who follow Christ are **called and chosen** by Him, and **faithful** to Him (Revelation 19:7-8, Revelation 19:14).**

Chapter 17 Verses 12-14 References	Chapter 17 Verses 12-14 References Commentary

Vv. 12-14

Revelation 16:14 For they are <u>spirits of demons</u>, <u>performing</u> signs, *which* go out to the kings of the earth and of the whole world, to gather them to the <u>battle</u> of that <u>great day of God Almighty</u>.

Revelation 19:19 And I saw the <u>beast</u>, the <u>kings of the earth</u>, and their armies, <u>gathered together</u> <u>to make war against</u> Him who sat on the horse <u>and against His army</u>."

Revelation 19:7-8 ⁷"Let us be glad and rejoice and give Him glory, for the marriage of the Lamb has come, and His <u>wife</u> has made herself ready." ⁸And to her it was granted to be arrayed in <u>fine linen, clean and bright</u>, for the fine linen is the <u>righteous</u> acts of the saints.

Revelation 19:14 And <u>the armies</u> in heaven, <u>clothed in fine linen</u>, <u>white</u> and clean, followed Him on white horses.

Vv. 12-14

<u>Revelation 16:14</u>: *The **spirits** are **of demons, performing** miracles to deceive the world's rulers, and to lure them to a climactic **battle** on the **great day of God Almighty**.*

<u>Revelation 19:19</u>: the **beast** is the Antichrist who gathers **together the kings of the earth—*one world government*—to make war against** the Lord Jesus **and against His army**.

<u>Revelation 19:7-8</u>: **The **wife** or the bride of Christ is the Church. The **fine linen, clean and bright**, represents the **righteous**ness of the church, which has now been judged and purified at the judgment seat of Christ.**

<u>Revelation 19:14</u>: *Riding white horses and **clothed in white linen** depicting their righteousness, **the armies** may be made up of heavenly Jerusalem angels, the raptured Church, and spirits of the Old Testament and Tribulation saints. <u>But it is noteworthy that they are not required to fight</u>* (2 Chronicles 20:23 *For the people of Ammon and Moab stood up against the inhabitants of Mount Seir to utterly kill and destroy them. And when they had made an end of the inhabitants of Seir, <u>they helped to destroy one another</u>*.). *The Lord Jesus defeats His foes unaided.*

¹⁵Then he said to me, "The waters which you saw, where the harlot sits, are peoples, multitudes, nations, and tongues. ¹⁶And the ten horns which you saw on the beast, these will hate the harlot [the false teaching *church* with which the ten kings had been associated], make her desolate and naked, eat her flesh and burn her with fire. ¹⁷For God has put it into their hearts to fulfill His purpose, to be of one mind, and to give their kingdom to the beast, until the words of God are fulfilled. ¹⁸And the woman whom you saw is that great city [the MYSTERY BABYLON with headquarters perhaps in Rome] which reigns over the kings of the earth."

[**Definition, purpose, history and possible future of the "Holy Roman Empire":** Webster's 1828 English Language Dictionary says: "An empire is the territories, regions or countries under the jurisdiction of an emperor." The nations outside the empire are called kingdoms. The purpose of becoming an empire was globalization: giving supreme dominion, sovereignty, and imperial power to the emperor. The "Roman Empire" existed from 31 BC till AD 476, but the "*Holy Roman Empire*" began in AD 962 and lasted until Martin Luther's time in mid AD 1500. For those 600 years, (only 500 years ago) the Popes claimed the right to install the most powerful rulers on the European Continent. In the world today we are seeing once again the powerful influence of the Pope. His Headquarters is the Vatican in Rome. Although the Reformation of the church has had great influence, the papacy's power, at times, seems to be regaining strength. The coming prophesied empire could have different political and military Headquarters than for the *religious* control center.]

17:15-18

The waters on which the **harlot sits, are peoples, multitudes, nations, and tongues** [languages] indicates the harlot *church's* worldwide influence and authority. But the **ten horns**—that is, the new Roman Empire which included the ten kings in verse 12 who ruled for a **short time**, realize they have been tricked by the influence of the **harlot** *church*. **The ten kings, only by the **will** of God (verse 17), strip the **harlot**, consume her, and **burn her with fire**. After overthrowing the harlot *church*, the kings will turn their total devotion and worship to the **beast** himself (Revelation 13:12; Revelation 17:13; Daniel 11:36-39). The ten kings will be God's instrument to destroy the harlot Babylon (Revelation 16:19; Revelation 18:5-6; Revelation 19:2b).** It is probable that the reason for all the kings and their nations destroying the **great city** is because of all the idol worship instead of giving total dedication to the Antichrist false messiah. Chapter 18 discloses the destruction of the **woman** or harlot as being pictured as a celebrated downfall of a **great city**. As mentioned before, this refers to the harlot *church* which is not only a vast religious system but perhaps the greatest commercial establishment in the world. It apparently controls the world market.

Chapter 17 Verses 15-18 **References**	**Chapter 17 Verses 15-18** **References Commentary**

Vv. 15-18

Revelation 13:12 And he exercises all the authority of the first beast in his presence, and causes the earth and those who dwell in it to worship the first beast, whose deadly wound was healed.

Revelation 17:13 "These are of one mind, and they will give their power and authority to the beast.

Daniel 11:36-37 [36]"Then the king shall do according to his own will: he shall exalt and magnify himself above every god, shall speak blasphemies against the God of gods, and shall prosper till the wrath has been accomplished; for what has been determined shall be done. [37]He shall regard neither the God of his fathers nor the desire of women, nor regard any god, for he shall exalt himself above *them* all."

Revelation 16:19 Now the great city was divided into three parts, and the cities of the nations fell. And great Babylon was remembered before God, to give her the cup of the wine of the fierceness of His wrath.
Revelation 18:5-6 [5]"For her sins have reached to heaven, and God has remembered her iniquities. [6]Render to her just as she rendered to you, and repay her double according to her works; in the cup which she has mixed, mix double for her."
Revelation 19:2b "He has avenged the blood of His servants *shed* by her [the harlot]."

Vv. 15-18

Revelation 13:12: The False Prophet works closely with the Antichrist, organizing an international campaign for the worship of the Antichrist, and making an image (huge idol illustration) of the Antichrist to show the Antichrist was wounded—and lived.

Revelation 17:13: *The ten kings unanimously yield **their power and authority** to the Roman **beast** for him to have worldwide control* (one world government). (2 Thessalonians 2:4)

Daniel 11:36-37: *The Antichrist will **prosper** till God's **wrath** against Israel is **accomplished**.* Verse 37 could be giving us a glimpse of the reason for the world's recent insisting on "politically correct" enforcement of sexual and gender orientation indoctrination. However, God is in control, and His plan will prevail, come what may.

Revelation 16:19, 18:5-6 and 19:2b: **Babylon** is possibly Rome or Roman Empire nations, whose sins God will no longer put up with, because His judgments of her harlotry *are* righteous...and vengeance is His. (Deuteronomy 32:35; Romans 12:19)

Babylon the Great is Fallen

*Chapter 18 is like a funeral song for the death of a great commercial city. Babylon refers to the harlot *church* which is not only a vast religious system but perhaps the greatest commercial establishment in the world. It apparently controls the world market.*

¹After these things I saw another <u>angel</u> coming down <u>from heaven</u>, having great authority, and the earth was illuminated with his glory. ²And he cried mightily with a loud voice, saying, "<u>Babylon the great is fallen</u>, is fallen, and has become a dwelling place of <u>demons</u>, a prison for <u>every foul spirit</u>, and a cage for every unclean and hated bird! [A prophecy that was made about two hundred years before the ancient Babylon's fall: **Isaiah 21:9b** *"Babylon is fallen, is fallen! And all the carved images of her gods He has broken to the ground."*] ³For all the nations have drunk of the wine of the wrath of her <u>fornication</u>, the kings of the earth have committed <u>fornication</u> with her, and the <u>merchants of the earth</u> have become rich through the abundance of her luxury."

18:1-3

The nations committed **fornication** not only against God, but also against the Antichrist false messiah; it is of absolute vital importance to note what this **fornication** means: they have worshiped those idols instead of our only one true God—having a relationship of devotion and adoration to created objects instead of their Creator. The ten kings would finally realize their people here in the Tribulation Period were being deceived to worship idols instead of the Antichrist, so they would then wipe out the harlot *church*. The harlot system when having been destroyed brings down an **angel from heaven** to earth who loudly makes the announcement **Babylon the great is fallen** (<u>Isaiah 13:1</u>, <u>Isaiah 13:9</u>, <u>Isaiah 13:19</u>; <u>Revelation 17:1-2</u>), and describes the total destruction including **demons** and **every foul spirit** being imprisoned. The entire Chapter of Isaiah 13 is Isaiah's prophecy of the fall of Babylon. **The **merchants of the earth** had become wealthy through the apostate, idolatrous system, possibly centered in Rome.**

Vv. 1-3
Isaiah 13:1 The burden [prophecy] against <u>Babylon</u> which Isāiah the son of Āmoz saw.
Isaiah 13:9 Behold, the <u>day of the LORD comes</u>, cruel, with both wrath and fierce anger, to lay the <u>land</u> desolate; and He will <u>destroy</u> its <u>sinners</u> from it.
Isaiah 13:19 And Babylon, the glory of kingdoms, the beauty of the Chaldēans' pride, <u>will be</u> as when God overthrew Sodom and Gomorrah.

Vv. 1-3
<u>Isaiah 13:1, Isaiah 13:9, Isaiah 13:19</u>: *Chapter 13 of Isaiah is the first of eleven Chapters containing prophecies against Gentile nations. The first is **Babylon**, the world power that crushed Assyria*— the nation that had exiled the northern kingdom, Israel. *The Babylonians defeated the Assyrians in about 609 B.C.* The Babylonians later exiled the southern Jewish kingdom of Judah. But here in Chapter 13 we learn the *Babylonians were subsequently conquered by the Medes and Persians (in 539 B.C.) However, some of the prophecies look beyond that event to the final destruction of **Babylon** at the close of the Great Tribulation as we have seen in Revelation 17 and now see here in Chapter 18.* **The day of the LORD comes** to **destroy** the whole **land** and its **sinners** in Isaiah 13:9.

Revelation 17:1-2 ¹Then one of the seven angels who had the seven bowls came and talked with me, saying to me, "Come, I will show you the judgment of the great harlot who sits on many waters [many peoples and religions of idol worship], ²with whom the kings of the earth committed fornication, and the inhabitants of the earth were made drunk with the wine of her fornication."

<u>Revelation 17:1-2</u>: The city **Babylon** in Chapter 18 is the same as the whore or harlot in Chapter 17, and the summary of God's judgment is the same.

⁴And I heard <u>another voice from heaven</u> saying, "<u>Come out of</u> her, my people, lest you share in her sins, and lest you receive of <u>her plagues</u>. ⁵For <u>her sins have reached to heaven</u>, and God has remembered her iniquities. ⁶Render to her just as she rendered to you, and repay her <u>double</u> according to her works; in the cup which she has mixed, mix <u>double</u> for her. ⁷In the measure that she glorified herself and lived luxuriously, in the same measure give <u>her torment</u> and <u>sorrow</u>; for she says in her heart, 'I sit *as* <u>queen</u>, <u>and</u> am no <u>widow</u>, and will not see <u>sorrow</u>.' ⁸Therefore her plagues will come in one day—<u>death and mourning and famine</u>. And she will be utterly burned <u>with fire</u>, for strong *is* the <u>Lord God</u> who judges her.

18:4-8

The newly sanctified believers must be separate from the harlot system of sin, or else they could receive some of **her plagues.** *Another voice from heaven** warns God's people to **come out of** the doomed system on the eve of its <u>Armageddon</u> destruction.* The connection with the ancient city of Babylon is given in verse 5: **her sins** *have piled up* **to heaven**. **The **double** judgment emphasizes <u>full punishment</u> (<u>Jeremiah 16:14-18</u>; <u>Jeremiah 17:17-18</u>; <u>Jeremiah 50:29-32</u>). Arrogantly she sees herself as **queen and** not a **widow** and thinks she is safe from **sorrow**. As she exalts herself she will be quickly humbled (<u>Luke 14:11</u>)** with **death, mourning and famine**, and the **Lord God** *will punish her **with fire**.*

Chapter 18 Verses 4-8
References

Vv. 4-8
Jeremiah 16:14-18 [14]"Therefore behold, the days are coming," says the LORD, "that it shall no more be said, 'The LORD lives who brought up the children of Israel from the land of Egypt,' [15]"but, 'The LORD lives who brought up the children of Israel from the land of the north and from all the lands where He had driven them.' For I will bring them back into their land which I gave to their fathers. [16]Behold, I will send for many fishermen," says the LORD, "and they shall fish them; and afterward I will send for many hunters, and they shall hunt them from every mountain and every hill, and out of the holes of the rocks. [17]For My eyes *are* on all their ways; they are not hidden from My face, nor is their iniquity hidden from My eyes. [18]And first I will repay double for their iniquity and their sin, because they have defiled My land; they have filled My inheritance with the carcasses of their detestable and abominable idols."

Jeremiah 17:17-18 [17]Do not be a terror to me; You are my hope in the day of doom. [18]Let them be ashamed who persecute me, but do not let me be put to shame; let them be dismayed, but do not let me be dismayed. Bring on them the day of doom, and destroy them with double destruction!

Jeremiah 50:29-32 and Luke 14:11

-CONTINUED ON NEXT PAGE UNDER REFERENCES!-

Chapter 18 Verses 4-8
References Commentary

Vv. 4-8
Jeremiah 16:14-18: **God provides a reassuring hope to Jeremiah. After Judah had paid for its sins and the divine purposes have been realized** (much like the 144,000 will realize right after the Church is raptured), **God will re-gather His people to the land in a deliverance from the nations that surpasses that of Israel's rescue from **Egypt.****

Jeremiah 17:17-18: **Jeremiah pleas for vindication and help. He prays not to be rescued from the persecution but to be delivered through it (James 1:2-4; 1 Peter 1:3-7; Peter 4:12-19).** He also prays for **double** punishment for his and God's enemies as we also read of in Revelation 18:6.

-CONTINUED ON NEXT PAGE UNDER REFERENCES COMMENTARY!-

Chapter 18 Verses 4-8

-VERSES 4-8 REPEATED
FROM PREVIOUS PAGE -

⁴And I heard <u>another voice from heaven</u> saying, "<u>Come out of</u> her, my people, lest you share in her sins, and lest you receive of <u>her plagues</u>. ⁵For <u>her sins have reached to heaven</u>, and God has remembered her iniquities. ⁶Render to her just as she rendered to you, and repay her <u>double</u> according to her works; in the cup which she has mixed, mix <u>double</u> for her. ⁷In the measure that she glorified herself and lived luxuriously, in the same measure give <u>her torment</u> and <u>sorrow</u>; for she says in her heart, 'I sit *as* <u>queen, and</u> am no <u>widow</u>, and will not see <u>sorrow</u>.' ⁸Therefore her plagues will come in one day—<u>death and mourning and famine</u>. And she will be utterly burned <u>with fire</u>, for strong *is* the <u>Lord God</u> who judges her.

Chapter 18 Verses 4-8
Commentary

-COMMENTARY 18:4-8 REPEATED
FROM PREVIOUS PAGE-

18:4-8

The newly sanctified believers must be separate from the harlot system of sin, or else they could receive some of **her plagues. *Another voice from heaven** warns God's people to **come out of** the doomed system on the eve of its <u>Armageddon</u> destruction.* The connection with the ancient city of Babylon is given in verse 5: **her sins** *have piled up* **to heaven**. **The **double** judgment emphasizes <u>full punishment</u> (<u>Jeremiah 16:14-18</u>; <u>Jeremiah 17:17-18</u>; <u>Jeremiah 50:29-32</u>). Arrogantly she sees herself as **queen and** not a **widow** and thinks she is safe from **sorrow**. As she exalts herself she will be quickly humbled (<u>Luke 14:11</u>)** with **death, mourning and famine**, and the **Lord God** *will punish her **with fire**.*

Chapter 18 Verses 9-13

⁹The <u>kings</u> of the earth who committed fornication and lived luxuriously with her will weep and lament for her, when they see the smoke of her burning, ¹⁰<u>standing at a distance</u> for fear of <u>her torment</u>, saying, '<u>Alas</u>, <u>alas</u>, that great city Babylon, that mighty city! For in one hour your judgment has come.' ¹¹And the <u>merchants</u> of the earth will weep and mourn over her, for no one buys their merchandise anymore: ¹²merchandise of gold and silver, precious stones and pearls, fine linen and purple, silk and scarlet, every kind of citron wood, every kind of object of ivory, every kind of object of most precious wood, bronze, iron, and marble; ¹³and cinnamon and incense, fragrant oil and frankincense, wine and oil, fine flour and wheat, cattle and sheep, horses and chariots, and bodies and <u>souls of men</u>.

Chapter 18 Verses 9-13
Commentary

18:9-13

The **kings**, **merchants** and seamen lament over the fallen city, because *of the loss of pleasure and luxury. **Standing at a distance**, they marvel at the extent of **her torment** and the <u>suddenness of her end</u>. Their hope of gain is gone, the trafficking in the **souls of men** and all the worldwide products are gone.* Now all that wealth has suddenly come to nothing.

-CONTINUED FROM PREVIOUS PAGE-

-CONTINUED FROM PREVIOUS PAGE-

Vv. 4-8

Jeremiah 50:29-32 [29]Call together the archers against Babylon. All you who bend the bow, encamp against it all around; let none of them escape. Repay her according to her work; according to all she has done, do to her; for she has been proud against the LORD, against the Holy One of Israel. [30]Therefore her young men shall fall in the streets, and all her men of war shall be cut off in that day," says the LORD. [31]"Behold, I *am* against you, O most <u>haughty one</u>!" says the Lord GOD of hosts; "For your day has come, the time *that* I will punish you. [32]The most proud shall stumble and fall, and no one will raise him up; I will kindle a fire in his cities, and it will devour all around him."

Vv. 4-8

In <u>Jeremiah 50:29-32</u> God's wrath against Babylon is further described. Our God is a jealous God and He is the One who takes vengeance.

Luke 14:11 "For <u>whoever exalts himself will be humbled,</u> and he who humbles himself will be exalted."

In <u>Luke 14:11</u> the **haughty one** will be humbled. Some of today's churches have those in leadership positions who cause their flock to look up to them as though they were not part of the flock themselves. We have <u>all</u> sinned and fallen short of the glory of God. *Jesus taught that it is better to be advanced to a place of honor than to grasp that place and later have to relinquish it. He Himself is the living example of self-renunciation (Philippians 2:5-8). He humbled Himself and God exalted Him.* **Whoever exalts himself will be humbled** by God (Matthew 23:12; <u>Luke 14:11</u>; Luke 18:14).

¹⁴"The fruit that your soul longed for has gone from you, and all the things which are rich and splendid have gone from you, and you shall find them <u>no more at all</u>. ¹⁵The merchants of these things, who became rich by her, will stand at a distance for fear of her torment, weeping and wailing, ¹⁶and saying, 'Alas, <u>alas</u>, that great city that was clothed in fine linen, purple, and scarlet, and adorned with gold and precious stones and pearls!

18:14-16

The kings and merchants shall never again find the riches for which their souls so deeply longed. They will simply continue to weep and lament until their final judgment. The words **alas, alas** are used back to back twice, on three occasions, in verses 10, 16, and 19. This means the people who are left are about to experience immeasurable grief; the worst type of <u>woe</u>. This <u>doubled woe</u>—**Alas, alas**—is an exclamation of exceedingly terrible, dreadful grief, sorrow, misery: heavy calamity.

¹⁷For in one hour such great riches came to nothing.' Every shipmaster, all who travel by ship, sailors, and as many as trade on the sea, stood at a distance ¹⁸and cried out when they saw the smoke of her burning, saying, 'What *is* like this great city?' ¹⁹They threw dust on their heads and cried out, weeping and wailing, and saying, 'Alas, <u>alas</u>, that great city, in which all who had ships on the sea became rich by her wealth! For in one hour she is made desolate.'

18:17-19

Ezekiel prophesied the details that match these verses (<u>Ezekiel 27:29-36</u>). Jeremiah also compares the lamenting (<u>Lamentations 2:10</u>). Either Ezekiel or Jeremiah was a probable author of 1ˢᵗ and 2ⁿᵈ Kings. The LORD was provoked to wrath by King Manasseh of Judah (<u>2 Kings 21:10-13</u>).

Vv. 17-19

Ezekiel 27:29-36 [29]"All who handle the oar, the mariners, all the pilots of the sea will come down from their ships *and* stand on the shore. [30]They will make their voice heard because of you; they will cry bitterly and cast dust on their heads; they will roll about in ashes. [31]They will shave themselves completely bald because of you, gird themselves with sackcloth, and weep for you with bitterness of heart *and* bitter wailing. [32]In their wailing for you they will take up a lamentation, and lament for you: 'What *city is* like Tyre [on the Mediterranean coast in today's southern Lebanon, about 70 km south of Beirut and on the edge of Israel's northern coastal border], destroyed in the midst of the sea? [33]When your wares went out by sea, you satisfied many people; you enriched the kings of the earth with your many luxury goods and your merchandise. [34]But you are broken by the seas in the depths of the waters; your merchandise and the entire company will fall in your midst. [35]All the inhabitants of the isles will be astonished at you; their kings will be greatly afraid, and *their* countenance will be troubled. [36]The merchants among the peoples will hiss at you; you will become a horror, and *be* no more forever."

Lamentations 2:10 and **2 Kings 21:10-13**

Vv. 17-19

<u>Ezekiel 27:29-36</u>: Ezekiel 27 *verses 10-11 inform us that Tyre's army, includes soldiers from Persia, Lydia, and Libya. Then verses 12-27 describe the vastness of Tyre's commerce in luxury goods. But it was to be wrecked by an east wind (the Babylonians). The other nations would be seriously shaken by the fall of the city.* This compares to the fall of the great city Babylon in the future Battle of Armageddon.

-CONTINUED ON NEXT PAGE
UNDER REFERENCES!-

-CONTINUED ON NEXT PAGE UNDER
REFERENCES COMMENTARY!-

-VERSES 17-19 REPEATED
FROM PREVIOUS PAGE -

-COMMENTARY 18:17-19 REPEATED
FROM PREVIOUS PAGE-

18:17-19

Ezekiel prophesied the details that match these verses (Ezekiel 27:29-36). Jeremiah also compares the lamenting (Lamentations 2:10). Either Ezekiel or Jeremiah was a probable author of 1st and 2nd Kings. The LORD was provoked to wrath by King Manasseh of Judah (2 Kings 21:10-13).

¹⁷For in one hour such great riches came to nothing.' Every shipmaster, all who travel by ship, sailors, and as many as trade on the sea, stood at a distance ¹⁸and cried out when they saw the smoke of her burning, saying, 'What *is* like this great city?' ¹⁹They threw dust on their heads and cried out, weeping and wailing, and saying, 'Alas, alas, that great city, in which all who had ships on the sea became rich by her wealth! For in one hour she is made desolate.'

Chapter 18 Verses 20-24

Chapter 18 Verses 20-24
Commentary

18:20-24

But while all the godless tears are being shed on earth, there is great rejoicing in **heaven**. At last **God has avenged** His *saints* (verse 20 NKJV margin), **apostles**, and **prophets**. The **stone** cast **into the sea** in verse 21 depicts the **city** of Babylon's total end.

²⁰Rejoice over her, O heaven, and you holy apostles and prophets, for God has avenged you on her!" ²¹Then a mighty angel took up a stone like a great millstone and threw *it* into the sea, saying, "Thus with violence the great city Babylon shall be thrown down, and shall not be found anymore. ²²The sound of harpists, musicians, flutists, and trumpeters shall not be heard in you anymore. No craftsman of any craft shall be found in you anymore, and the sound of a millstone shall not be heard in you anymore. ²³The light of a lamp shall not shine in you anymore, and the voice of bridegroom and bride shall not be heard in you anymore. For your merchants were the great men of the earth, for by your sorcery all the nations were deceived. ²⁴And in her was found the blood of prophets and saints, and of all who were slain on the earth."

**Three main reasons are given for her destruction:
1) arrogance,
2) deception of the nations, and
3) persecution and martyrdom of God's people.**
There will be no more merriment in the great city, for by her "**sorcery all the nations were deceived. And in her was found the blood of prophets and saints, and of all who were slain on the earth.**" In these verses is the *sixfold* repetition of the phrase **shall not be anymore;** with the likes of **shall be found no more at all** in the KJV; emphasizes God's wrath to the point of total annihilation. **The Babylonian system began in Genesis 10, and has continued uninterrupted in one form or another to the present day. But one day it will suddenly "sink," never to return.** However, the eternal suffering for those who have rejected the righteous Judge who loves them will have just begun.

-CONTINUED FROM PREVIOUS PAGE-

-CONTINUED FROM PREVIOUS PAGE-

18:17-19

Lamentations 2:10 The elders of the daughter of Zion sit on the ground *and* keep silence; they throw dust on their heads and gird themselves with sackcloth. The virgins of Jerusalem bow their heads to the ground.

18:17-19

Lamentations 2:10: **All of these actions express the depths of grief (cf. 2 Kings 19:1:** *And so it was, when King Hezekiah heard it* [the bad news given to him by the chief of the household, the scribe and the recorder—*all three men with their clothes torn* {2 Kings 18:37}], *that he tore his clothes, covered himself with sackcloth, and went into the house of the LORD.* **Job 2:8, 12:** *⁸And he took for himself a potsherd* [a fragment of a broken, baked, clay pot that Job used to scrape the sores covering his body] *with which to scrape himself while he sat in the midst of the ashes.*)

2 Kings 21:10-13 ¹⁰And the LORD spoke by His servants the prophets, saying, ¹¹"Because Manasseh king of Judah has done these abominations (he has acted more wickedly than all the Amorītes who *were* before him, and has also made Judah sin with his idols), ¹²therefore thus says the LORD God of Israel: 'Behold, *I* am bringing *such* calamity upon Jerusalem and Judah, that whoever hears of it, both his ears will tingle.¹³And I will stretch over Jerusalem the measuring line of Samaria and the plummet of the house of Āhab; I will wipe Jerusalem as *one* wipes a dish, wiping *it* and turning *it* upside down.'"

2 Kings 21:10-13: This passage gives evidence that the LORD God does not put up with sin. *Manasseh** had led the people into such terrible **abominations** that God stretched **the measuring line** and used **the plummet**, both of which symbolize judgment. His people would be led off into captivity in Babylon because they had provoked the LORD so grievously.*

We still cannot say with any certainty exactly what city or region the great Babylon will be in the end times. But Babylon possibly consists of more than just one city; it could even include nations. No matter what, the prophecy will be fulfilled.

[The center of Rome is about 20 km {about 12 mi.} off the Mediterranean coast of western Italy. The edge of the metropolis city then stretches nearly to the coast. If Rome were to be destroyed by all that has been prophesied, the smoke rising up would be easily visible by the sailors on the sea.]

The Marriage of the Church to the Lamb
More on Second Coming of Christ
and His Millennial Kingdom

19:1-20:9

begin the climax of the Book of Revelation. But first, the first five verses of Chapter 19 which show the heaven's response to the judgment of the harlot.

¹After these things I heard a loud voice of a great multitude in heaven, saying, "Alleluia! Salvation and glory and honor and power *belong* to the Lord our God! ²For true and righteous *are* His judgments, because He has judged the great harlot who corrupted the earth with her fornication; and He has avenged on her the blood of His servants *shed* by her." ³Again they said, "Alleluia! Her smoke rises up forever and ever!" ⁴And the twenty-four elders and the four living creatures fell down and worshiped God who sat on the throne, saying, "Amen! Alleluia!" ⁵Then a voice came from the throne, saying, "Praise our God, all you His servants and those who fear Him, both small and great!"

19:1-5

****After these things** a **great multitude in heaven** praises the Lord for His righteous punishment of the great harlot and avenging the **blood** of martyrs. The word **Alleluia** is the Greek equivalent of *hallelujah*, and means "Praise Yahweh" or "Praise the Lord" (Psalm 106:1, 106:48d; 111:1; 112:1; 113:1, 113:9c; 117:1, 117:2c; 135:1a, 135:21c; Psalm 146-150). The eternal **smoke** symbolizes the permanence of Babylon's destruction. **Amen** derives from a Hebrew word meaning "to be firm," and may be translated "truly" or "so be it."**

Vv. 1-5

Psalm 106:1 PRAISE the LORD! Oh, give thanks to the LORD, for *He is* good! For His mercy *endures* forever.

Psalm 106:48d Praise the LORD!

Psalm 111:1 PRAISE the LORD! I will praise the LORD with *my* whole heart, in the assembly of the upright and *in* the congregation.

Psalm 112:1 PRAISE the LORD! Blessed *is* the man *who* fears the LORD, *who* delights greatly in His commandments.

Psalm 113:1 PRAISE the LORD! Praise, O servants of the LORD, praise the name of the LORD!

Psalm 113:9c Praise the LORD!

Psalm 117:1 PRAISE the LORD, all you Gentiles! Laud Him, all you peoples!

Psalm 117:2c Praise the LORD!

Psalm 135:1a PRAISE the LORD! Praise the name of the LORD; praise *Him*, O you servants of the LORD!

Psalm 135:21c Praise the LORD!

Vv. 1-5

Psalm 106:1, 106:48d; 111:1; 112:1; 113:1, 113:9c; 117:1, 117:2c; 135:1a, 135:21c all say:
Praise the LORD!

And the last 5 Psalms, 146 to 150, all begin and end with **Praise the LORD!**

The word *alleluia* is the Greek equivalent of *hallelujah*, and means "Praise Yahweh," or "Praise Jehovah," or "Praise God Almighty," or "Praise the Lord."

19:6-7

⁶And I heard, as it were, the voice of a <u>great multitude</u>, as <u>the sound of many waters</u> and as the sound of mighty thunderings, saying, "<u>Alleluia! For the Lord God Omnipotent reigns</u>! ⁷Let us be glad and rejoice and give Him glory for <u>the marriage of the Lamb</u> <u>has come</u>, and His <u>wife</u> has made herself ready."

*Another loud song breaks out of heaven with a great **Alleluia! For the Lord God Omnipotent reigns**.* **God's power is endless!** *<u>The Tribulation is past</u>. Babylon has been judged.* ****The marriage of the Lamb** takes place in heaven at the end of the Tribulation (verse 7). The **wife** or the bride of Christ is the Church (<u>Matthew 22:2-3</u>; <u>2 Corinthians 11:2</u>; <u>Ephesians 5:25-27</u>).

19:8

⁸And to her it was granted to be arrayed in <u>fine linen, clean and bright</u>, for the fine linen is the <u>righteous</u> <u>acts</u> of the saints.

The **fine linen, clean and bright**, represents the **righteous acts** of the Church, which has already been judged and purified at the judgment seat of Christ (<u>1 Corinthians 3:13-15</u>; <u>2 Corinthians 5:10</u>).**

Vv. 6-7

Matthew 22:2-3 ²"The kingdom of heaven is like a certain king who arranged a marriage for his son, ³ and sent out his servants to call those who were invited to the wedding; and they were not willing to come."

2 Corinthians 11:2 For I am jealous for you with godly jealousy. For I have betrothed you to one husband, that I may present you as a chaste virgin to Christ.

Ephesians 5:25-27 ²⁵Husbands, love your wives, just as Christ also loved the church and gave Himself for her, ²⁶that He might sanctify and cleanse her with the washing of water by the word, ²⁷that He might present her to Himself a glorious church, not having spot or wrinkle or any such thing, but that she should be holy and without blemish.

Ephesians 5:30-32... ³⁰For we are members of His body, of His flesh and of His bones. ³¹"For this reason a man shall leave his father and mother and be joined to his wife, and the two shall become one flesh." ³²This is a great mystery, but I speak concerning Christ and the church.

Vv. 6-7

Matthew 22:2-3: **Rejection of the invitation to attend constitutes disloyalty to the King, as well as discourtesy to the Son, and accounts for the forthcoming severe treatment.**

2 Corinthians 11:2: *Paul undoubtedly felt a personal responsibility for the spiritual welfare of the Corinthian saints. His desire was that in a coming day—at the Rapture—he could present the bride to the Lord Jesus, uncorrupted by prevalent false teachings.*

Going to Ephesians 5:25-27, *it has been well said that no wife would mind being submissive to a husband who loves her as much as **Christ** loves **the church**. He demonstrated His love for **the church** by giving **Himself for her** in His sacrificial death on the cross. He paid the greatest price in order to purchase a bride for Himself.*

Ephesians 5:30-32 speaks volumes concerning His love for us. Whatever affects the members affects the Head also. It is unimaginable for Him to allow His precious bride to experience the deception attempts and the wrath of any part of the Seven-year Tribulation.

V. 8

1 Corinthians 3:13-15 ¹³each one's work will become clear; for the Day will declare it, because it will be revealed by fire; and the fire will test each one's work, of what sort it is. ¹⁴If anyone's work which he has built on *it* endures, he will receive a reward. ¹⁵If anyone's work is burned, he will suffer loss; but he himself will be saved, yet so as through fire.

2 Corinthians 5:10 For we must all appear before the judgment seat of Christ, that each one may receive the things *done* in the body, according to what he has done, whether good or bad.

V. 8

In 1 Corinthians 3:13-15 ***Day** refers to the judgment seat of Christ when all service for the Lord will be reviewed. Service that has brought glory to God and blessing to man, like gold, silver, and precious stones, will not be affected by the fire. On the other hand, that which has caused trouble among the people of God or failed to edify will nearly be consumed.*

In 2 Corinthians 5:10 *not only the *amount* of our service, but also its *quality*, and even the very *motives* that prompted it will be brought into review. It will not be a matter of whether we are saved or not; that is already an assured fact. But it is a matter of reward or loss of same.*

⁹Then he said to me, "Write "Blessed *are* those who are <u>called</u> to <u>the marriage supper of the Lamb</u>!" And he said to me, "These are the true sayings of God." ¹⁰And I fell at his feet to <u>worship</u> him. But he said to me, "See that *you do* not *do that*! I am your fellow servant, and of your brethren who have the <u>testimony</u> of <u>Jesus</u>. <u>Worship</u> God! For the <u>testimony</u> of <u>Jesus</u> is the <u>spirit of prophecy</u>."

19:9-10

The marriage supper of the Lamb **will take place on earth** when all believers are gathered for the Millennial reign (verse 9).

The Jewish **marriage consisted of three major elements:

First, the <u>betrothal</u> (engagement) takes place on earth during the <u>Church Age</u>,

second, the <u>wedding</u> will take place in heaven following the Tribulation (verse 7), and

third, the **marriage** feast will take place on earth following Christ's return with the believers (verses 11-14).

Called: Those who are invited to the **marriage supper** include Old Testament Israel and possibly the rest of the redeemed who will turn to Christ during the Tribulation (<u>Revelation 7:14b</u>; Jeremiah 31:31-34♦; <u>Romans 11:25-27</u>).**

Worship: *John falls before the angel's **feet**, but is forbidden. Only God is to be worshiped* (**Revelation 22:8-9; <u>Acts 10:25-26</u>**).

Spirit of prophecy: **The person and message of **Jesus** is the essence of all true **prophecy**.** *The purpose of all true **prophecy** is to bear **testimony** to the Person and work of Jesus Christ.*

¹¹Now I saw heaven opened, and behold, a <u>white horse</u>. And He who sat on him *was* called <u>Faithful and True</u>, and <u>in righteousness He judges</u> and makes war. ¹²<u>His eyes</u> *were* <u>like a flame of fire</u>, and on His head *were* many crowns. He had a name written that no one knew except Himself.

19:11-12

Verses 11-12 depict the return of Christ to earth. (Revelation 20:4; Matthew 25:1-13; <u>Zechariah 13:9</u>; <u>Luke 14:16</u>, <u>Luke 14:18a</u>, <u>Luke 14:24</u>). *When Christ is first seen back on earth He is riding a **white horse**—a war **horse**—since <u>He is coming</u> to conquer His enemies. He is **Faithful** to His promises **and True** to His own character. **His eyes** are **like a flame of fire**, suggesting the penetrating power of His **righteous judgment.** Only He wears the diadem (crown) of royalty and His mysteries will never be comprehended by any created being.*

♦These verses also speak of the Millennial reign and the wedding supper.

Vv. 9-10
Revelation 7:14b "These are the ones who come out of the great <u>tribulation</u>, and washed their robes and made them white in the blood of the Lamb."

Vv. 9-10
In Revelation 5:11, tens of thousands who had already been raptured will witness a new **great multitude** in <u>Revelation 7:14b</u> arriving before the throne. The ones who have been raptured are able to see the many Jews and Gentiles who'll be saved <u>during the Tribulation</u>.

Romans 11:25-27 ²⁵For I do not desire, brethren, that you should be ignorant of this <u>mystery</u>, lest you should be wise in your own opinion, that <u>blindness in part</u> has happened to Israel <u>until</u> the <u>full</u>ness of the Gentiles has come in. ²⁶And so all Israel will be saved, as it is written: *"The Deliverer will come out of Zion, and He will turn away ungodliness from Jacob;* ²⁷*For this is My covenant with them, when I take away their sins."*

In <u>Romans 11:25-27</u> *Paul writes that the future restoration of Israel is an assured fact, but it has been a **mystery**. Some of Israel (**in part**) have been blinded (the unbelieving ones). The **blindness** is temporary. It will continue only **until** the Church has become <u>full</u> with the last believer from every nation. And then, the Rapture will happen! The <u>completed</u> Body of Christ will be taken home. Israel's judicial **blindness** will then be removed.*

Acts 10:25-26 ²⁵As Peter was coming in, Cornelius met him and fell down at his feet and worshiped *him*. ²⁶But Peter lifted him up, saying, "Stand up; I myself am also a man."

<u>Acts 10:25-26</u>: God desires we worship no one other than Himself—the One true God (Exodus 20:3, Exodus 20:5; Deuteronomy 5:7, 9; Hosea 13:4).

Vv. 11-12
Zechariah 13:9 "I will bring <u>one</u>-third through the fire, will refine them as <u>silver</u> is refined, and test them as <u>gold</u> is tested. They will call on My name, and I will answer them. I will say, 'This *is* My people'; and each one will say, 'The LORD is my God.'"

Vv. 11-12
In <u>Zechariah 13:9</u> *although two-thirds of the nation of Israel will die during the Great Tribulation, **one-third** will be preserved. This remnant will be refined like **silver** and **gold**.*

Luke 14:16 Then He said to him, "A certain man gave a great supper and invited many,
Luke 14:18a But they all with one *accord* began to make excuses. The first said to him, 'I have <u>bought a piece of ground</u>, and I must go and see it. I ask you to have me excused.'
Luke 14:24 For I say to you that none of those men who were invited shall taste my supper.

In <u>Luke 14:16, 14:18a and 14:24</u> *our Lord is saying that wonderful as it may be to eat bread in the kingdom of God, the sad fact is that many of those who are invited make all kinds of foolish excuses for their failure to accept His invitation. The one who had **bought a piece of ground** was putting material things ahead of the gracious invitation.*

End of the Battle of Armageddon
and the Great Tribulation

¹³He was <u>clothed with a robe dipped in blood</u>, and His name is called The <u>Word of God</u>.

19:13

*Clothed in a robe dipped in blood, not the blood He shed on Calvary's cross, but the **blood** of His enemies whom He tramples in the winepress of the wrath of God* (<u>Isaiah 63:3</u>). **The name Word of God expresses Christ as the revelation of God Himself (<u>John 1:1</u>, <u>John 1:14a</u>; <u>1 John 1:1</u>). In His first advent, Jesus especially revealed the love and grace of God (<u>John 1:17</u>; <u>Romans 5:8</u>). In His second advent, He will reveal the holiness, justice, and judgment of God (<u>Hebrews 4:12</u>).** Giving one's word expresses truth. By Christ being the **Word**, *God has fully expressed Himself to man.*

V. 13

Isaiah 63:3 I have trodden the winepress alone, and from the peoples no one *was* with Me. For I have trodden them in My anger, and trampled them in My fury; their blood is sprinkled upon My garments, and I have stained all My robes.

John 1:1 In the beginning was the Word, and the Word was with God, and the Word was God.

John 1:14a And the Word became flesh and dwelt among us

1 John 1:1 THAT which was from the beginning, which we have heard, which we have seen with our eyes, which we have looked upon, and our hands have handled, concerning the Word of life—

John 1:17 For the law was given through Moses, *but* grace and truth came through Jesus Christ.

Romans 5:8 But God demonstrates His own <u>love</u> toward us, in that while we were still sinners, Christ <u>died for us</u>.

Hebrews 4:12 For the <u>word of God *is* living</u> and powerful, and sharper than any two-edged sword, piercing even to the division of soul and spirit, and of joints and marrow, and is a discerner of the thoughts and intents of the heart.

V. 13

<u>Isaiah 63:3</u>: Instead of accepting the forgiveness by the shed blood of Jesus Christ, Isaiah prophesied that their stubbornness would result in their own blood staining the Lord's garment.

<u>John 1:1, 1:14a</u>: *This is the first of many clear statements in this Gospel that *Jesus Christ is God*.* He had always existed as the Son of God with the Father in heaven who now chose to send the Son into the world in a human body.

<u>1 John 1:1</u>: *The doctrinal foundation of all true fellowship is the Person of the Lord Jesus Christ. There can be no true fellowship with those who hold false views concerning Him.*

<u>John 1:17</u>: The **law** *was given to show men they were sinners, but it could not save them from their sins.* The punishment for sin is death. The Savior took that punishment for all, and all who believe so are saved.

<u>Romans 5:8</u>: God showed us His marvelous **love** for sinners by dying for us. He **died for us** before we accepted His free offer to save us.

<u>Hebrews 4:12</u>: *This verse refers not to the Living Word, Jesus, but to the living, written word, the Bible. This **word of God is living**—constantly and actively alive. It is the **word** that judges us, not we who judge the **word**.*

¹⁴And <u>the armies</u> in heaven, <u>clothed in</u> fine <u>linen</u>, <u>white</u> and <u>clean</u>, followed Him on white horses. ¹⁵Now out of His mouth goes a sharp <u>sword</u>, that with it He should strike the nations. And He Himself will <u>rule</u> them <u>with a rod of iron</u>. He Himself treads <u>the winepress of the fierceness and wrath of Almighty God</u>. ¹⁶And He has on *His* robe and on His thigh a name written:

<u>KING OF KINGS AND LORD OF LORDS</u>.

19:14-16

Riding white horses and **Clothed in white linen** depicting their righteousness, ****the armies** may be made up of the heavenly angels, the raptured Church, spirits of the Old Testament and Tribulation saints (Hebrews 12: 22-24♦)**. Verse 14 dismisses any notion that the saints who have <u>already been</u> in heaven and have <u>already been</u> **clothed in fine linen, white and clean**, would *still be waiting for the Second Coming to be raptured.* That the Rapture happens *after* the Tribulation is an example of false, deceiving teaching (<u>2 Thessalonians 2:1-2a, 2:3-4a</u>). *<u>But it is noteworthy that they are not required to fight</u>* (<u>2 Chronicles 20:23</u>). *The Lord Jesus defeats His foes unaided.* **The **sword** from His mouth depicts judgment through His spoken Word (Revelation 1:16; 2:12, 16, Isaiah 11:4)** *He will **rule** the nations **with a rod of iron** and tread **the winepress of fierceness and wrath of Almighty God**. Our Lord Jesus is the Supreme Ruler; all others must submit to His reign.* He is **KING OF KINGS AND LORD OF LORDS** (**<u>Revelation 17:14a</u>; <u>Deuteronomy 10:17</u>; <u>Daniel 2:47a</u>; <u>1 Timothy 6:14b-15</u>**).

In verse 15 the Lord Jesus Christ is pointed out to be Almighty God for the seventh time in this Book.

♦These verses also have to do with the subject matter.

Vv. 14-16

2 Thessalonians 2:1-2a, c ¹Now, brethren, concerning the coming of our Lord Jesus Christ and our gathering together to Him [being taken up to Him in the air], we ask you, ²ᵃnot to be soon shaken in mind or troubled, ²ᶜas though the day of Christ had come.

2 Thessalonians 2:3-4a ³Let no one deceive you by any means; for *that Day will not come* unless the falling away comes first, and the man of sin is revealed, the son of perdition, ⁴ᵃwho opposes and exalts himself above all that is called God or that is worshiped, so that he sits as God...

Vv. 14-16

The Thessalonians had mistakenly thought the Day of the Lord—the judgment in the Tribulation—had already begun. The Rapture had to take place first (2 Thessalonians 2:1-2a, c; 2:3-4a).

2 Thessalonians 2:7-8a confirms that not only the falling away must happen, but also the Spirit indwelled evangelizing Church must be taken up out of the way: *⁷For the mystery of lawlessness is already at work; only He who now restrains will do so until He is taken out of the way. ⁸ᵃAnd then the lawless one will be revealed.* *After the Church has been raptured, the Antichrist will be revealed, and he will continue his mad, seven-year career until Christ then returns to this earth.* *The **lie** in 2 Thessalonians 2:11, is the Antichrist's claim to be God.*

2 Chronicles 20:23 For the people of Ammon and Mōab stood up against the inhabitants of Mount Sēir to utterly kill and destroy *them*. And when they had made an end of the inhabitants of Sēir, they helped <u>to destroy</u> <u>one another</u>.

2 Chronicles 20:23: *God confounded the enemy and stirred them up **to destroy one another**.*

Revelation 17:14a "These will make war with the <u>Lamb</u>, and the Lamb will overcome them, for He is <u>Lord of lords and King of kings</u>;"

Revelation 17:14a: The ten kingdoms will meet their demise in this *battle of Armageddon*, because the **Lamb** is **Lord of lords and King of kings**. Those who follow Christ are called and chosen by Him, and are faithful to Him (Revelation 19:7-8, Revelation 19:14).

Deuteronomy 10:17 "For the LORD your God *is* God of gods and Lord of lords, the great God, mighty and awesome, who shows no partiality nor takes a bribe.

Deuteronomy 10:17: **In Mesopotamian literature, only kings showed concern for the welfare of widows and orphans, but God urged Israel to show kindness to such people** (verses 18-19) because God shows no partiality (Romans 2:11).

Daniel 2:47a The king answered Daniel, and said, "Truly your God *is* the God of gods, the Lord of kings,"

Daniel 2:47a: *God gave Daniel the wisdom to impress King Nebuchadnezzar to the point that the king made Daniel ruler over the whole province of Babylon.*

1 Timothy 6:14b-15 ¹⁴ᵇuntil our Lord Jesus Christ's appearing, ¹⁵which He will manifest in His own time, *He <u>who is</u> the blessed and only Potentate* [Sovereign], the King of kings and Lord of lords,

1 Timothy 6:14b-15: When the Lord Jesus Christ comes back to reign on earth, men will realize **who <u>is</u> the blessed and <u>only</u> Potentate** (Sovereign King).

¹⁷Then I saw an angel standing in the sun; and he cried with a loud voice, saying to all <u>the birds</u> that fly in the midst of heaven, "Come and gather together for <u>the supper of the great God</u>, ¹⁸that you may eat the flesh of kings, the flesh of captains, the flesh of mighty men, the flesh of horses and of those who sit on them, and the flesh of all *people,* free and slave, both small and great."

¹⁹And I saw the <u>beast</u> [the Antichrist], <u>the kings of the earth</u>, and their armies, gathered together <u>to make war against</u> Him who sat on the horse <u>and against His army</u>. ²⁰Then the <u>beast</u> was <u>captured</u>, and with him <u>the false prophet</u> who worked signs in his presence, by which he deceived those who received the mark of the beast and those who worshiped his image. These two were cast <u>alive into the lake of fire burning with brimstone</u>. ²¹And the rest were <u>killed with the sword</u> which proceeded from the mouth of Him who sat on the horse. And all the <u>birds</u> were filled with their flesh.

19:17-18

The supper of the great God is different from the marriage supper of the Lamb (Revelation 19:9). Here, God calls **the birds**—vultures—to gather to **eat the flesh** of all unbelievers who have died in the <u>Battle of Armageddon</u> (Revelation 16:14♦, Revelation 16:16♦; Revelation 19:21♦; <u>Ezekiel 39:17a, 39:18a</u>).**

19:19-21

The **beast** is the Antichrist who gathers **together the kings of the earth—*one world government's military*—to make war against** the Lord Jesus **and against His army**. *But it is a futile attempt. Both the Antichrist **beast** and **the false prophet** will be **captured** and hurled **alive into the lake of fire burning with brimstone**. The rest of the unbelievers are **killed with the sword** of the Lord. The **sword** refers to the word of God (Ephesians 6:17♦; 2 Thessalonians 2:8; <u>Hebrews 4:12a</u>; <u>Revelation 1:16a</u>; <u>Revelation 2:12</u>, <u>Revelation 2:16</u>).* **The remaining unbelieving survivors of <u>the Battle of Armageddon which ends the Tribulation Period</u> will be judged by Christ and also sentenced to everlasting fire** (<u>Isaiah 66:24b</u>; <u>Jeremiah 7:20b</u>; <u>Ezekiel 20:47b, 20:48b</u>; **Matthew 25:41, 46**♦; Mark 9:43-48♦; <u>Jude 7b</u>). Christ's *Second Coming* was the theme of the Bible's first prophecy (Jude 14-15♦♦), and of the last message of our Lord Jesus Christ being quoted (Revelation 22:20♦♦).

♦These verses also have to do with the subject matter.
♦♦These verses reveal the first and last prophecies in all the Scriptures.

Chapter 19 Verses 17-21
References

Chapter 19 Verses 17-21
References Commentary

Vv. 17-18

Ezekiel 39:17a "As for you, son of man" [Ezekiel], thus says the Lord GOD, "Speak to every sort of bird and to every beast of the field:
Ezekiel 39:18a "You shall eat the flesh of the mighty, drink the blood of the princes of the earth,"

Vv. 17-18

<u>Ezekiel 39:17a, 39:18a</u>: *The dead bodies of the horses and riders (Ezekiel 39:20) will provide a great feast for birds and beasts of prey.*

Vv. 19-21

Hebrews 4:12a For the word of God *is* living and powerful, and sharper than any two-edged <u>sword</u>,

Revelation 1:16a He had in His right hand <u>seven stars</u>, out of His mouth went a sharp two-edged sword,

Revelation 2:12 "And to the angel [messenger] of the church in Pergamos write, 'These things says He who has the sharp two-edged sword:'"
Revelation 2:16 "<u>Repent</u>, or else I will come to you quickly and will fight against them with the sword of My mouth."

Isaiah 66:24b "And their fire is not quenched"
Jeremiah 7:20b "And it <u>will burn and not be quenched</u>."
Ezekiel 20:47b "The <u>blazing flame shall not be quenched</u>."
Ezekiel 20:48b "it shall not be quenched."

Jude 7b suffering the vengeance of <u>eternal fire</u>.

Vv. 19-21

<u>Hebrews 4:12</u>: The Bible is alive, cutting like a sharp **two-edged sword**.

<u>Revelation 1:16a</u>: The **seven stars** are the seven churches. At this point in Revelation this verse could be pointing out the difference between the faithful, universal raptured Church and the apostate disobedient churches.

<u>Revelation 2:12, 2:16</u>: **The Pergamos church is urged to **repent** of the toleration and sins from false teachers, before Christ judges them Himself. The church should discipline itself and not tolerate false teaching and immorality within.** (1 Corinthians 5:11-13)

<u>Isaiah 66:24b, Jeremiah 7:20b, Ezekiel 20:47b, 48b</u>: These four verses all agree: **their fire is not quenched**. *God desires obedience, not rituals.* Disobedience is sin. *In Mark 9, Jesus uses Isaiah's solemn words three times!* "*Their worm does not die and their fire is not quenched.*"

In <u>Jude 7b</u> God's judgment on sexual sin and offensiveness to Christ's followers is severe: <u>eternal fire</u>.

Reigning with Christ
The Great White Throne

¹Then I saw an angel coming down from heaven, having the key to the bottomless pit and a great chain in his hand. ²He laid hold of <u>the dragon, that serpent of old</u>, who is *the* Devil and <u>Satan</u>, and bound him for a thousand years; ³and he cast him into the <u>bottomless pit</u>, and shut him up, and set a seal on him, so that he should deceive the nations no more till the thousand years were finished. But after these things he must be released for <u>a little while</u>.

20:1-3

The Devil, Satan, that is **the dragon, that serpent of old**, will not join the Antichrist and False Prophet in the lake of fire until after he is released from 1,000 years of being imprisoned in the **bottomless pit**. His "release" (repeated in Revelation 20:7-10) will be for only **a little while**. Satan's demons—or fallen angels—are also in the pit with Satan (<u>Isaiah 24:21-23</u>).

⁴And I saw thrones, and they sat on them, and judgment was committed to them. Then I *saw* the souls of those who had been beheaded for their witness to Jesus and for the word of God, who had not worshiped <u>the beast</u> or his image, and <u>had not received *his* mark</u> on their foreheads or on their hands. And they lived and reigned with Christ for a <u>thousand</u> years. ⁵But <u>the rest of the dead</u> did not live again until the thousand years were finished. This *is* the first resurrection. ⁶Blessed and holy *is* he who has <u>part</u> in <u>the first resurrection</u>. Over such the second death has no power, but they <u>shall be priests of God and of Christ</u>, and shall reign with Him a thousand years.

20:4-6

The saints of the Church Age *and* the martyrs who **had refused to take the mark** of **the beast... shall be priests of God and of Christ** during His <u>thousand</u> year reign.

There are three phases to **the first resurrection:
1) <u>Christ's resurrection</u>—the first fruits
   (<u>1 Corinthians 15:20, 15:23</u>; <u>Revelation 1:5</u>);
2) The <u>Church's resurrection</u>
   (<u>Romans 11:25</u>; <u>1 Thessalonians 4:16-17</u>);
   <u>Revelation 4:1</u>; 5:9a, <u>5:11</u>)
3) <u>Old Testament and Tribulation saints' resurrections</u>.** These saints are from the <u>third</u> **part** of the **first resurrection**.
   (<u>Revelation 6:9b-10</u>; <u>Revelation 7:14b</u>)

After the 1,000 year reign, the **rest of **the *unbelieving* dead** will be raised in the <u>second resurrection</u> and be sentenced to their <u>second death</u> and cast into the lake of fire (Revelation 20:13-15).**

Vv. 1-3

Isaiah 24:21-23 [21]It shall come to pass in that day *that* the LORD will punish on high the host of exalted ones, and on the earth the kings of the earth. [22]They will be gathered together, *as* prisoners are gathered in the pit [dungeon], and will be shut up in the prison; after many days they will be punished. [23]Then the moon will be disgraced and the sun ashamed; for the LORD of hosts will reign on Mount Zion and in Jerusalem and before His elders, gloriously.

Vv. 1-3

Isaiah 24:21-23: **The LORD will punish the host on high of exalted ones** means above the earth (**Satanic powers**), *and* He will also punish **the kings on earth**. **Notice the obvious parallel after many days** to Revelation 20:1-3—**they will be gathered in the pit**...**after many days** where Satan is bound in the bottomless pit for a thousand years.**

Vv. 4-6

1 Corinthians 15:20 But now Christ is risen from the dead, *and* has become the firstfruits of those who have fallen asleep [died].
1 Corinthians 15:23 But each one in his own order: Christ the firstfruits, afterward those *who are* Christ's at His coming.

Vv. 4-6

1 Corinthians 15:20, 1 Corinthians 15:23: Christ is the first to be raised from the dead to remain alive forever into eternity. His resurrection is the first part of what is called THE FIRST RESURRECTION. Believers of the Church Age (which we are now experiencing) will be the second part of "The First Resurrection." All who believed prior to the Church Age and all who will be saved after the Church Age during the Tribulation will be the third part of "The First Resurrection." "The Second Resurrection" will consist of the masses of unbelievers who will face the Lord Jesus at the Great White Throne before experiencing their second death and the lake of fire (Revelation 20:13-15).

Revelation 1:5; 1 Thessalonians 4:16-17; Revelation 4:1; 5:11; 6:9b-10; 7:14b

-CONTINUED ON NEXT PAGE UNDER REFERENCES!-

-CONTINUED ON NEXT PAGE UNDER REFERENCES COMMENTARY!-

-VERSES 4-6 REPEATED FROM PREVIOUS PAGE -

-COMMENTARY 20:4-6 REPEATED FROM PREVIOUS PAGE-

⁴And I saw thrones, and they sat on them, and judgment was committed to them. Then I *saw* the souls of those who had been beheaded for their witness to Jesus and for the word of God, who had not worshiped <u>the beast</u> or his image, and <u>had not received *his* mark</u> on their foreheads or on their hands. And they lived and reigned with Christ for a thousand years. ⁵But <u>the rest of the dead</u> did not live again until the thousand years were finished. This *is* the first resurrection. ⁶Blessed and holy *is* he who has part in <u>the first resurrection</u>. Over such the second death has no power, but they <u>shall be priests of God and of Christ</u>, and shall reign with Him a thousand years.

20:4-6

The saints of the Church Age *and* the martyrs who **had refused to take the mark** of **the beast...shall be priests of God and of Christ** during His 1,000 year reign.

There are three phases to **the first resurrection:
1) <u>Christ's resurrection</u>—the first fruits (<u>1 Corinthians 15:20, 23</u>; <u>Revelation 1:5</u>);
2) The <u>Church's resurrection</u> (Romans 11:25; <u>1 Thessalonians 4:16-17</u>); <u>Revelation 4:1</u>; 5:9a, <u>5:11</u>)
3) <u>Old Testament and Tribulation saints' resurrections</u>.** These saints are from the <u>third part</u> of the **first resurrection**. (<u>Revelation 6:9b-10</u>; <u>Revelation 7:14b</u>)

After the 1,000 year reign, the **rest of **the *unbelieving* dead** will be raised in the <u>second resurrection</u> and be sentenced to their <u>second death</u> and cast into the lake of fire (Revelation 20:13-15).**

-CONTINUED FROM PREVIOUS PAGE-

-CONTINUED FROM PREVIOUS PAGE-

Vv. 4-6

Vv. 4-6

Revelation 1:5 and from Jesus Christ, the faithful witness, the <u>firstborn from the dead</u>, and the <u>ruler over the kings of the earth</u>. To Him who <u>loved us and washed us from our sins in His own blood</u>,

In <u>Revelation 1:5</u> the Lord Jesus Christ **is the firstfruits of the first resurrection,** (the first to be raised and to remain alive forever) and the **ruler over the kings of the earth**. He **loved us**, **washed us from our sins in His own blood**, redeemed us, and even in the next verse (6) makes us kings and priests.

1 Thessalonians 4:16-17 [16]For the Lord Himself will descend from heaven with a shout, with the voice of an archangel, and with <u>the trumpet of God</u>. And the dead in Christ will rise first. [17]Then we who are alive *and* remain shall be caught up together with them in the clouds to meet the Lord in the air. And thus we shall always be with the Lord.

In <u>1 Thessalonians 4:16-17</u> *the exact order of events at Christ's coming to rapture His saints is given. **The trumpet of God** is the same as the **last trumpet** of 1 Corinthians 15:51-52:* [51]*Behold, I tell you a mystery: We shall not all sleep* [die], *but we shall all be changed—*[52]*in a moment, in the twinkling of an eye, at the <u>last trumpet</u>. For the trumpet will sound, and the dead will be raised incorruptible, and we shall be changed.*

Revelation 4:1 After these things I looked, and behold, a door *standing* open in heaven. And the first voice which I heard *was* like a trumpet speaking with me, saying, "Come up here, and I will show you things which must take place after this."

Revelation 5:11 ...Then I looked, and I heard the voice of many angels around the throne, the living creatures, and the elders; and the number of them was ten thousand times ten thousand, and thousands of thousands,

<u>Revelation 4:1 and 5:11</u> began the chronological order of events from the Rapture of the Church to the saints' [living creatures] voices praising the Lord Jesus Christ for having redeemed them by His blood (Revelation 5:10). Chapter 6 presented the appearance of the Antichrist coming in on his white horse and followed with the red, black, and pale horses which represent his seven-year career. Chapter 7 gives the arrival of the saved 144,000 Jews. All is in Scriptural agreement.

Revelation 6:9b-10 [9b]I saw under the altar the souls of those who had been slain for the word of God and for the testimony which they held. [10]And they cried with a loud voice, saying, "How long, O Lord, holy and true, until You judge and avenge our blood on those who dwell on the earth?" (Zechariah 1:12)

<u>Revelation 6:9b-10</u> quotes what Old Testament prophet Zechariah said in Zechariah 1:12, thus, since John the writer of Revelation, seeing the souls of those Old Testament saints provides proof that they will indeed be raised.

Revelation 7:14b "These are the ones who come out of the great tribulation, and washed their robes and made them white in the blood of the Lamb.

<u>Revelation 7:14</u> specifies that there will be those who become believers during the Great Tribulation. They will be in the third part of the First Resurrection. Only the Church will be married to the Lamb, but the Old Testament saints and Great Tribulation believers will attend the marriage supper. Revelation 19:7; Revelation 19:9.

⁷Now when the thousand years have expired, <u>Satan will be released from his prison</u> ⁸and <u>will go out to deceive</u> <u>the nations</u> which are in the four corners of the earth, <u>Gog and Māgog</u>, to gather them together to battle, whose number *is* as the sand of the sea. ⁹They went up on the breadth of the earth and surrounded the camp of the saints and <u>the beloved city</u>. And <u>fire</u> came <u>down from God out of heaven</u> and devoured them. ¹⁰The devil, who deceived them, was <u>cast into the lake of fire</u> and brimstone where <u>the beast</u> <u>and the false prophet</u> *are*. <u>And they will be tormented day and night forever and ever.</u>

20:7-10

Unbelieving Tribulation survivors will enter the Millennium in unresurrected, natural bodies, bringing offspring who will reproduce during the 1,000 years. Since these people are not "born again" and have the old nature of Adam they will therefore commit to sin. At the end of the Millennium **Satan shall be **released from his** **prison** and **will go out to deceive** all **the nations** of the earth. **Gog and Magog** here possibly refer to the nations of the world in general and are *after* the Millennium. (But in <u>Ezekiel 38**:2-3; 38:15a,</u> <u>38:16</u> and Chapter 39 {very similar to Revelation 19:17-18} Gog and Magog are *pre-millennial* and possibly refer to only a great land north of Israel in Ezekiel's time.) *With the army of ungodly rebels, the devil marches against <u>Jerusalem</u>, **the beloved city**. But **fire** comes **down from God out of heaven** and consumes them* (<u>Ezekiel 39:3-6,</u> <u>39:8</u>). **The devil** himself is **cast into the lake of fire** to join **the beast** [Antichrist] **and the false prophet. And they will be tormented day and night forever and ever.**

¹¹Then I saw a <u>great white throne</u> and Him who sat on it, <u>from whose face the earth and the heaven fled away</u>. And there was found no place for them. ¹²And I saw the dead, small and great, standing before God, and books were opened. And another book was opened, which is *the Book* of Life. And the dead were judged according to their <u>works</u>, by the things which were written in the books. ¹³The sea gave up the dead who were in it, and <u>Death</u> and <u>Hādēs</u> delivered up the dead who were in them. And they were judged, each one according to his <u>works</u>. ¹⁴Then Death and Hādēs <u>were cast into the lake of fire</u>. This is the second death. ¹⁵And anyone not <u>found written in the Book of Life</u> was cast into the lake of fire.

20:11-15

*The Lord Jesus is the Judge (<u>John 5:22</u>, <u>John 5:27</u>) on the **great white throne**. The expression **from whose face the earth and the heaven fled away** indicates that this judgment takes place after the destruction of the present earth and stars (<u>2 Peter 3:10</u>). **Hādēs** will have given up the souls of all the rest of the dead who died in unbelief—bodies and souls will be reunited to be judged. No one who appears at this judgment is registered in **the Book of Life**, but record of his evil **works** determines the degree of punishment.* There would be no further need for **Death** or **Hādēs**, both **were cast into the lake of fire** with all the unsaved, since no one's name was **found written in the Book of Life.**

Vv. 7-10

Ezekiel 38:2-3 ²"Son of man [Ezekiel], set your face against Gog, of the land of Māgog, the prince of Rosh, Mēshech, and Tūbal, and prophecy against him, ³and say, 'Thus says the Lord GOD: "Behold, I *am* against you, O <u>Gog</u>, <u>the prince of Rosh</u>, <u>Mēshech</u>, and <u>Tūbal</u>"....
Ezekiel 38:15a "Then you will come from your place out of the far north, you and many peoples with you,"...
Ezekiel 38:16 "You will come up against My people Israel like a cloud, to cover the land. It will be in the <u>latter days</u> that I will bring you against My land, so that the nations may know Me, when I am hallowed in you, O <u>Gog</u>, before their eyes.

Ezekiel 39:3-6 ³"Then I will knock the bow out of your left hand, and cause the arrows to fall out of your right hand. ⁴You shall fall upon the <u>mountains of Israel</u>, you and all your troops and the peoples who *are* with you; I will give you to <u>birds of prey</u> of every sort and <u>to the beasts</u> of the field <u>to be devoured</u>. ⁵You shall fall on the open field; for I have spoken," says the Lord GOD. ⁶And I will send fire on Magog and on those who live in security in the coastlands. Then they shall know that I *am* the Lord. …
Ezekiel 39:8 Surely it is coming, and it shall be done," says the Lord GOD. "This *is* the day of which I have spoken.

Vv. 11-15

John 5:22 "For the Father judges no one, but has committed all judgment to the Son."...
John 5:27 "and has given Him authority to execute judgment also, because He is the Son of Man."

2 Peter 3:10 But <u>the day of the Lord</u> will come as a thief in the night, in which the heavens will pass away with a great noise, and the elements will melt with fervent heat; both the earth and the works that are in it will be burned up.

Vv. 7-10

<u>Ezekiel 38:2-3; Ezekiel 38:15a, Ezekiel 38:16</u>: *Ezekiel Chapters 38 and 39 predict the destruction of Israel's future enemies. God will lure **Gog** and his allies to gather their troops. Some have said that **Gog, the prince of Rosh, Mēshech, and Tūbal**, could be the ancient names from which come Russia, Moscow, and Tobolsk* (2,000 km East of Moscow). *This is a fascinating possibility, but by no means proven.* God is using whoever it is—similar to the way He used those who exiled Israel and Judah to get the attention of the Israelites and to punish them for having worshiped idols, sexual immorality, and forsaking God. However, this time He will be using the enemy to lure them to their destruction.

<u>Ezekiel 39:3-6, Ezekiel 39:8</u>: *The hordes of enemy troops will meet utter destruction on **the mountains of Israel**.*

Vv. 11-15

<u>John 5:22, John 5:27</u>: Since Christ is God with the Father, He is able *to judge by discerning the thoughts and motives of men's hearts.*

<u>2 Peter 3:10</u>: **The day of the Lord** *refers to any period when God acts in judgment*—in this case of all unbelievers at the Great White Throne.

New Heaven and New Earth
Eternal State and Final Judgment
Following the Millennium

21:1-2

¹Now I saw a <u>new heaven and</u> a <u>new earth</u>, for the first heaven and <u>the first earth had passed away</u>. Also there was no more sea. ²Then I, John, saw the holy city, <u>New Jerusalem</u>, coming down out of heaven from God, <u>prepared</u> as a <u>bride</u> adorned for her husband.

Isaiah predicts the **new heaven and new earth (<u>Isaiah 65:17-19</u>; <u>Isaiah 66:22</u>). The first heaven and the first earth are replaced by a new heaven and a new earth because **the first earth had passed away**. The present universe will thus be cleansed from all the effects of sin** (<u>2 Peter 3:7</u>, <u>2 Peter 3:11-12</u>). **Anything that defiles, or causes an abomination or** even **a lie** will be completely excluded from entering (Revelation 21:27). **The New Jerusalem is prepared** as the habitation of the **bride** of Christ.** *The distinction between the Church as the Bride, the Lamb's wife (Revelation 21:9), Israel (Revelation 21:12), and the Gentile nations (Revelation 21:24), is maintained throughout.*

21:3-5

³And I heard a loud voice from heaven saying, "Behold, <u>the tabernacle of God</u> *is* <u>with men</u>, and He will dwell with them, and they shall be His people. <u>God</u> Himself will be <u>with them</u> *and be* their God. ⁴And God will wipe away every tear from their eyes; there shall be <u>no more death</u>, <u>nor sorrow</u>, <u>nor crying</u>. There shall be no more <u>pain</u>, <u>for the former things have passed away</u>." ⁵Then He who sat on the throne said, "Behold, I <u>make all things new</u>." And He said to me, "Write, for these words are true and faithful."

The tabernacle of God is with men means **God** will forever **dwell with** His people. We *will enjoy communion with Him closer than ever dreamed of.* There shall be **no more** tears**, death, nor sorrow, nor crying,** nor **pain, for the former things have passed away.** God will **make all things new** including our bodies. <u>Philippians 3:20b-21a</u> tells us that **the Savior, the Lord Jesus Christ, will transform our lowly body that it may be conformed to his glorious body**...(<u>John 1:3</u>)

Vv. 1-2

Isaiah 65:17-19 [17]"For behold, I create new heavens and a new earth; and the former shall not be remembered or come to mind. [18]But be glad and rejoice forever in what I create; for behold, I create Jerusalem *as* a rejoicing, and her people a joy. [19]I will rejoice in Jerusalem, and joy in My people; the voice of weeping shall no longer be heard in her, nor the voice of crying."

Isaiah 66:22 "For as the new heavens and the new earth which I will make shall remain before Me," says the LORD, "so shall your descendants and your name remain.

2 Peter 3:7 But the heavens and the earth *which* are now preserved by the same word, are <u>reserved for fire until the day of judgment</u> and perdition of ungodly men.
2 Peter 3:11-12 [11]Therefore, since all these things will be dissolved, what manner *of persons* ought you to <u>be in holy conduct and godliness,</u> [12]looking for and hastening the coming of the day of God, because of which the heavens will be dissolved, being on fire, and the elements will melt with fervent heat?

Vv. 1-2

Isaiah 65:17-19: There are actually three heavens:
1) The earth's atmosphere and blue sky,
2) the stars of the universe and the galaxies
3) the heaven of God's throne.
Since the earth and stars will be destroyed, God will replace them. Paul writes of God's heaven: 2 Corinthians 12:2b: *God knows—such a one was caught up to the third heaven.*

Isaiah 66:22: God will rejoice for our having joy in the new earth which will last for all eternity.

2 Peter 3:7, 2 Peter 3:11-12: **Just as God once destroyed the world by water, so it is now **reserved for fire until the day of judgment**.** What kind of persons should we **be in holy conduct and godliness**, since our Savior shed His blood to forgive us and died for us to avoid undergoing eternal grief and suffering and, instead, to have this new eternal, joyful life?

Vv. 3-5

Philippians 3:20b-21a [20b]eagerly wait for the Savior, the Lord Jesus Christ, [21a]who will transform our lowly body that it may be conformed to His glorious body,

Vv. 3-5

Philippians 3:20b-21a: God's Word promises us a new, glorious body. If believers should die before the Rapture, their souls and spirits will be with the Lord at the moment of death (2 Corinthians 5:8). <u>Upon being raptured</u> either from the grave or from this present life, we will also be given a new, glorious body (Philippians 3:21).

John 1:3 All things were made through Him, and without Him nothing was made that was made.

In John 1:3 the Son, the Second Person of God, obeyed every desire of the Father. The Father is quoted speaking of His Son: Hebrews 1:10: "*You, LORD, in the beginning laid the foundation of the earth, and the heavens are the work of Your hands.*"

⁶And He said to me, "It is done! I am the Alpha and the Omega, the Beginning and the End. I will give of the fountain of the water of life freely to him who thirsts.

21:6

God's eternal purpose **is done. He is the origin and source of all things (Isaiah 41:4; Isaiah 44:6; Isaiah 46:4a; Isaiah 48:12). He is also the goal or aim of all things** (John 18:6; **Romans 10:4**; Romans 11:36). He is *the One who began creation and the One who finishes*
(John 1:3: *All things were made through Him, and without Him nothing was made that was made.*
Colossians 1:16-17: *¹⁶For by Him all things were created that are in heaven and that are on earth, visible and invisible, whether thrones or dominions or principalities or powers. All things were created through Him and for Him. ¹⁷And He is before all things, and in Him all things consist.*);
*He is the Eternal One. It is He who gives **the water of life*** (John 4:14; salvation with eternal sustenance and provision) *__freely to__ whoever **thirsts** for it* (Revelation 22:17).

V. 6

Isaiah 41:4 "Who has performed and done *it*, calling the generations from the beginning? 'I, <u>the LORD</u>, am the first; and with the last <u>I *am* He</u>.'"
Isaiah 44:6 "Thus says the LORD, <u>the King of Israel</u>, and his Redeemer, the LORD of hosts: 'I *am* the First and I *am* the Last; besides Me *there is* no God.'"
Isaiah 46:4a "Even to *your* old age, <u>I *am* He</u>,"
Isaiah 48:12 "Listen to Me, O Jacob, and Israel, My called: <u>I *am* He</u>, I *am* the First, I *am* also the Last."

V. 6

<u>Isaiah 41:4; Isaiah 44:6; Isaiah 46:4a; Isaiah 48:12</u>:
The LORD, the King of Israel, *challenges any so-called god to predict the future as He does. His people* (Israel back then; and all believers today) *need not fear any challenge to His supremacy.*

John 18:6 Now when He said to them, **"I am He,"** they drew back and fell to the ground.

In <u>John 18:6</u> *for a brief moment, the Lord Jesus revealed Himself to them as **I *AM***, Almighty God. This was an overpowering statement!*

Romans 10:4 For Christ *is* the end of the law for righteousness to everyone who <u>believes</u> [We obtain our righteousness from Him by <u>believing</u> in Him].

<u>Romans 10:4</u>: The Law <u>convicts</u> us, it does <u>*not* save</u> us.

Romans 11:36 For of Him and through Him and to Him *are* all things, to whom *be* <u>glory</u> forever. Amen.

<u>Romans 11:36</u>: *The <u>Almighty</u> is the Object for which everything has been created. Everything is designed to bring **glory** to Him.*

John 4:14 "but whoever drinks of the water that I shall give him will never thirst. But the water that I shall give him will become in him a fountain of water springing up <u>into everlasting life</u>."

<u>John 4:14</u>: *All that earth can provide is not sufficient to fill the human heart. The pleasures of this world are for a few short years, but the pleasures which Christ provides go on **into everlasting life**.*

Revelation 22:17 And the Spirit and the bride say, "Come!" And let him who hears say, "<u>Come</u>!" And let him who thirsts come. Whoever desires, let him take <u>the water of life</u> freely.

In <u>Revelation 22:17</u> **the water of life** refers to salvation. This verse can also refer to the believers' prayers for Christ to **Come** (for Him to return to the air and rapture us—that is, take us up to Himself).

21:7

⁷He who overcomes shall inherit all things, and I will be his God and he shall be My son.

He who overcomes is he who has overcome man's way in the world and believes Jesus is the Son of God (1 John 5:4-5).

21:8

⁸But the cowardly, unbelieving, abominable, murderers, sexually immoral, sorcerers, idolaters, and all liars shall have their part in the lake which burns with fire and brimstone, which is the second death."

But those who continue to reject Him by their life-style of sin, will feel their second death and be cast into the lake of fire (Revelation 20:14-15; Luke 16:19-31).

21:9-17

⁹Then one of the seven angels who had the seven bowls filled with the seven last plagues came to me and talked with me, saying, "Come, I will show you the bride, the Lamb's wife." ¹⁰And he carried me away in the Spirit to a great and high mountain, and showed me the great city, the holy Jerusalem, descending out of heaven from God, ¹¹having the glory of God. Her light *was* like a most precious stone, like a jasper stone, clear as crystal. ¹²Also she had a great and high wall with twelve gates, and twelve angels at the gates, and names written on them, which are *the names* of the twelve tribes of the children of Israel: ¹³three gates on the east, three gates on the north, three gates on the south, and three gates on the west. ¹⁴Now the wall of the city had twelve foundations, and on them were the names of the twelve apostles of the Lamb. ¹⁵And he who talked with me had a gold reed to measure the city, its gates, and its wall. ¹⁶The city is laid out as a square; its length is as great as its breadth. And he measured the city with the reed: twelve thousand furlongs [1,380 miles in all]. Its length, breadth, and height are equal. ¹⁷Then he measured its wall: one hundred *and* forty-four cubits, *according* to the measure of a man, that is, of an angel.

These verses describe the beauty and glory of the **holy Jerusalem. **The bride, the Lamb's wife** is perhaps a reference to the Church being the new city's principle inhabitant. Saved **Israel** is also present. The effect of the beautiful colors of precious stones is a magnificent city of brilliant gold adorned with gems of every color.** **The names of the twelve apostles of the Lamb** will be on the **twelve foundations** of the wall. The size will be 140 **cubits, length, breadth, and height** all being **equal**. This is about 1,380 miles cubed.

V. 7

1 John 5:4-5 ⁴For whatever is born of God overcomes the world. And this is the victory that has overcome the world—our faith. ⁵Who is he who overcomes the world, but he who believes that Jesus is the Son of God?

V. 7

1 John 5:4-5: *The world system is a monstrous scheme of temptation, always trying to drag us away from God and from what is eternal, and seeking to occupy us with what is temporary and sensual. The believer is able to rise above the perishing things of this world and see things in their true, eternal perspective.*

V. 8

Revelation 20:14-15 ¹⁴Then Death and Hādēs were cast into the lake of fire. This is the second death [the lake of fire]. ¹⁵And anyone not found written in the Book of Life was cast into the lake of fire.

V. 8

Revelation 20:14-15: ***Hādēs,** or hell, is a disembodied state of *conscious* punishment for unbelievers awaiting the Great White Throne. **Hādēs** for believers is a state of blessedness in paradise, awaiting the resurrection and glorification of the body.* The Lake of Fire is the final, eternal prison of the unbeliever.

The New Jerusalem's Brilliance

21:18-20

18The construction of its wall was *of* jasper; and the city *was* pure gold, like clear glass. 19The foundations of the wall of the city *were* adorned with all kinds of precious stones; the first foundation *was* jasper, the second sapphire, the third chalcedony, the fourth emerald, 20the fifth sardonyx, the sixth sardius, the seventh chrysolite, the eighth beryl, the ninth topaz, the tenth chrysoprase, the eleventh jacinth, and the twelfth amethyst.

*The **jasper** green **wall** and the **pure gold city** create an image of magnificence and brilliance. **The** twelve **foundations** adorned with twelve **precious stones** are similar to those of the breastplate of the high priest who represented the twelve tribes of Israel.* Each **foundation** had its own special colored **precious stone**: **jasper**-green, **sapphire**-blue, **chalcedony**-green, **emerald**-green, **sardonyx**-red and white, **sardius**-blood-red, **chrysolite**-yellow or gold, **beryl**-green, **topaz**-greenish gold or yellow, **chrysoprase**-green, **jacinth**-bluish purple, and **amethyst**-purple quartz.**

21:21

21The twelve gates *were* twelve pearls: each individual gate was of one pearl. And the street of the city *was* pure gold, like transparent glass.

*The twelve gates** are **twelve pearls**, a reminder that the church is the pearl of great price for which the Savior sold all that He had (Matthew 13:45-46).* **The street of the city** *was* **pure gold, like transparent glass**.

V. 21

Matthew 13:45-46 ⁴⁵ "Again, the kingdom of heaven is like a <u>merchant</u> seeking beautiful pearls, ⁴⁶ who, when he had found one <u>pearl of great price</u>, went and sold all that he had and bought it."

V. 21

In <u>Matthew 13:45-46</u> *the **merchant** is the Lord Jesus. The **pearl of great**, tremendous **price** is the Church. The Savior gave His all to purchase the Church.*

²²But I saw <u>no temple</u> in it, for the Lord God Almighty and the Lamb are its temple. ²³The city had <u>no</u> need of the <u>sun</u> or of the <u>moon</u> to shine in it, for <u>the glory of God</u> illuminated it. <u>The Lamb</u> <u>is</u> its <u>light</u>.

21:22-23

****No temple** is necessary since both the Father and the Son will be present and revealed in their fullest.** *There is **no sun** or **moon** because **the glory of God** illuminates it, and **the Lamb is** the lamp* (**<u>Exodus 3:3-4</u>; <u>Exodus 24:15-18</u>; <u>Exodus 33:14-16</u>; <u>Luke 2:9</u>; <u>Luke 9:29</u>; <u>Hebrews 1:3</u>**).

Revelation 21 verse 22 speaks of the Lord God Almighty for the eighth time, but possibly in this instance to either the Father or the Triune God. But the previous seven times were specifically saying that the Lord Jesus Christ is Almighty God with the Father and the Holy Spirit.

Vv. 22-23

Vv. 22-23

Exodus 3:3-4 ³Then Moses said, "I will now turn aside and see this great sight, why the **bush** does not burn." ⁴So when the LORD saw that he turned aside to look, God called to him from the midst of the bush and said, "Moses, Moses!" And he [Moses] said, "Here I am."

In <u>Exodus 3:3-4</u> *the burning **bush** that is not consumed suggests the glory of God.*

Exodus 24:15-18 ¹⁵Then Moses went up into the mountain, and a cloud covered the mountain. ¹⁶Now the glory of the LORD rested on Mount Sinai, and the cloud covered it six days. And on the seventh day He called to Moses out of the midst of the cloud. ¹⁷The sight of the glory of the LORD <u>was like a consuming fire</u> on the top of the mountain <u>in the eyes of</u> the children of <u>Israel</u>. ¹⁸So Moses went into the midst of the cloud and went up into the mountain. And Moses was on the mountain forty days and forty nights.

<u>Exodus 24:15-18</u>: Verse 18 *informs us that Moses was to remain on top of the mountain for forty days and forty nights. Forty is the number of testing or probation.* **In the eyes of ... Israel**, the **sight...was like a consuming fire**. Since Moses did not descend from the mountain for forty days, the Israelites gave up on him, saying in Exodus 32:1b: *"we do not know what has become of him."* So they talked Aaron into making a "golden calf" to worship! We need to listen to this example and be patient and wait upon the Lord (Psalm 27:14: *Wait on the LORD; be of good courage, and He shall strengthen your heart; wait, I say, on the LORD!*).

Exodus 33:14-16 ¹⁴And He said, "My <u>Presence</u> will go *with you*, and I will give you rest." ¹⁵Then he [Moses] said to Him, "If Your <u>Presence</u> does not go *with us*, do not bring us up from here. ¹⁶For how then will it be known that Your people and I have <u>found grace in</u> Your <u>sight</u>, except You <u>go with us</u>? So we shall be separate, Your people and I, from all the people who *are* upon the face of the earth."

In <u>Exodus 33:14-16</u> *Moses insisted that nothing short of God's **Presence** with them would do. Like Noah, Moses had **found grace in** the Lord's **sight** and received his request for God to **go with us**. "Safety does not consist in the absence of danger but in the **Presence** of God."*

Luke 2:9; Luke 9:29; Hebrews 1:3

-CONTINUED ON NEXT PAGE UNDER REFERENCES!-

-CONTINUED ON NEXT PAGE UNDER REFERENCES COMMENTARY!-

²²But I saw <u>no temple</u> in it, for the Lord God Almighty and the Lamb are its temple. ²³The city had <u>no</u> need of the <u>sun</u> or of the <u>moon</u> to shine in it, for <u>the glory of God</u> illuminated it. <u>The Lamb</u> <u>is</u> its <u>light</u>.

21:22-23

No temple is necessary since both the Father and the Son will be present and revealed in their fullest.** *There is **no sun** or **moon** because **the glory of God** illuminates it, and **the Lamb is** the lamp* (**<u>Exodus 3:3-4</u>; <u>Exodus 24:15-18</u>; <u>Exodus 33:14-16</u>; <u>Luke 2:9</u>; <u>9:29</u>; <u>Hebrews 1:3</u>**).

Chapter 21 Verses 24-26

Chapter 21 Verses 24-26
Commentary

²⁴And the <u>nations of those who are saved shall walk in its light, and the kings of the earth bring their glory and honor into it</u>. ²⁵Its <u>gates</u> shall not be shut at all by day (there shall be <u>no night</u> there). ²⁶And they shall bring the glory and the honor of the <u>nations</u> into it.

21:24-26

Since the **glory of God in the New Jerusalem will **light** the earth,** the Gentile **nations of those who are saved shall walk in its light, and the kings of the earth bring their glory and honor into it**. *The new Jerusalem has no closed **gates**, because there is perfect security and freedom of access* (<u>Isaiah 60:11</u>). *There is **no night**—no darkness—there. There is no sin present. It is a land of righteousness and fadeless day.* **The **nations**, ruled by various kings and levels of earthly authority, will honor the heavenly city as the dwelling place of God.**

-CONTINUED FROM PREVIOUS PAGE-

-CONTINUED FROM PREVIOUS PAGE-

Vv. 22-23

Luke 2:9 And behold, <u>an angel of the Lord</u> stood before them, and the <u>glory of the Lord</u> <u>shone</u> <u>around them</u>, and they were greatly afraid.

Vv. 22-23

In <u>Luke 2:9</u> at Christ's incarnate birth **an angel of the Lord** *came to the shepherds, and a bright, glorious light **shone** all **around them**.* The <u>glory of the Lord</u> is never extinguished—not from His appearances in the Old Testament, not from His coming in the flesh, and not for forever in eternity future.

Luke 9:29 As He [Jesus] prayed, the appearance of His face was altered, and His robe *became* white *and* glistening.

In <u>Luke 9:29</u> this bright radiance preceded the glory which will be His during His coming kingdom.

Hebrews 1:3 who being the brightness *of His* glory and the express image of His person, and upholding all things by the word of His power, when He had by Himself purged our sins, sat down at the right hand of the Majesty on high,

In <u>Hebrews 1:3</u> *the Lord Jesus Christ is the outshining **of** God's **glory**. All the perfections found in God the Father are also found in His Son. Jesus Christ is the radiance **of His glory**. All the moral and spiritual glories of <u>God Almighty</u> are seen in Him.*

Chapter 21 Verses 24-26
References

Chapter 21 Verses 24-26
References Commentary

Vv. 24-26

Isaiah 60:11 "Therefore your <u>gates</u> shall be <u>open</u> continually; they shall not be shut <u>day</u> or <u>night</u> that *men* may bring to you the <u>wealth</u> of the Gentiles, and their <u>kings</u> in procession,

Vv. 24-26

<u>Isaiah 60:11</u>: *No need to lock the city **gates** because there is no danger. On the contrary, it is important to keep them **open** because **kings** and cart loads of **wealth** are arriving **day** and **night**.* (Revelation 21:25 and Revelation 22:5 say *there shall be no night there* [Greek: *nux*: no absence of light] see Revelation 21:23.

²⁷But there <u>shall by no means enter it anything that</u> <u>defiles, or causes an abomination or a lie, but only</u> <u>those who are written in the Lamb's Book of Life</u>.

21:27
Only redeemed and glorified people will have access to or dwell in the New Jerusalem (Revelation 21:8; <u>Revelation 22:15</u>; <u>Isaiah 52:1</u>; <u>Ezekiel 44:9</u>; <u>1 Corinthians 6:9-10</u>; <u>2 Peter 3:13b</u>). **By no means shall anything that defiles, or causes an abomination or a lie, enter** the city, **but only those who are written in the Lamb's Book of Life**.

(The number *twelve* is seen twenty-one times in this Book and seven times in this Chapter. It is commonly understood to stand for *government* or administration.)

V. 27

Revelation 22:15 But outside *are* <u>dogs</u> [metaphorically, ungodly, immoral males] and sorcerers and sexually immoral and murderers and idolaters, and whoever loves and practices a lie.

V. 27

<u>Revelation 22:15</u> tells us this: Forever excluded from heaven will be these wicked ones who perform abominations to God. *__Dogs__ here may refer to male prostitutes (Deuteronomy 23:18), unclean Gentiles (Matthew 15:26), or Judaizers (Philippians 3:2).*

Isaiah 52:1 Awake, awake! Put on your strength, O Zion; put on your beautiful garments, O Jerusalem, <u>the holy city</u>! For the <u>uncircumcised and the unclean</u> shall no longer come to you.

<u>Isaiah 52:1</u>: **The throne of God's deliverance for His people now reaches its greatest expression in the Servant of the Lord who will suffer for the sins of His people. The prophet foresees the Millennium, when Jerusalem will once again be **the holy city**, and the **uncircumcised and the unclean** (unrighteous) will no longer enter her gates.**

Ezekiel 44:9 Thus says the Lord GOD: "No <u>foreigner</u>, uncircumcised in heart or uncircumcised in flesh, shall enter My sanctuary, including any foreigner who *is* among the children of Israel."

In <u>Ezekiel 44:9</u> the use of any **foreigner** (unsaved ones today) in fellowshipping with the Lord is forbidden.

1 Corinthians 6:9-10 ⁹Do you not know that the unrighteous will not inherit the kingdom of God? Do not be deceived. Neither fornicators, nor idolaters, nor adulterers, nor homosexuals [NKJV margin: those submitting to homosexuals], nor sodomites [male homosexuals], ¹⁰nor thieves, nor covetous, nor drunkards, nor revilers, nor extortioners will inherit the kingdom of God.

In <u>1 Corinthians 6:9-10</u> *People who *practice* such sins are not Christians*:
1 John 3:9: *Whoever has been born of God does not* [practice] *sin, for His seed remains in him, and he cannot sin, because he has been born of God.* The indwelling Holy Spirit within each and every true believer causes the believer to overcome such temptations.
1 Corinthians 10:13: *No temptation has overtaken you except such as is common to man; but God is faithful, who will not allow you to be tempted beyond what you are able, but with the temptation will also make the way of escape, that you may be able to bear it.*

2 Peter 3:13b we, according to His promise, look for new heavens and a new earth...

In <u>2 Peter 3:13b</u> God has never broken a promise and He cannot lie: Titus 1:2: *in hope of eternal life which God, who cannot lie, promised before time began.*

Eternal Abundance of Life

¹And he showed me <u>a pure river of water of life</u> [the ever fresh and fruitful influence of the Holy Spirit], clear as crystal, proceeding <u>from</u> the throne of God and <u>of</u> the Lamb. ²In <u>the middle</u> of its <u>street</u>, and <u>on either side of the river</u>, *was* <u>the tree of life</u>, which bore <u>twelve</u> fruits, each *tree* yielding its fruit every month. <u>The leaves of the tree</u> *were* <u>for the healing of the nations</u>.

22:1-2

***A pure river of water of life** flows **<u>from</u> the throne of God and <u>of</u> the Lamb** through **the middle of** the street. **On either side of the river** grows **the tree of life** with its **twelve** kinds of fruit, no longer forbidden* (Ezekiel 47:12). Abundant life and continuous provisions of the New Jerusalem is depicted. **The leaves of the tree** are **for the healing of the nations** *is a figurative way of saying they will enjoy perpetual health.*

³And there shall be no more <u>curse</u>, but the throne <u>of</u> God <u>and</u> <u>of</u> the Lamb shall be in it [God is present, in Person!], and His servants shall serve Him.

22:3

The effects on Satan of the post-Edenic **curse (<u>Genesis 3:14</u>) will be totally gone <u>forever</u>. God's saints will serve God (<u>Revelation 7:15</u>) and **reign** with Him **forever** (<u>Daniel 7:18</u>; <u>Daniel 7:27</u>).**

V. 3

Genesis 3:14 So the LORD God said to the serpent: "Because you have done this, you *are* <u>cursed</u> more than all cattle, and more than every beast of the field; on your belly you shall go, and you shall eat dust all the days of your life.

Revelation 7:15 "Therefore they are before the throne of God, and <u>serve</u> Him day and night in His temple. And He who sits on the throne will dwell among them.

Daniel 7:18 '<u>But</u> the <u>saints of the Most High</u> shall receive <u>the kingdom</u>, and possess the kingdom forever, even forever and ever.'
Daniel 7:27 'Then the kingdom and dominion, and the greatness of the kingdoms under the whole heaven, shall be given to the people, the <u>saints of the Most High</u>. His <u>kingdom</u> *is* an everlasting <u>kingdom</u>, and all dominions <u>shall serve and obey Him</u>.'

V. 3

<u>Genesis 3:14</u>: As a result of Adam and Eve's eating, all of creation was **cursed**, but the <u>serpent</u> was uniquely **cursed** by representing all that is odious, disgusting and low. Reptiles are branded and avoided with fear.

<u>Revelation 7:15</u>: **The principal activity of believers, who were redeemed back to God for eternity, will be to gladly **serve** God.**

<u>Daniel 7:18, Daniel 7:27</u>: The word ***But*** begins the verse because Daniel foresees the four kingdoms nearer his time to eventually be succeeded by **the kingdom** of **the Most High** and of His **saints** who **shall serve and obey Him.**

[4]They shall see His face, and His name *shall be* on their foreheads. [5]There shall be no night there: They need no lamp nor light of the sun, for the Lord God gives them light. And they shall reign forever and ever.

22:4-5

The greatest blessing of eternity is that **they shall see His face (Matthew 5:8; Hebrews 12:14). Though this is now present day impossible for an unglorified human being (Exodus 33:20), it will occur in the eternal state. The **name** of God **on their foreheads** shows constant focus on God, allegiance and devotion (Revelation 3:12; Exodus 28:38). Since in the New Jerusalem God is always present, His glory makes all other sources of **light** unnecessary (Revelation 21:23; Isaiah 60:19; Zechariah 14:7).**

Vv. 4-5
Matthew 5:8 "Blessed *are* the pure in heart, for they shall see God."

Vv. 4-5
Matthew 5:8: *A pure-hearted person is one whose motives are not mixed, whose thoughts are holy, whose conscience is clean.*

Hebrews 12:14 Pursue peace with all *people*, and holiness, without which no one will see the Lord:

Hebrews 12:14: *Martin Luther said, "My holiness is in heaven." Christ is our holiness, that is, as far as our standing before God is concerned.*

Exodus 33:20 But He said, "You cannot see My face; for no man shall see Me, and live."

Exodus 33:20: *No one can look upon the unveiled glory of God; He dwells "in unapproachable light" (1 Timothy 6:16).*

Revelation 3:12 "He who overcomes, I will make him <u>a pillar</u> in the temple of My God, and he shall go out no more. I will write on him the name of My God and the name of the city of My <u>God, the New Jerusalem,</u> which comes down out of heaven from My God. And *I will write on him* My <u>new name.</u>"

Revelation 3:12: *That the believer will be **a pillar** certainly carries the thought of strength, honor, and permanent security. He shall never leave this place of safety and joy, and he will belong to **God, the New Jerusalem**, and the **new name** of the Lord Jesus.*

Exodus 28:38 "So it shall be on Aaron's forehead, that Aaron may bear <u>the iniquity of the holy things</u> which the children of Israel hallow in all their holy gifts; and it shall always be on his forehead, that they may be accepted before the LORD."

Exodus 28:38: *The miter on Aaron's forehead served as a reminder for **the iniquity** (sins) **of the holy things**—a prompt that even our most sacred acts are stained with sin.*

Isaiah 60:19 "<u>The sun</u> shall no longer be your light by day, nor for brightness shall the <u>moon</u> give light to you; but <u>the LORD will</u> be to you an everlasting <u>light</u>, and your God your glory.

Isaiah 60:19: *The light of **the sun** and **moon** will no longer be necessary in Jerusalem, since the glory of **the LORD will** provide all necessary **light**. Darkness will vanish and Israel's (and in Isaiah 60:20 our) **mourning shall be ended**.*

Zechariah 14:7 It shall be one day which is known to the LORD—neither day nor night. But <u>at evening</u> time it shall happen *that* it will be <u>light</u>.

Zechariah 14:7: The preceding verse, Zechariah 14:6, speaks of no light—only darkness, but subsequently verse 14:9 provides the context that when the light occurs **at evening**, the LORD shall be King over all the earth—His Millennial reign.

⁶Then he said to me, "These words *are* faithful and true." And the Lord God of the holy prophets <u>sent His angel</u> to show His servants the things which <u>must shortly take place</u>. ⁷"Behold, I am coming <u>quickly</u>! Blessed *is* he who keeps the <u>words</u> of the prophecy of this book."

22:6-7

We are reminded by the interpreting angel that **the Lord God sent His angel to show us the many events that **must shortly take place** (take place after the Rapture: See Revelation 4:1). These **words** definitely refer to the entire Book of Revelation, but, perhaps also appropriately, to the *entire Bible*: Acts 20:27: *"For I have not shunned to declare to you the whole counsel of God."* **Quickly** here refers to the imminent return of Christ to rapture His Church (1 Thessalonians 4:16-17). The Rapture can occur at any time. The blessing [reward] is for those who have been prepared by reading, absorbing, digesting, and applying the words of this Book (Revelation 1:3) and obeying the commands for repentance, faith, and perseverance.** We can do this by living in the hope of His Coming to the clouds to take us up to be with Him forever.

⁸Now I, John, saw and heard these things. And when I heard and saw, I <u>fell down</u> to worship before the <u>feet</u> of the <u>angel</u> who showed me these things. ⁹Then he said to me, "See *that you do* not *do that.* For I am your fellow servant, and of your brethren the prophets, and of those who keep the words of this book. <u>Worship God</u>." ¹⁰And he said to me, "<u>Do not seal the words of the prophecy of this book</u> for the time is at hand. ¹¹He who is <u>unjust</u>, let him be <u>unjust</u> still; he who is <u>filthy</u>, let him be <u>filthy</u> still; he who is righteous, let him be righteous still; he who is holy, let him be holy still."

22:8-11

*When John **fell down** at the angel's **feet**, he was forbidden to do so. The **angel** was only a created being; only God is to be worshiped* (Acts 5:29b; Revelation 19:10b). Since the prophecies of this Book are not yet fulfilled, John is not to **seal** it up—and neither are we to *seal it up*. The Book must be left for a little longer since the fulfillment *is near*. **Daniel was told *to* "seal" up his Book since *the end* was still in the *distant* future (Daniel 12:4). **The time is at hand** tells us His return is *imminent*. Verse 11 is a statement of fact and a warning. When the time of fulfillment comes—when Christ comes for us—the deliberate choice of each person will have fixed his eternal fate.** Whether **unjust** or **filthy**, the offer expires when the Lord returns in His Second Coming after the Seven-year Tribulation Period. The **righteous** and **holy** will continue. The offer allowing us to avoid the Tribulation or wrath expires at the Rapture (Romans 5:9; 1 Thessalonians 1:10; 1 Thessalonians 5:9).

Vv. 6-7

1 Thessalonians 4:16-17 [16]For the Lord Himself will descend from heaven with a shout, with the voice of an archangel, and with the trumpet of God. And the dead in Christ will rise first [17]Then we who are alive *and* remain shall be caught up together with them in the clouds to meet the Lord in the air. And thus we shall always be with the Lord.

Vv. 6-7

1 Thessalonians 4:16-17: This passage gives a beautiful description of the nearly instantaneous sequence of events of the Rapture.

Revelation 1:3 Blessed *is* he who reads and those who hear the words of this prophecy, and keep those things which are written in it; for the time *is* near.

Revelation 1:3: *It was obviously God's intention that this Book should be read in the assembly meeting because he promised a special blessing to the one **who reads** it aloud and to all **those** in the assembly **who hear** it and take it to heart. The reason: **The time** for the fulfillment of the prophecies is **near**.*

Vv. 8-11

Acts 5:29b "We ought to obey God rather than men."

Vv. 8-11

Acts 5:29b: Those who do things man's way instead of God's way will find themselves on a slippery slope. We need to follow God's prescription His purpose—not ours. (Acts 4:19)

Revelation 19:10b "Worship God! For the testimony of Jesus is the spirit of prophecy."

Revelation 19:10b: The very first Commandment: Deuteronomy 5:7: *"You shall have no other gods before Me."*
And the second Commandment:
Deuteronomy 5:9: *"you shall not bow down to them nor serve them. For I, the LORD your God, am a jealous God."*

Daniel 12:4 "But you, Daniel, shut up the words, and seal the book until the time of the end; many shall run to and fro, and knowledge shall increase."

Daniel 12:4: **It was impossible to understand the significance of these prophecies in Daniel's own day, but God indicated that at **the time of the end; many** would seek to understand these predictions and be able to do so**—as we are now doing.

[12] "And behold, I am coming quickly, and My reward *is* with Me, to give to every one according to his work.

22:12

Reward is always based on **work (Jeremiah 17:10; Romans 2:5b-6; 1 Peter 1:17). For believers, there is the judgment seat of Christ (2 Corinthians 5:10); for Old Testament saints see Daniel 12:2. For unbelievers there are various judgments culminating with the Great White Throne judgment (Revelation 20:11-15). Matthew 25:31-46**♦ and Revelation 19:20♦ also point out the Lord's judgments.

(♦see Scriptures on following set of pages under "Commentary").

Vv. 12

Jeremiah 17:10 "I, the LORD, search the heart, *I* test the mind, even to give every man according to his ways, according to the fruit of his doings."

Romans 2:5b-6 [5b]in the day of wrath and revelation of the righteous judgment of God, [6]who *will render to each one according to his deeds*"

1 Peter 1:17 And if you call on the Father, who without partiality judges according to each one's work, conduct yourselves throughout the time of your stay *here* in fear;

2 Corinthians. 5:10 For we must all appear before the judgment seat of Christ, that each one may receive the things *done* in the body, according to what he has done, whether good or bad.

Daniel 12:2 and **Revelation 20:11-15**

-CONTINUED ON NEXT PAGE UNDER REFERENCES!-

Vv. 12

Jeremiah 17:10: **Man cannot trust his own heart, but must leave all to God who alone knows the heart and judges all men fairly.**

Romans 2:5b-6: **In the day of...judgment** at the Rapture and at the Great White Throne *the **judgment of God** *will be seen to be absolutely* **righteous**, without prejudice or injustice of any kind.*

1 Peter 1:17: we should live with a respectful fear of displeasing the **Father**.

2 Corinthians 5:10: **The judgment seat of Christ** *will reveal our lives of service for Christ exactly as we have **done, whether good or bad**. Not only the *amount* of service, but also its *quality*, and the *motives* that prompted it will be revealed* when we appear **before...Christ** at His **judgment seat**...

-CONTINUED ON NEXT PAGE UNDER REFERENCES COMMENTARY!-

CONTINUED FROM PREVIOUS PAGE

♦**Matthew 25:31-41** *[31]"When the Son of Man comes in His glory, and all the holy angels with Him, then He will sit on the throne of His glory. [32]All the nations will be gathered before Him, and He will separate them one from another, as a shepherd divides his sheep. [33]And He will set the sheep on His right hand, but the goats on the left. [34]Then the King will say to those on His right hand, 'Come, you blessed of My Father, inherit the kingdom prepared for you from the foundation of the world: [35]for I was hungry and you gave Me food; I was thirsty and you gave Me drink; I was a stranger and you took Me in; [36]I was naked and you clothed Me; I was sick and you visited Me; I was in prison and you came to Me.' [37]Then the righteous will answer Him, saying, 'Lord, when did we see You hungry and feed You, or thirsty and give You drink? [38]When did we see You a stranger and take You in, or naked and clothe You? [39]Or when did we see You sick, or in prison, and come to You?' [40]And the King will answer and say to them, 'Assuredly, I say to you, inasmuch as you did it to one of the least of these My brethren, you did it to Me.' [41]Then He will also say to those on the left hand, 'Depart from Me, you cursed, into the everlasting fire prepared for the devil and his angels:"*

♦**Revelation 19:20** *Then the beast was captured, and with him the false prophet who worked signs in his presence, by which he deceived those who received the mark of the beast and those who worshiped his image. These two were cast alive into the lake of fire burning with brimstone.*

CONTINUED FROM PREVIOUS PAGE

CONTINUED FROM PREVIOUS PAGE

Daniel 12:2 And many of those who sleep in the dust of the earth shall awake, some to <u>everlasting life</u>, some to shame *and* <u>everlasting contempt</u>.

In <u>Daniel 12:2</u> **after the Great Tribulation there will be two more resurrection events, one of the righteous to **everlasting life** and another of the unrighteous to **everlasting contempt**. These two resurrections are separated by Christ's 1,000 year reign** and more—back to His own resurrection, the Rapture of His Church prior to the Tribulation period, and then resurrection of the Old Testament saints and surviving converts after the Tribulation. Then will come His Millennial reign, and then, post-Millennial, the unsaved will be resurrected to bow their knees to Him at the Great White Throne.

Revelation 20:11-15 ¹¹Then I saw a <u>great white throne</u> and Him who sat on it, from whose face the earth and the heaven fled away. And there was found no place for them. ¹²And I saw the dead, small and great, standing before God, and books were opened. And another book was opened, which is *the Book* of Life. And the dead were judged according to their <u>works</u>, by the things which were written in the books. ¹³The sea gave up the dead who were in it, and Death and Hādēs delivered up the dead who were in them. And they were judged, each one according to his <u>works</u>. ¹⁴Then Death and Hādēs were cast into the lake of fire. This is the second death. ¹⁵And anyone not found written in the Book of Life was cast into the lake of fire.

In <u>Revelation 20:11-15</u> *no one who appears at **the great white throne** judgment is registered in **the Book of Life**. The fact that his name is missing *condemns* him, but the record of his evil **works** determines the *degree* of punishment.*

22:13

¹³I am the Alpha and the Omega, *the* Beginning and *the* End, the First and the Last."

The three designations of verse 13 are virtually equivalent in meaning. By applying them to Himself, Christ claims unlimited, eternal equality with God (Revelation 1:8, Revelation 1:17; Revelation 2:8). Philippians 2:6 agrees: [*Christ Jesus*] *who, being in the form of God, did not consider it robbery to be equal with God.*

22:14

¹⁴Blessed *are* those who do His commandments, that they may have the right to the tree of life, and may enter through the gates into the city.

Verse 14 does not teach being saved by works, but rather works as the fruit and proof of having been saved. The Lord Jesus Christ did the works to save us on the cross at Calvary. Father God views all true believers as having the righteousness of God Himself by their having genuine faith in the Lord Jesus Christ. (Romans 3:21-22) **But those who do His commandments** are believers now with Christ (Revelation 12:17; Revelation 14:12; 1 John 3:10; 1 John 5:3). Only believers can have heavenly citizenship in the eternal dwelling place of God and redeemed mankind.

V. 13

Revelation 1:8 "I am the Alpha and the Omega, *the* Beginning and *the* End," says the Lord, "who is and who was and who is to come, the <u>Almighty</u>."
Revelation 1:17 And when I saw Him, I fell at His feet as dead. But He laid His right hand on me, saying to me, "Do not be afraid; I am <u>the First and the Last</u>."
Revelation 2:8 "And to the angel of the church in Smyrna write, 'These things says the First and the Last, who was dead, and came to life:'"

V. 13

<u>Revelation 1:8; Revelation 1:17; Revelation 2:8</u>: *The Lord Jesus reveals Himself as **the First and the Last**, a title of <u>Jehovah</u>, the One and only <u>God</u> (Isaiah 44:6; Isaiah 48:12).*

V. 14

Revelation 12:17 And the dragon was enraged with the woman, and he went <u>to make war with</u> the rest of her offspring, who keep the <u>commandments of God</u> and have the testimony of Jesus Christ.
Revelation 14:12 Here is the patience of the saints; here *are* those who keep the commandments of God and the faith of Jesus.

V. 14

<u>Revelation 12:17; Revelation 14:12</u>: It outrages Satan so much when believers express their love and devotion to **God** by obeying His **commandments** that he wants **to make war with** us!

1 John 3:10 In this the children of God and the children of the devil are manifest [revealed]: Whoever does <u>not practice righteousness</u> is <u>not of God</u>, nor *is* he who does not love his brother.
1 John 5:3 For this is the love of God, that we keep His commandments. And His commandments are not burdensome.

In <u>1 John 3:10</u> and <u>1 John 5:3</u> *those who do not **practice righteousness** are **not of God**. There is no in-between ground. There are none who are half and half. God's children are known by their righteous lives.* One should take note that the word **practice** is of utmost importance here. True believers <u>practice righteousness</u> and although God sees us as having His righteousness, we still have a sin nature. But the indwelling Spirit helps us to quickly recognize our faults so we can sincerely ask for forgiveness and turn back to doing things God's way.

¹⁵But <u>outside</u> *are* <u>dogs</u> and sorcerers and sexually immoral and murderers and idolaters, and whoever loves and practices a lie.

22:15

All unbelievers are outside. *Dogs* here probably refers to male prostitutes (<u>Deuteronomy 23:18</u>), unclean Gentiles (<u>Matthew 7:6a</u>), or Judaizers (<u>Philippians 3:2</u>).* The ones who <u>practice</u> unrighteousness and do not sincerely repent and seek forgiveness are not going to see their names found in the Book of Life.

V. 15

Deuteronomy 23:18 "You shall not bring the wages of a <u>harlot</u> or the price of a <u>dog</u> to the house of the LORD your God for any vowed offering, for both of these *are* an abomination to the LORD your God."

V. 15

In <u>Deuteronomy 23:18</u> a **harlot**[2] is a whore[2]—a female prostitute[2], **and **dog** in the sense used here is probably referring to a male prostitute. God does not accept the wages that were taken by means of immorality—things that are an abomination—detestable to Him.**

Matthew7:6a "Do not give what is holy to the dogs;"

In <u>Matthew 7:6a</u> just as God does not accept reprehensible gifts, He also does not approve of giving things that are holy to the people who are practicing shameful and disgraceful living. God separates all sin from Himself, and He retains all of those who have accepted His Truth.

Philippians 3:2 Beware of <u>dogs</u>, beware of <u>evil workers</u>, beware of the mutilation!

<u>Philippians 3:2</u>: *here the term **dogs** refers to false teachers—**evil workers** who *profess* to be true believers. They attempt to gain admission into Christian fellowship in order to spread their false teachings. The result of their work can only be evil.*

16 "I, Jesus, have sent My angel to testify to you these things in the <u>churches</u>. I am the Root and the Offspring of David, <u>the Bright and Morning Star</u>."

22:16

*As to His deity, the Lord Jesus is David's <u>*Creator*</u>; as to His humanity, He is David's <u>*Descendent*</u>* (**<u>Isaiah 11:1-5</u>; <u>Romans 1:3</u>**<u>-4</u>). *The bright and morning star** appears <u>before</u> the <u>sun</u> rises. Christ will <u>first come</u> to the Church as **the Bright and Morning Star**, that is, at the Rapture of the **Church**.* The **Church** has not been mentioned since the last word in Chapter 3; reason being: the **Church** was not present on earth during the Tribulation period. <u>Later</u> marking the end of Tribulation, *He will come to the earth as the Sun of Righteousness to reign over the earth with healing of the nations in His wings (<u>Malachi 4:2</u>).* Those who <u>fear</u> <u>God's name</u> will triumph over their foes (Malachi 4:3).

V. 16

Isaiah 11:1-5 ¹There shall come forth a Rod [Shoot] from the stem [stock or trunk] of Jesse [David's earthly father], and a Branch [Jesus] shall grow out of his [Jesse's] roots. ²The Spirit of the LORD shall rest upon Him, the Spirit of wisdom and understanding, the Spirit of counsel and might, the Spirit of knowledge and of the fear of the LORD. ³His delight *is* in the fear of the LORD, and He shall not judge by the sight of His eyes, nor decide by the hearing of His ears; ⁴but with righteousness He shall judge the poor, and decide with equity for the meek of the earth; He shall strike the earth with the rod of his mouth, and with the breath of His lips He shall slay the wicked. ⁵Righteousness shall be the belt of His loins, and faithfulness the belt of His waist.

V. 16

Isaiah 11:1-5: *Chapter 11 verse 4 of Isaiah carries us forward to the Second Coming of Christ.*

Romans 1:3-4 ³concerning His <u>Son Jesus Christ our Lord, who</u> was born of the seed of David <u>according to the flesh,</u> ⁴*and* <u>declared *to be* the Son of God with power</u> <u>according to the Spirit</u> of holiness, <u>by the resurrection from the dead.</u>

Romans 1:3-4: *The Gospel is the good news concerning God's **Son, Jesus Christ our Lord, who** is a descendant **of David according to the flesh** (that is, as far as His humanity is concerned;* Luke 3:23-31 informs us that David's son Nathan, leads from Adam to **Hēli**—the father of Mary— the father-in-law of Joseph {Luke 3:23, like much of Scripture includes *in-laws* as parents}.) *The words **according to the flesh** imply that our Lord is more than a Man.* He is also fully **God**. Jesus is **declared to be...God**—that is, the Second Person of God— **the Son of God**—equally <u>Almighty</u> God—**with** the **power...**of **God...by the resurrection from the dead. The Spirit of** holiness confirms the righteousness of the Lord Jesus—the righteousness that only God is capable of directly achieving.

Malachi 4:2 But to you <u>who fear</u> My <u>name</u> the Sun of Righteousness shall arise with healing in His wings; and you shall go out and grow fat like stall-fed calves.

Malachi 4:2: Those **who fear** God's **name** will overcome the world and triumph over the worldly foes.

¹⁷And the Spirit and the bride say, "Come!" And let him who hears say, "Come!" And let him who thirsts come. Whoever desires, let him take the water of life freely.

22:17

Revelation 22:17 speaks of **the Holy **Spirit** who works through the Church to evangelize by taking the Gospel to the world. The **water of life** is eternal life, available freely by faith in Christ (Revelation 7:17; Revelation 21:6b; John 4:14; John 7:37-38).** By the world possibly noticing the Spirit in the bride and evangelizing and saying, "Come!" the Antichrist is restrained from appearing.

V. 17

Revelation 7:17 for the Lamb who is in the midst of the throne will shepherd them and lead them to living fountains of waters. And God will wipe away every tear from their eyes."

Revelation 21:6b "I will give of the fountain of the water of life freely to him who thirsts."

John 4:14 "but whoever drinks of the <u>water</u> that I shall give him will never thirst. But the <u>water</u> that I shall give him will become in him a fountain of <u>water</u> springing up <u>into everlasting life</u>."

John 7:37-38 [37]On the last day, that great *day* of the feast, Jesus stood and cried out, saying, **"If anyone thirsts, <u>let him come to Me </u>and <u>drink</u>.** [38]He who believes in Me, as the Scripture has said, out of his heart will flow rivers of living <u>water</u>."

V. 17

<u>Revelation 7:17; Revelation 21:6b; John 4:14; John 7:37-38</u>: These verses are all in agreement that **water of life** is the free gift of God's grace, for all who believe, to save them from the punishment of their sins and save them from wrath and give them salvation—<u>eternal life</u>. "All that earth can provide is not sufficient to fill the human heart. The pleasures of this world are for a few short years, but the pleasures which Christ provides go on **into everlasting life**." **If anyone thirsts** means any person who realizes he is lost and needs spiritual influence to find his way to life. The Savior invited the thirsting soul to come to Him—not to the church, the preacher, the waters of baptism, or to the breaking of bread. Jesus said, **"Let him come to Me."** "No one or nothing else will do. *To **drink** here means to accept Christ—to believe in Him— to know that He will save you. It means to take Him into our lives as we would take a glass of water into our bodies"* (William MacDonald).

¹⁸For I testify to everyone who hears the words of the prophecy of <u>this book</u>: If <u>anyone</u> adds to these things, God will add to him <u>the plagues</u> that are written in this book; ¹⁹and if <u>anyone</u> <u>takes away from the words</u> of the book of <u>this prophecy</u>, God shall take away his part from the Book of Life, from the holy city, and *from* the things which are written in this book.

22:18-19

*If anyone adds to the things written in **this book** of Revelation, they will suffer **the plagues** described in it. Since the subjects in this book are woven throughout the Bible, verse 18, in effect, condemns any tampering with God's Word* (**<u>Deuteronomy 4:2</u>; <u>Deuteronomy 12:32</u>; <u>Proverbs 30:6</u>; <u>Galatians 1:6-9</u>**; <u>Joshua 1:7</u>; <u>Ecclesiastes 3:14</u>;). In verse 19: *A similar judgment is pronounced on **anyone** who **takes away from the words of this prophecy**. This may not apply to minor differences of interpretation, but to an outright attack on the inspiration and completeness of the Bible.*

22:20-21

²⁰He who testifies to these things says, **"Surely I am coming quickly."** Amen. Even so, come, Lord Jesus! ²¹<u>The grace of our Lord Jesus Christ</u> *be* <u>with you all. Amen.</u>

The final promise of Christ in the Bible is our hope: that His return is imminent (Revelation 22:7; Revelation 22:12). The answer to the problems of life is found in the return of the sovereign Son of God. The benediction in verse 21 is best understood when the margin of the NKJV is considered: **The grace of our Lord Jesus Christ be *with all the saints*. Amen.**"

Vv. 18-19

Deuteronomy 4:2 "You shall not add to the word which I command you, nor take from it, that you may keep the commandments of the LORD your God which I command you."

Deuteronomy 12:32 "Whatever I command you, be careful to observe it; you shall not add to it nor take away from it."

Proverbs 30:6 Do not add to His words, lest He rebuke you, and you be found a liar.

Galatians 1:6-9 [6]I marvel that you are turning away so soon from Him who called you in the grace of Christ, to a different gospel, [7]which is not another; but there are some who trouble you and want to pervert the gospel of Christ. [8]But even if we, or an angel from heaven, preach any other gospel to you than what we have preached to you, let him be accursed. [9]As we have said before, so now I say again, if anyone preaches any other gospel to you than what you have received, let him be accursed.

Ecclesiastes 3:14 I know that whatever God does, it shall be forever. Nothing can be added to it, and nothing taken from it. God does *it*, that men should fear before Him.

Vv. 18-19

Deuteronomy 4:2; Deuteronomy 12:32: Proverbs 30:6: Galatians 1:6-9; Ecclesiastes 3:14: These verses are all in agreement that if anyone willfully changes God's Word in any way from His original intention they will be **accursed**.

Revelation 22:18-19 effectively summarize not only the Book, *The Revelation of Jesus Christ*, but also the whole Bible and the entire counsel of God. What we have learned is that the Word of God just continues to reinforce His Truth each time we read and understand more. We have so much more to learn from our Lord's wisdom, and we should never stop hungering and thirsting. When we seek Him we not only find Him for our salvation, but we also find more wisdom from His absolute, flawless Truth.

Jesus Christ is Revealed; He is Lord God Almighty

In this Book of *The Revelation of Jesus Christ* it must not go unnoticed that the Lord Jesus Christ is referred to as God Almighty or One of the Persons of Almighty God at least seven times.

1. Revelation 1:8 **"who is and who was and who is to come, the Almighty"**
2. Revelation 4:8 "Lord God Almighty, Who was and is and is to come!"
3. Also speaks of equality with the Trinity and exhibits unity.
4. Revelation 11:17 "Lord God Almighty, the One who is and who was and who is to come"
5. Revelation 15:3 "Lord God Almighty!" ... "O King of the saints!"
6. Revelation 16:7 "Lord God Almighty, true and righteous *are* Your judgments."
7. Revelation 16:14 "the battle of that great day of God Almighty"
8. Revelation 19:15 Speaks of His wrath being that of "Almighty God"

DANIEL'S PROPHECY TIMELINE

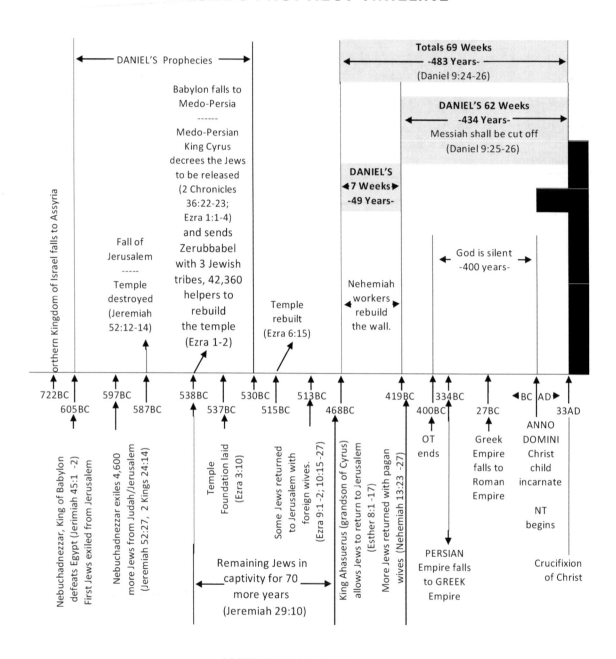

Totals 69 Weeks
-483 Years-
(Daniel 9:24-26)

DANIEL'S Prophecies

DANIEL'S 62 Weeks
-434 Years-
Messiah shall be cut off
(Daniel 9:25-26)

DANIEL'S
◄**7 Weeks**►
-49 Years-

Babylon falls to
Medo-Persia

Medo-Persian
King Cyrus
decrees the Jews
to be released
(2 Chronicles
36:22-23;
Ezra 1:1-4)
and sends
Zerubbabel
with 3 Jewish
tribes, 42,360
helpers to
rebuild
the temple
(Ezra 1-2)

God is silent
-400 years-

Fall of
Jerusalem

Temple
destroyed
(Jeremiah
52:12-14)

Temple
rebuilt
(Ezra 6:15)

Nehemiah
workers
rebuild
the wall.

Northern Kingdom of Israel falls to Assyria

| 722BC | | 597BC | | 538BC | | 530BC | | 513BC | | 419BC | | 334BC | | ◄BC AD► | |
| 605BC | | 587BC | | 537BC | | 515BC | | 468BC | | 400BC | | 27BC | | 33AD | |

OT
ends

Greek
Empire
falls to
Roman
Empire

ANNO
DOMINI
Christ
child
incarnate

NT
begins

Nebuchadnezzar, King of Babylon
defeats Egypt (Jerimiah 45:1 -2)
First Jews exiled from Jerusalem

Nebuchadnezzar exiles 4,600
more Jews from Judah/Jerusalem
(Jeremiah 52:27, 2 Kings 24:14)

Temple
Foundation laid
(Ezra 3:10)

Some Jews returned
to Jerusalem with
foreign wives.
(Ezra 9:1 -2; 10:15 -27)

King Ahasuerus (grandson of Cyrus)
allows Jews to return to Jerusalem
(Esther 8:1 -17)

More Jews returned with pagan
wives (Nehemiah 13:23 -27)

Remaining Jews in
captivity for 70
more years
(Jeremiah 29:10)

PERSIAN
Empire falls
to GREEK
Empire

Crucifixion
of Christ

COMPARE TO TIMELINE ABOVE

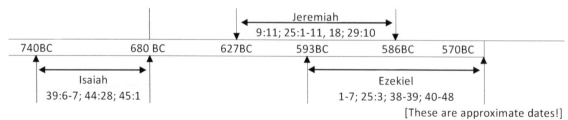

Jeremiah
9:11; 25:1-11, 18; 29:10

| 740BC | | 680 BC | | 627BC | | 593BC | | 586BC | | 570BC |

Isaiah
39:6-7; 44:28; 45:1

Ezekiel
1-7; 25:3; 38-39; 40-48

[These are approximate dates!]

BIBLE PROPHECY TIMELINE

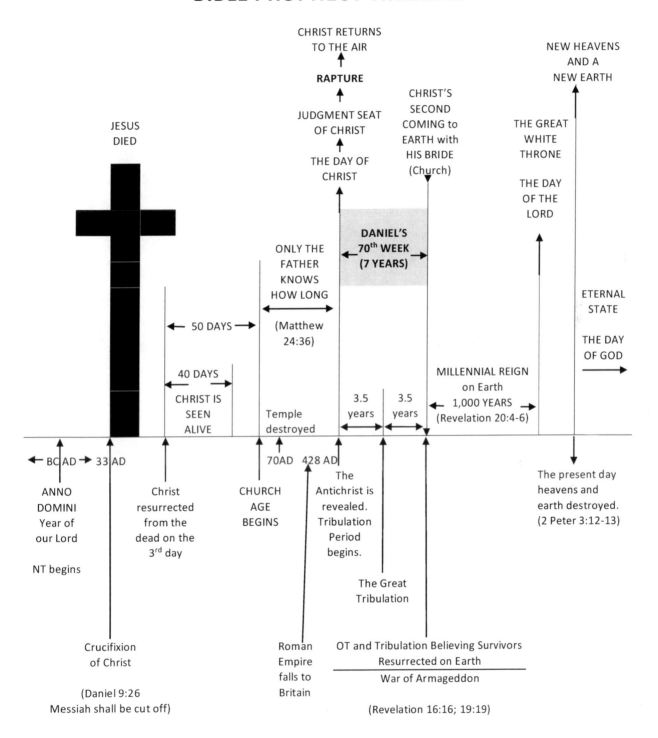

CHRIST RETURNS
TO THE AIR

RAPTURE

NEW HEAVENS
AND A
NEW EARTH

JUDGMENT SEAT
OF CHRIST

CHRIST'S
SECOND
COMING to
EARTH with
HIS BRIDE
(Church)

JESUS
DIED

THE DAY OF
CHRIST

THE GREAT
WHITE
THRONE

THE DAY
OF THE
LORD

ONLY THE
FATHER
KNOWS
HOW LONG

**DANIEL'S
70th WEEK
(7 YEARS)**

(Matthew
24:36)

ETERNAL
STATE

THE DAY
OF GOD

50 DAYS

40 DAYS

MILLENNIAL REIGN
on Earth
1,000 YEARS
(Revelation 20:4-6)

CHRIST IS
SEEN
ALIVE

Temple
destroyed

3.5
years

3.5
years

BC AD → 33 AD

70AD   428 AD

ANNO
DOMINI
Year of
our Lord

NT begins

Christ
resurrected
from the
dead on the
3rd day

CHURCH
AGE
BEGINS

The
Antichrist is
revealed.
Tribulation
Period
begins.

The present day
heavens and
earth destroyed.
(2 Peter 3:12-13)

The Great
Tribulation

Crucifixion
of Christ

Roman
Empire
falls to
Britain

OT and Tribulation Believing Survivors
Resurrected on Earth

War of Armageddon

(Daniel 9:26
Messiah shall be cut off)

(Revelation 16:16; 19:19)

Printed in the United States
By Bookmasters